THE LIFE AND TIMES OF
MAXWELL SMART

THE LIFE AND TIMES OF
MAXWELL
SMART

DONNA McCROHAN

St. Martin's Press   New York

Design by Karin Batten

Library of Congress Cataloging-in-Publication Data

McCrohan, Donna.
  The life and times of Maxwell Smart / by Donna McCrohan.
    p. cm.
  ISBN 0–312–00030–8 (pbk.)
  1. Get smart (Television program) I. Title.
PN1992.77.G4773M33   1988
791.45'72—dc19   87–38243

First Edition

10 9 8 7 6 5 4 3 2 1

To Leonard Stern

who carved his name on my funny bone
before I could even spell my name,
long before I learned to recognize his.

ACKNOWLEDGMENTS

The best thing about writing a *Get Smart* book is the chance to spend time with so many people you're really glad to know. One could do worse than to sit within earshot of Leonard Stern and Alan Spencer, the Obi Wan Kenobi and Luke Skywalker of comedy. May the force—and the Schwartz—be with them, on Schwartz's Island or wherever it may lead.

Don Adams is a doll. Barbara Feldon is, too. Very special thanks to them, and to all the marvelous people who have helped me every step of the way: Donna Anderson, Reza Badiyi, John Behrens, Bruce Bilson, Pat O'Leary Burkette, Alan Burns, Stan Burns, Ricky Byars, Michael Capes, Marc Chevalier, Pat Colvig, Bill Dana, Michael Dann, Jane Dulo, Ann Elder, Charles Falzon, Alexander and Howard Frank, Danny Fuchs, Jeff Fuerst, William Gaines, Dick Gautier, Chris Hayward, Buck Henry, John Javna, Bob Karvelas, Stacy Keach, Christine Keeling, Dave Ketchum, James Komack, Bernie Kopell, David Krinsky, Rose Maione, Denise Marcil, Mike Marmer, Jeremiah McAward, Jo McDaniel, Mary Helen McMahon, Dan Melnick, Robert Miller, Stuart Moore, Howard Morris, Gary Nelson, Burt Nodella, Bill Parkhurst, Angelique Pettyjohn, Colleen Plummer, Ted Rich, Karen Richardson, Henry Rogers, Freda Rosen, Jay Sandrich, Edgar Scherick, William Schallert, Herbert Schlosser, Avery Schreiber, Elroy Schwartz, Sherwood Schwartz, Isobel Silden, Ron Simon, Barbara Stuart, Fred Willard, and Tracy Yeager.

And I can hardly contain my gratitude to my editor, Brian De Fiore, and his two assistants named Chris. One could do worse than to have Brian for an editor, but it's hard to imagine that one could do better.

—Donna McCrohan
New York, 1988

CONTENTS

FOREWORD

"Now you realize, Max, that once KAOS learns of your mission, they'll stop at nothing. You will be in imminent danger and constant jeopardy, facing death at every turn."

These words, seemingly uttered over a thousand times to CONTROL agent Maxwell Smart, would invariably bring about his ridiculously smug response: "And *loving* it."

The Chief's warning also carries grim validity to those outside the high-risk realm of espionage. In the even riskier world of network television, the Chief's precautions also apply to any producer endeavoring to achieve success through a satirical situation comedy.

A satirical sitcom faces "imminent danger" the second it reaches the pilot stage. If it somehow manages to leap this first hurdle and find a place on a network's schedule, the "constant jeopardy" of decent ratings is the next foe to overcome. A tough fight, made virtually suicidal when a series has the misfortune of being labeled "different."

Ask any creative person in television and they'll tell you that looming cancellation and "facing death" share no difference whatsoever.

In that vast video graveyard of short lived tv shows, the countless bodies of satire sitcoms are strewn everywhere. The casualties encompass every era. Their life spans range from a mere six weeks to an optimistic thirteen, and amongst the dearly departed rest series that leave behind millions of mourning loved ones.

(Those loved ones being tv viewers seeking alternatives to the traditional situation comedy format of a family sitting around the breakfast table exchanging wisecracks on the temperature of mayonnaise.)

Of course, it would be foolhardy to presume that all attempts at parody were struck down in their prime time. I'm not so sure whether Captain Nice should have flown for years, or if Buddy needed to keep running into a syndication afterlife.

Did Mr. Terrific live up to his name? Was Henry Phyffe more than a flash in the pan? Were Holmes and Yoyo discharged maybe too quickly? Time will *never* tell.

Still, I can fondly recall some fleeting weeks when a captain named Quark brought mirth to the galaxy. A time When Things Were Rotten in jolly ol' Nottingham, and the men of Police Squad tackled a brief assignment to make you laugh aloud in your living room.

One television memory of mine remains indelible. I remember the date, September 18, 1965. The night was Saturday and I was the very ripe old age of six when I first met Maxwell Smart.

For five hilarious years, Max and lovely agent 99 battled the dastardly forces of KAOS. Week after week I was enthralled. Goodness and niceness triumphed over evil.

Behind the scenes, another triumph had occurred. A group of extraordinarily talented people had bravely defied the conventions of the tv medium. The result was a landmark series whose breakthrough radically altered popular comedy. *Get Smart,* the first and only successful satirical sitcom.

Get Smart's innovative blend of sustained social and political satire, zany slapstick, character comedy along with frequent black humor paved the way for such subsequent shows as *All in the Family, M*A*S*H, Saturday Night Live,* and the current *Moonlighting.*

It's certainly satisfying to know that Donna McCrohan has provided us with an extensively researched and highly affectionate chronicle of a brilliant television series, *Get Smart.*

I feel personally indebted to Don Adams, Dan Melnick, Mel Brooks, Buck Henry, and most especially that resident genius Leonard Stern. They, along with countless others, pulled off a minor miracle in the entertainment industry. Five years of their *Smart* handiwork helped shape my perceptions of comedy, and fueled me to seek a career in the field I presently enjoy being a part of.

I wonder if there's anything I could do to repay them?

Would you believe I'm gonna run out and buy them all new cars?

Would you believe . . . new car *stereos?*

How about just dropping them a nice "thank you" note?

Sorry about that,

—Alan Spencer,
creator/executive producer,
Sledge Hammer!

INTRODUCTION

"The unkempt hippie of today will be the mutual-fund salesman of tomorrow."

—Don Rickles in *Playboy,* 1968

To people over a certain age, the *Get Smart* era seems like only yesterday, and that yesterday, known as the Sixties, promised every enlightenment left to unfold on the face of the earth. In that era, viewers looked back on the Fifties, compared the two decades point for point, and saw exactly how much the world had changed and what had inspired the changes.

They could also look ahead to the future and guess, wonder, posit, but the future itself they could not know. Watching *Get Smart*, they could laugh, pick up its gag lines, and recognize its place in a new media trend of wit and irreverence. Yet they couldn't foretell what the show's two creators, Mel Brooks and Buck Henry, and such others in the credits as producer Jay Sandrich and KAOS kingpin Bernie Kopell, were on their way to

Max (Don Adams) and 99 (Barbara Feldon), spies. *Courtesy of Howard Frank Archives/Personality Photos, Inc.*

becoming: Mel Brooks of *The Producers, Blazing Saddles, Spaceballs.* Buck Henry

1

of *The Graduate* and *Saturday Night Live*. Jay Sandrich of *Soap, The Mary Tyler Moore Show*, and *The Cosby Show*, and Bernie Kopell as a recognized sex symbol among middle-aged viewers of *The Love Boat*.

Few if any, when *Get Smart* dawned in 1965, would have envisioned a *Soap*, a *Producers*, or a *Saturday Night Live* at all. Viewers, as a rule, view. They don't dissect with the purpose of prediction. They assume they're watching end products, neither seeking nor discerning the germs of what will be. Why? Because viewers see themselves as end products. You can bet that the first families gaping at their clunky Motorola consoles in the early Fifties, or hearkening unto their clunky Stromberg-Carlson radios two decades before, felt undeniably modern. The beneficiaries of history, not its charming artifacts.

It happens, though. Every year, every decade, every generation. Now becomes then with alarming rapidity. *Get Smart*—would you believe?—is nearly a quarter-century old.

And so, to people under a certain age—people born into a world of astronauts and satellite communications, *Soap, The Producers*, and *Saturday Night Live*—*Get Smart* may seem to smack of yesterday. Like Mom relating her teeny-bopper moments of swooning over the Beatles, and Junior's flabbergasted reaction: "Wow! Mom remembers Paul Mc-Cartney before Wings!"

Ironically, when it comes to *Get Smart*, Mom and Junior share the same blindspot. Mom's probably forgotten

what Junior most likely never knew—that when it first hit the airwaves, *Smart* had no TV rivals for candor (except the news), nor for originality (except the failures). It smarted off at sacred cows as no situation comedy had before; assumed a level of intelligence and reference well beyond what standard sitcom fare decreed; turned to the times and the headlines as no other sitcom dared to, long before *All in the Family* gave new meaning to daring on TV.

It offered, in the words of Mel Brooks, "the *only* witty show on TV today. Other shows on TV haven't a modicum of wit. They may be funny [here he cited *Lucy*] but we have a great deal of wit, both in the writing and the direction."

Ultimately, by making a higher-level audacity possible, *Get Smart* made possible the more extreme brazenness of other shows. *Smart* embodied a reaction to everything before we knew anything, yet we thought there was nothing we didn't know. One generation's state-of-the-art brains paved the way for the next's:

The Sixties declared a "love generation," denounced the impersonal, then saw no contradiction when they popularized computer dating.

The Sixties invented "Love-ins," with a whole issue of the *Saturday Evening Post* being dedicated to "Love In America." Love wore on, wore thin, some say wore out. By 1977, we happily packed love off to sea on *The Love Boat*.

The Sixties launched a nostalgia craze—Bogart, Thirties musicals, and the like—and our love affair with the future lost ground to our love affair with the past.

The cutting edge of relevant sitcom characterization loomed largest in Bob Denver's beatnik Maynard G. Krebs on *The Many Loves of Dobie Gillis* (1959–1963).

The Sixties average Joe did not loudly lampoon the government, for fear neighbors would think he had dropped out, turned on, tuned in, and sold out to the enemy.

The baby boomers, whose parents told them above all to get an education, got an education about education. They smartened up about getting smart, and considered taking night courses in TV repair.

Credit cards belonged to the very privileged very few, while the many still bartered with grubby money.

Swanson introduced three new varieties in TV dinners: franks and beans, spaghetti and meatballs, and hash.

When *Get Smart* premiered in 1965, guitar sales were up by 300 percent over ten years; Elizabeth Taylor and Elvis Presley tied as highest-paid movie idols; Jane Fonda had not so much as starred in *Barbarella*, let alone denounced the government's Vietnam policy; and, according to the Associated Press in September of the year, [Ronald] "Reagan has not even announced that he will be a candidate for Governor [of California], but Republican moderates are already trying to organize a stop-Reagan movement."

The Sixties, by Eighties yardsticks, still had a lot to learn. About frozen foods. About politics. About comedy with an edge. Many of the Sixties' top TV teachers enrolled in Get Smart U.

Unlike the great predecessor sitcoms whose gifted writers earned their stripes primarily as radio or movie scripters, *Get Smart* fell heir to the first generation of TV writers whose background consisted essentially in writing for TV. Moreover, *Smart's* writers hailed less from domestic and situation comedy than from those highwater marks of satiric commentary brilliance represented by *The Steve Allen Show,* Sid Caesar's *Your Show of Shows* and *Caesar's Hour, That Was The Week That Was,* and *The Bullwinkle Show. Smart's* executive producer, Leonard Stern, combined the best of both traditions, having moved from writing award-winning classic *Honeymooners* scripts to head writing and directing for Steve Allen.

To the sitcom, a form previously enamored of the family, they brought the means to treat espionage, politics, and terrorism. The hero ditched cozy hearth and humble home for a bachelor flat with a booby-trapped fireplace. Where *The Andy Griffith Show* (1960–1968) based plots on finding mason jars for Aunt Bee and putting up pickles, *Get Smart's* writers relished the ramifications of stashing those pickles and jars in fallout shelters, or using the ingredients of a salami sandwich to propel a rocket to the moon.

They united behind a concept, ideas, and the times, which may not seem extraordinary until compared with earlier classics. Lucy and Desi produced, starred in, and propelled *I Love Lucy.* Jackie Gleason produced, starred in, dreamed up, and in his youth lived *The Honeymooners*. So personally did Ozzie Nelson take his televised escapades that his TV self didn't have a job. As his office once explained it, "because the show is based on true life and the stories mainly based on true happenings, Ozzie decided way back in the beginning, that it would be better not to invent a job as that would take away from the truthfulness of the show. He also felt that he couldn't be an actor going to work at the studio every day, as that would take away from the feeling the show gives that their family was the family 'next door' anywhere in the USA."

Smart sprang forth from many heads but not a single life. Its biography is many biographies that not only converged, but converged upon something, that something being a special point in time. *Smart* could not have been launched in the Fifties, nor in the Seventies either. Nor would it have been *Smart* without Mel Brooks, Buck Henry, Leonard Stern, Don Adams, Barbara Feldon, and a handful of others, not one of whom ever set out to be a government spy.

A cache of *Get Smart* collectibles from the Alan Spencer collection. *Courtesy of Alan Spencer.* (The rarest of *Get Smart* collectibles is rumoured to be a 45-rpm record made by Barbara Feldon. Says she, "I sang a song called '99' on one side, and one called 'Max' on the other. I don't remember anything else about it except wishing it would go away.")

1

THE SMARTIAN CHRONICLES

"The change of ownership had been a gradual one but I was sure that something more than cigarettes was changing hands."

—Len Deighton, *Spy Story*

Get Smart's opening credits read, "created by Mel Brooks with Buck Henry." Mel Brooks, for his part, was created some thirty-nine years earlier, by his parents Max and Kitty Brookman Kaminsky, who lived on Powell Street in New York.

Melvin, youngest of four boys, lost his father at the age of two. His mother and he became pals: "My mother had this exuberant joy of living, and she infected me with that. By the time my other brothers were old enough to work, she could stay at home and she was my company. There was Kitty and Mel and we

Mel Brooks as a child (in *High Anxiety*, 1977).

got to know each other, and she really was responsible for the growth of my imagination."

Responsible too were the endless Saturday movie matinees to which Melvin and much of his generation unfailingly flocked. A dime bought admission to a serial, cartoon, short, newsreel, trailers, and two feature films.

Beyond Melvin's imagination stirred the trappings of real life. In his early teens, while still in high school, he worked as a busboy, drummer, and funny guy for a Catskills resort; at seventeen he went to Virginia Military Institute; he enlisted in the Armed Forces, and completed basic training just in time to welcome the end of the Second World War.

During his Catskills tenure, Brooks met another resort entertainer, a gifted saxophonist named Sid Caesar. Caesar had gone on to a role in the movie *Tars and Spars,* and from it to host TV's *The Admiral Broadway Revue,* a spectacular comedy-variety program characterized by such madness as an opera spoof à la showman-songwriter Billy Rose, entitled "No, No Rigoletto." Brooks joined the show—the result, according to Caesar, of "a three-year campaign of incredible *chutzpah* and persistence."

At one point, recalls Brooks, Caesar invited him to stop by the theater, so he went to the stage door, introduced himself, and got the heave: "His manager, Leo Pillot, was at the door. Pillot said, 'Throw him out.' So these two big ushers picked me up by the scruff of my neck and the seat of my pants and literally tossed me into the alley. I said, 'You're crazy. You can't do this to Mel Brooks. I'm potentially very important.'" Then Caesar heard the noise and let Brooks in.

Reportedly, Brooks's first contribution to *The Admiral Broadway Revue* came about from desperation. A sketch, "The Professor and the Jungle Boy," an hour shy of air time, needed help. The Jungle Boy had to explain how he got breakfast in the wilds, but nothing funny developed. Caesar, who still regarded Brooks as something of a groupie, dragged him into the fray: "Do something. Write." Brooks invented the Cry of the Crazy Crow, which rescued the skit, and swung him $50/week (unofficially, off the payroll with no screen credit) and a subsequent position on Caesar's immortal *Your Show of Shows.*

Your Show of Shows, NBC's ninety-minute Saturday night triumph of comedic excellence, ran from 1950 to 1954 (to be succeeded by *Caesar's Hour,* more of the ingenious same). The program literally changed the way America entertained itself. Instead of going out on Saturday nights, people stayed in.

Of its magic, Caesar has noted, "I'm not putting down the performances in *Your Show of Shows*—mine or anyone else's—but the key to our amazing success unquestionably was the writing." By the time the show became *Caesar's Hour,* the now legendary writing team included, among others, Carl Reiner, Woody Allen, Neil Simon, Mel Tolkin, Larry Gelbart, Selma Diamond, and Mel Brooks.

Writing sessions made history. Caesar sat in on them, presiding from a gold throne given him by Larry Gelbart. Writers burned desks, threw each other's shoes out the window, and knocked dents in the walls. Brooks, says Caesar, "exasperated them all because he would sit around, coolly reading the *Wall Street Journal*, and then come in with the one punch line we all were searching for. Mel's childhood nickname was Mibbie, so we had a Mibbie doll, with which Mel could be hanged in effigy when he exasperated the others." On one occasion, Caesar pontifically placed his hand on Brooks's head and intoned, "I own this." Brooks responded by slipping a hand into Caesar's pocket, removing Caesar's wallet, and observing, "I own this."

When General David Sarnoff, head of NBC, was holding a very important meeting, Mel Brooks barged in uninvited, threw himself onto a long conference table, slid across its full length, and met Sarnoff nose-to-nose. At an Emmy ceremony, when the award for best comedy writing went to the *Phil Silvers Show* (1955–1959)—a remarkably regular occurrence during the years *Bilko* ran—Brooks jumped onto a table and railed, "Coleman Jacoby and Arnie Rosen won an Emmy and Mel Brooks didn't! Nietzsche was right! There is no God!"

After *Caesar's Hour* went off the air, Brooks bewailed its demise which left him "no vehicle for my passion." (Since *The Lawrence Welk Show* had played opposite Caesar, Mel Brooks felt special pride when *Get Smart* later played opposite Welk, and put a huge dent in Welk's audience). Post-Caesar, Brooks turned to such fare as Jerry Lewis and Victor Borge specials, convinced that the market for comedy had shifted from the glory days he'd known. When Judge Vincent A. Lupiano asked him, in 1961, why he couldn't keep up his $1,000 per week alimony payments to ex-wife Florence Baum, Brooks cited a trend in viewing that favored news, documentaries, and Westerns over comedies. "Yet," observed the judge, "he admits that his total earnings for the year 1960 were $87,000, though $46,900 came, not from television, but as a comedy writer for a Jerry Lewis motion picture. . . . These are gross figures, of course."

The humor market notwithstanding, Mel Brooks remained the proverbial stitch. At parties, he and Caesar-days cohort Carl Reiner improvised interviews along the lines of the *Show of Shows* "Nonentities in the News" routine. Reiner played the reporter. Brooks evolved into the 2,000-year-old man, a sort of philosophical Jewish codger. The exchange emerged in 1960 as an LP, *2,000 Years with Carl Reiner and Mel Brooks*, followed by *2,001 Years with Carl Reiner and Mel Brooks, Carl Reiner and Mel Brooks at the Cannes Film Festival*, and a commercial for Ballantine Beer in which he portrayed the 2,500-year-old brewmaster (the extra half-millenium added to allow for numbering Cleopatra and Caesar among his acquaintances). Ballantine gave him a new interlocutor, a young and relatively unknown performer named Dick Cavett. Said Brooks of the teaming, "He's innocent and guileless, and he just aches to be cut to pieces. He reacts beautifully during the interviews, especially when I call him 'company rat.'" Brooks's commercial included the ad-lib, "My tongue just threw a party for my mouth," eliciting raves from copywriter Alex Kroll: "That's why you have a Mel Brooks. Because he can give you that flash of genius. He doesn't use punch lines so much as he uses startling nonsequiturs which get better with repeated hearings." Fan clubs for the 2,500-year-old brewmaster began to form.

The old man launched young Brooks on a new career, as a performer, panelist, talk-show raconteur. With several millions of his record sold, people stopped him on the street, in elevators, in Chock Full o'Nuts. "Aren't you Mel Brooks?" Appearing on Johnny Carson's first *Tonight* show on October 1, 1962, he ad-libbed Rudy Vallee, Tony Bennett, and Joan Crawford into the shade.

The same years found Buck Henry experimenting in social satire as a pure improvisational form.

Henry had grown up in New York as Buck Henry Zuckerman, the son of Air Force general Paul Zuckerman (who later became a prominent Wall Street stock broker) and former Mack Sennett bathing beauty Ruth Taylor. He attended private schools and Dartmouth College, at sixteen landed a part as one of the sons in the national touring company of *Life with Father*, then served as a panelist on the TV show *Who Said That?*, and was drafted into the U.S. Army. During the Korean War, he toured Germany with the Seventh Army Repertory Company in a musical comedy written by, directed by, and starring himself.

Returning to civilian life, Henry ap-peared in the national company of *No Time For Sergeants*, accumulated several years of rejection slips as a writer, then gained wide exposure pretending to be weirdo G. Clifford Prout when he and Alan Abel formed the Society for Indecency to Naked Animals (SINA). As Prout, he denounced the moral fiber of any nation too lax to clothe its barnyard friends—no wonder cows don't look at each other; they're too embarrassed. He tried, but failed, to put Fruit of the Looms on a baby elephant. Yet as Prout he wangled what, as Henry, he had not achieved—invitations to the major talk shows, and even the *CBS Evening News*. Since he played it straight, audiences had to judge his ironic intent. Walter Cronkite, CBS news anchorman, may have thought Prout a ninny, but at least thought him a sincere one, and missed the joke upon learning he'd been hoaxed.

In 1960, Buck Henry joined The Premise, New York's off-Broadway offshoot of the improvisational comedy trail blazed by Mike Nichols and Elaine May, Shelley Berman, David Shepherd, Paul Sills, and Viola Spolin at The Compass (later, The Second City) in Chicago. The company that Second City sent to New York took off when David Susskind saw them and featured them on his TV show. For a while, New York's Second City and The Premise played to capacity crowds within blocks of each other.

The Premise, founded by Compass alumnus Theodore J. Flicker, in a few short years pitted Flicker, Henry, George Segal, Godfrey Cambridge, Gene Hackman, Diana Sands, Joan Darling, Al Freedman, Jr., and Thomas Aldredge against the headlines and heady social climate of the day. Responding to audience suggestions for sketches—"the President," "the pill," "sewage"—the players gamely gave forth with instant, biting humor. Ground rules precluded stand-up jokes; the material had to flow from the human situation, from people interacting, from the real.

Henry's first screenplay, released as *The Troublemaker* in 1964, hilariously—though the box office seemed to think otherwise—furthered his Premise connections. Directed by Theodore Flicker and starring Aldredge, Darling, Flicker, Cambridge, Freedman, and Henry, it concerned a young man's efforts to open a coffee house in Greenwich Village. Henry attributes its lack of commercial success to the fact that "the world wasn't really waiting for the final definitive attack on the cabaret-licensing system in New York City."

Within six months of joining The Premise, Henry graduated to writing for Steve Allen's TV show, something he'd grown up wanting to do. Perennially silly, but invariably motivated by smarts, Allen regaled viewers with such memorable ongoing spots as "Letters to the Editor," "The Allen Report to the Nation," "The Question Man," "The Allen Bureau of Standards," "Mad-Libs," and "Man on the Street." "Man on the Street," an interview feature, introduced Don Knotts as the quaking Mr. Morrison, Bill Dana as José Jimenez, and Tom Poston as . . . uh . . . he never could remember his name.

On *Tonight*, Allen's amalgam of braintrust insanity brought to talk-format television what Sid Caesar did to variety. Wrote critic Larry Kart of Steve Allen in the *Chicago Tribune*, he was "the first [comedian] perhaps, to find ways of being funny on television that were peculiar to that medium, and as the virtual inventor of the television talk-show, Allen has shaped our lives more profoundly than Bob Hope, David Sarnoff, and Johnny Carson put together."

From Steve Allen, Henry went to Garry Moore's program, with its history of variety fare ranging from newcomer Carol Burnett as a regular to newcomer Johnny Carson doing his impression of Jack Benny to Eleanor Roosevelt holding Open Forum with the studio audience. In 1964, Buck Henry began writing for and appearing on *That Was The Week That Was*, which was to television satire what knives are to puncture wounds. Preceding *The Smothers Brothers Comedy Hour* by three years and *Rowan & Martin's Laugh-In* by four, *NBC's Saturday Night Live* by eleven, it managed for slightly over one year to weekly lambast the news of the previous week as TV comedy never had before. Joined by such performers as Nancy Ames, Bob Dishy, Phyllis Newman, and David Frost, and such writers as Gerald Gardner (author of political humor books) and Dee Caruso (co-editor of *Sick Magazine*), Henry discovered exactly how far the prevailing limits could be pushed. He commented after the series folded, "It was more often preempted than any show on TV—by the G.O.P. I don't believe TW3 hurt the Republicans any more than they hurt themselves. They were marching forward into the past."

An eye-opener, it won considerable praise, was sometimes blacked out in the South, and scared much of the nation half to death.

Elsewhere, nowhere near New York—his life evolving along lines no way parallel to the paths taken by Henry and Brooks—in the seedy corners of Zanzibar, in the seedy bars of Corfu, a third figure came into being. His roots: the generic spy.

The secret agent of WW II's years faced down danger, survived intrigue, made the best of bad situations, and unlike his WW I counterpart, smacked more of remorse than romance. The missions rarely dazzled. Often as not, the tools of the trade consisted of a matchbook (spies frequented dark offices and dark alleys) and a gun, with the protagonist no more the master of his destiny than a mouse in a maze. In Graham Greene's *The Confidential Agent* (1939), widely considered the model for the modern espionage novel, the unwilling hero, sickened with fear, compromises himself and his principles to assure the delivery of a vital supply of coal. ("Coal used to be called black diamonds before people discovered electricity. Well, in his own country it was more valuable than diamonds, and soon it would be as rare.")

Two decades later, world-weary and waxing ironic, Greene wrote *Our Man In Havana* (1958). In it, a vacuum cleaner salesman relocates to Cuba, and, hopeful of making ends meet to support his daughter, allows government agents to enlist him as a spy. He creates false operatives, milks his expense account, and thinly disguises vacuum cleaner plans, passing them off as designs for an enemy installation. Both sides buy the ruse, acting on his fabrications, and the bodies pile up. Even in humor, Greene wrote of spies whose underlying grim, bleak, resigned disenchantment bordered on despair.

The Fifties became the Sixties. The world war turned to cold war. Spies swapped their trenchcoats for Botany 500 suits. The Eisenhower era yielded to Kennedy's Camelot, and Kennedy's favorite author, previously little appreciated in the U.S., captured the world's imagination. The author, like Greene a former spy, was Ian Fleming. His creation: James Bond.

Bond novels suddenly catapulted onto best-seller lists. Bond movies raked in fortunes. Bond, like Graham Greene's agents, spied for the British government. Beyond that, they dwelt light years apart. Bond, a flawless superman, enjoyed his work, marshalling a zillion new skills to discharge it. Urbane bon vivant. World-class gambler. Rugged sportsman. Irresistible ladies' man. Enemy of incarnate evil. Rated double zero, with a license to kill. Revitalized by peril, dreading nothing so much as ennui. The stories, primarily espionage adventures, dolloped on a soupçon of tongue-in-cheek for good measure.

But—believed Dan Melnick, a partner in the production firm of Talent Associ-

Sean Connery strikes a characteristic pose as the movies' first James Bond.

ates—why stop at tongue-in-cheek when you can go for foot-in-mouth? The world of TV, he reasoned, had come of age—a big catchphrase of the era—and stood ready for a satire of James Bond.

Brave man, this Melnick, not quite thirty when the thought first struck. Satire, according to the reigning wisdom, didn't sell on TV, and that wasn't the only strike against him. As one partner of Talent Associates (the other being the aforementioned David Susskind, *cum laude* Harvard graduate, and host of the exposé-oriented interview program *Open End*), he had committed the unpardonable sin of succeeding with television drama in an industry that rarely recognizes the possibility of cross-over. Their critically acclaimed *East Side/West Side* (1963–1964), for instance, revolving around the crusades of social workers in the slums, set a standard for television

drama (including giving Cicely Tyson the first regular dramatic role for a black woman as someone other than a domestic). Their specials confirmed the value of television as an enlightening medium.

"We were doing all these high-tone dramatic specials, *Death of a Salesman, The Crucible, The Ages of Man,* and all those things, and I had the idea to do something commercial to pay the bills for the allegedly uncommercial dramas. Actually, we made an embarrassingly large amount of money doing the dramas, and got into enormous deficit financing problems with *Get Smart*, but it didn't start out to be that way.

"I had the idea to satirize the James Bond genre because I was already a fan of James Bond novels. Much earlier I'd tried to acquire the rights when I was a programming executive at ABC, but they were unavailable. Hubbell Robinson owned them as a television property and couldn't get them on the air.* They were bigger than life. There were no precedents. Then they got national attention when Kennedy started praising them, and the movies came out. I enjoyed the real James Bond, so when I thought of satirizing, it was a way to extend James Bond and to satirize the FBI and the CIA as well.

"But our reputation, our credential, came exclusively from the serious

---

*CBS did air an adaptation of *Casino Royale* as one episode of its *Climax* series. Barry Nelson portrayed an American James Bond. But his secret agent failed to capture the public imagination. By only a few years, he was ahead of his time.

Get Smart's answer to James Bond. *Courtesy of Howard Frank Archives/Personality Photos, Inc.*

sphere. The prejudices that existed in the networks were, if not as great as today, at least beginning to be. In other words, comedy did comedy and drama did drama. So although I'd grown up working on a lot of comedy shows, I had to get a credential. And the first thing I did, I went to Mike Nichols."

Nichols, a little past thirty, had spent the previous decade reshaping comedy,

first with The Compass improvisational troupe, and then on national scale with fellow Compass alumna Elaine May. *An Evening With Mike Nichols and Elaine May* floored Broadway in 1960, their *Improvisations With Music* became the first best-selling spoken comedy record, and their television appearances established them as the number one satirical duo in the country. The two split amicably in 1961, each going on to influence other aspects of the field.

Dan Melnick ran into Nichols's agent at a Chinese restaurant, learned Nichols had "a corridor of time" between assorted projects, phoned Nichols, who liked the idea, and set about negotiating with Nichols's agent: "Mike had this nine or ten or twelve week corridor. By the time we finished analyzing and making the deal, the corridor of time was gone, so it became academic. It became clear halfway through that this was never going to happen." Reported *Newsweek* later, Nichols would not have another corridor of time until 1971.*

So Dan Melnick "started looking around. I had to find people who were in New York because our headquarters were in New York—our West Coast operation started with *Get Smart*—so I contacted another chum, Mel Brooks. I could always tell when Mel came to the office because my office was way in the back, and I would hear laughter rolling back, getting closer and closer, because Mel would come in and stop at each desk and do ten minutes, fifteen minutes, with each secretary, and he wouldn't leave until he got a really big finish at each desk, then he'd move on to the next one."

Before Talent Associates, Dan Melnick had been head of programming of ABC. Pitching *Get Smart* as a Mel Brooks comedy spoofing James Bond, he

*When 1971 rolled around, Nichols had won raves for directing *Who's Afraid of Virginia Woolf?* (1966), *The Graduate* (1967), *Catch-22* (1970), and *Carnal Knowledge* (1971), which he also produced.

sought, from his ABC successor Ed Scherick, funding for a pilot. Previously, perhaps *because* he went to a successor, Melnick had only managed to sell to ABC one of TV's most popular and fondly-remembered-as-a-pickleheaded game shows, *Supermarket Sweepstakes* (in which competitors raced maniacally against a stopwatch through supermarket aisles, filling their carts in hopes of amassing the highest register total, which is what it took to win. When the show debuted, Melnick asked a friend, "How was the press?" The friend replied, "Not since the Germans used gas in World War I has there been such bad press").

ABC gave Talent Associates the money for a Bond-like screenplay, while Melnick came to a realization: "I thought Mel was very funny, and Mel thought the concept of satirizing Bond was funny. What I didn't know is that Mel didn't really sit down ever at a typewriter and write." (Explained Brooks to the *New York Herald Tribune* in 1965, "I never learned to type. When I worked on *Show of Shows,* I noticed that the one who typed got tied down. I wanted to be the one who ran around and acted it out.")

Melnick quickly concluded that "if this was ever going to be more than a series of very funny jokes and wild motions, if it was ever going to appear on paper with marginalia, someone else was going to have to get involved, so I called Buck Henry. When I first met him, he'd been appearing with The Premise, and we'd since become friendly and yes, he was interested in my idea. Of course, the big attraction was that I had, a few years earlier, gotten rid of the conference table in our conference room at 50th and Madison and replaced it with a pool table."

Buck Henry came aboard, and remembers Talent Associates as "a very interesting place. They were doing *East Side/West Side,* plays, exceptional work, and had gifted people around. So it was a good environment to shoot pool. That was important."

Melnick forged ahead: "Buck and Mel played great pool, major pool, whereas I played a miserable game. We worked over, I don't remember how long, but it must have been seven or eight months, two or three nights, sitting around and talking and assuming Buck was making notes, and any time we had a block of any sort, Buck or Mel would say, 'Let's shoot some dollar pool.' The cost of that pilot is, to me personally, $1,123 at a dollar a pop."

As Buck Henry told the *Los Angeles Times* a month before the show debuted, "We kept breaking off to duel on the green felt and it took us five times as long as it should have. But the more we kicked it around, the funnier it got—at least to us. We decided on a secret agent named Smart—Maxwell Smart—and gave him, as his most sterling quality, a remarkable lack of insight. Nevertheless, since he was our hero, he would always win out despite his inspired inefficiency. We also gave him a number, which all operatives must have."

They bestowed upon Max a number drawn straight from the lexicon of bartenders and bouncers—86—as in "86

that guy, he's had enough," and created a script which caused ABC to gaze longingly back upon *Supermarket Sweepstakes.*

Recalls Dan Melnick, "Talent Associates had a wonderful agent at that time, the last time we had an agent. His name was Dick Dorso. Dick is a great enthusiast and a great supporter, a man with lots of theories about television and pilots, and a really terrific analytical mind. And, as we got closer to delivery of the screenplay, Dick started saying, 'I've been having these meetings with the head of the network, and I don't think he's counting on this being really funny. I think he heard the bit about spies.'

"My blood went cold. Then I finally gave the script to Dorso to give to them, and he said, 'I'm really worried about it. I'm really worried about your relationship with these people, because they want something else.' I said, 'Dick, it's late in the day. If my relationship is going to go down the tubes, it's going to go down the tubes, but I can't change what I've done.' He suggested, 'Well, they have an idea if you put a dog in shows it improves them.' So we had this two week discussion-argument about how I wasn't going to put a dog in."

ABC, in essence, sought "warm and lovable." Not only a dog, but perhaps a mom for Max to take his troubles home to. "Maybe a nice mother in a print dress, with undulant fever," Brooks noted caustically. "We figured we'd try to make them happy. So we threw in a dog." An asthmatic dog—the canine equivalent of Maxwell Smart—not quite to ABC's taste. "I suppose," added Brooks, "they felt we might offend some important dogs." When someone later complained that unlike every other dog on television, this one couldn't run, Brooks countered with the fact that of course he couldn't: he had asthma.

The script, along with jabbing at government agents, concerned a terrorist take-over of the Statue of Liberty. ABC questioned its suitability for younger audiences. Edgar Scherick was quoted as having pronounced it "dirty and un-American," though Scherick has insisted that he never called it any such thing, nor ever asked for a dog. "I just didn't think it was funny. I didn't think Dan Melnick and David Susskind had a laugh between them. If Leonard Stern had been part of the package when I had it on the table, I might have decided differently."

ABC passed on it—as they would, a few short years later, having funded the pilot, on *All in the Family*. As they would, in another decade, on *The Cosby Show*. Wrote Hal Humphrey that December in the *Los Angeles Times*, "This attitude is not surprising from a network which for years has found success with Lawrence Welk, Donna Reed, and Ozzie and Harriet."

Comments Buck Henry, "The ABC rejection was our first stroke of luck."

But it did not, at the time, seem too lucky for Dan Melnick, who sensed in the script's rejection an implication that he had let them down. Sufficiently smarting to make the beau geste, he responded that if they simply thought the script wasn't good, those were the risks of the game. If however they thought Talent Associates hadn't delivered what it said it would, "then what we would like to do is return your check." *Like* overstated the matter, with the geste running far more beau than met the eye "because to return the check I had to go find some money to put in the bank."

Weighing the offer with businesslike dispatch, ABC opted to see its money again, requesting it before the end of the following day. Talent Associates scurried to find and rebate the figure, a massive $7,500. This move Melnick attributes to stubbornness and pride, "but it was the single best move we ever made, because it then gave us back the pilot as a so-called free ball, which we could sell to anybody. We didn't have to wait for an option period to run out."

By this point, Talent Associates had brought in Leonard Stern, to oversee the West Coast operation of Talent Associates—assuming there would be a *Get Smart* to launch a West Coast operation—and to eventually become TA's third partner. In the manner of Mel Brooks and Buck Henry, he came from, knew intimately, and had personally crafted, much of the best that smart comedy had to offer.

A former Hollywood screenwriter, Stern cut his TV teeth as a panelist on the incisive and biting *How To*. Co-written by Stern and moderator Roger Price, it put all end to doubt on such quandaries as how to steal a locomotive (take a small black bag and a screwdriver and walk away several thousand times) and how to open a beer can with a thumb tack (place the tack on top of the can and hit it with a large axe).

After *How To,* Stern went to work creating scripts for Jackie Gleason's *The Jackie Gleason Show* and its showpiece *The Honeymooners*—a classic without which no discussion of TV's Golden Age is incomplete. To date, the show has inspired four separate books extolling its far-reaching contributions to popular culture; and to a large degree, it wrote the book on television character comedy.

Writing for Gleason could be all consuming. Stern, on one occasion, cancelled theater tickets in order to finish a script, "and I heard a thump. I looked around. Another writer, Marvin Marx, had fainted from sheer exhaustion." Another time, Stern and writing partner Syd Zelinka, struggling with the script in an apartment, lit the fireplace without opening the flue, and proceeded to lose themselves in thought. Zelinka smoked a pipe. Gray clouds filled the room as the fireplace backed up. "To show you the intensity with which we worked—there was a banging on the door. It was the fire department. I'd been vaguely aware of the smoke but wrote it off as Syd's pipe. He was totally ignorant of it. The alarm went off in the building, but because we were concentrating on *The Honeymooners,* our senses had dulled completely."

From *The Honeymooners* and a Writers Guild Award for its "99,000 Answer" script, Stern left the simple sphere of a civil servant bus driver to focus on a wily army con artist, as an Emmy-winning writer for Phil Silvers's "Bilko" show,

Phil Silvers as Sgt. Ernie Bilko in *You'll Never Get Rich.*

You'll Never Get Rich (1955–1959). Bilko effectively transformed the motor pool into a private country club, while the series, presented as broad comedy, nonetheless scored on several satirical levels, depicting an army that not only tolerated a Sergeant Bilko in its ranks, but genuinely (shades of the Maxwell Smart phenomenon) depended on him.

From *Bilko,* Stern segued to the position of head writer for Steve Allen, introducing "Man on the Street," which accelerated the trend of topical humor; then to founding Heyday Productions, where he created, wrote, produced, and directed one of the funniest failed shows in the history of television (*I'm Dickens, He's Fenster,* 1962–1963).

Stern next immersed himself in *Get*

Leonard Stern flanked by John Astin (left) and Marty Ingels (right), of *I'm Dickens—He's Fenster. Courtesy of Howard Frank Archives/Personality Photos, Inc.*

Smart. Though ABC didn't want it, other, larger networks remained. Grant Tinker, later to be *the* Grant Tinker (of MTM Enterprises and NBC honcho fame), represented the voice of NBC programming on the West Coast. He first noticed *Smart* when, legend has it, someone thrust a copy of the script in his hand in front of the Beverly Hills Hotel shortly after a gang from Canada came down to blow up the Statue of Liberty.

The thought had briefly passed through Mel Brooks's mind to play agent 86 himself. But by the time they presented the property to ABC, it was to star Tom Poston. Poston, most visible today as George Utley on *Newhart*, back then captured the nation's affection as one of Steve Allen's Men On The

Street—the one who couldn't remember his name. This won him the Best Supporting Actor (Continuing Character) in a Comedy Series Emmy in 1959 and it, along with appeareances as a regular on *Pantomime Quiz* and *To Tell The Truth*, accounted for his considerable public favor.

However, NBC did not have Tom Poston under contract. They had Don Adams under contract, and fancied him for the title role.

Don Adams hailed originally from New York City. Born Donald James Yarmy in 1927—one of three kids of a Hungarian Jewish father and an Irish Catholic mother—he quickly earned the reputation as an embarrassingly "one-and-a-half-sewer" man at stickball, while his playmate Larry Storch (later of *The Larry Storch Show* and *F Troop*) had a three-sewer range, and their friend James Komack (who went on to write and direct *My Favorite Martian*, create and serve as executive producer of *Chico and the Man* and *Welcome Back, Kotter,* and to write for, direct, and appear in *Get Smart*) observed him to be "a funny runner." Of the company of future comedians, Komack long after reminisced, "You couldn't open your mouth without being topped.

"And I remember, for some reason, a lot of them did impressions. That was the big thing in our neighborhood. We'd go to a party at night, boys and girls, and instead of telling jokes, we'd sit around and guys would do impressions. Clark Gable, Jimmy Cagney, those voices. They'd develop them. Larry Storch did great impressions. His brother, Jay Storch, did too. A kid named Greenie Horowitz did a good Clark Gable, but he never went into show business. And Don Yarmy did impressions. That was in the West End neighborhood. Then, as they gravitated toward show business, that was downtown, they hung around with guys like Lenny Bruce, who did impressions."

Don Yarmy didn't like school: "That's where you mouth someone else's words, where you're a mimic, a brain picker. They ask a question and you answer. Right. Wrong. They were wasting my time. Ma tried her best, but I was the great truant of my day. Mr. Hooky. I was left back in the sixth grade. It was a miracle I ever finished. Three times a week, maybe four, I'd head for school and never make it. I'd end up on 42nd Street. I saw movies all the time. It was half my youth, my time in the movies. I saw Rhett Butler a hundred times.

"I thought Bogart was the suavest, sexiest, coolest man in the world. I loved all those rotten little guys, Cagney, Garfield, Widmark. Those little guys were tough, they were cool, and they were only about 5′8″." Yarmy grew to 5′9″.

Graduating from elementary school, he attempted high school at the behest of his restaurant-manager dad and, succumbing to impatience, quit school, left home, became a construction and steel worker, then lied about his age (sixteen) to join the Marines. This he did not do alone, but with his twin cousins Bill and Bob Karvelas, two beefy young football players from New York who moved to Pittsburgh when, says Bob, "a scout came up and saw us playing in Van Cortland Park. He talked my mother into enrolling us in high school in Pittsburgh—I think we were the only two guys paid to play high school ball—then Don came down to spend a weekend with us and stayed two years.

"When the war broke out, the three of us decided to join the Marine Corps. You had to be in great shape to get in the Marines. You had to bite an apple and have a perfect bite. We told Cuz, 'You know, we're football players. We have scholarships. We're big and strong. But they aren't going to take you. You weigh 120 pounds.'

"We took our physicals. Bill and I flunked out because we were ten pounds overweight, but Don passed. So what we decided to do—this is how close the three of us were in those days—we decided to go on a strict diet, lose our ten or twelve pounds, then all three of us got in the Marine Corps.

"The three of us went to boot camp together, and we went overseas together to Samoa, and that's where they split us up. Bill and I were standing on top of a mountain, while they were sending Don to Guadalcanal. We saw the ship pulling out and tears poured out of our eyes. I said, 'There goes Cuz. He's not gonna make it without us.' "

"Cuz" saw Guadalcanal, saw action, got shot, got blackwater fever (fatal in most cases), blew up like a balloon, and informed the corpsman who sat his deathwatch, "I'm not going any place." To the surprised delight of the Brothers

Don Adams on the *Get Smart* set ("Spy, Spy, Birdie"), flanked by the brothers Karvelas. **Robert Karvelas** (Larabee) is on the left. *Courtesy of Robert Karvelas.*

Karvelas, he survived the war—after a total of two and a half years in hospitals—and returned to the States to serve as a drill instructor.

After receiving an honorable discharge, Yarmy enrolled at the Terry Art Institute and became a commercial artist: "I was never very happy at that and not very good at it." Next he hitchhiked to Miami, met a New York friend named Jay Lawrence (formerly Jay Storch), and with him did impersonations at a club on the beach.

From Miami and on to the circuit of dumps, dives, and merely repellent bookings synonymous with the saloon circuit, he developed his style, his act, and a certain reluctance to persist under such soul-squelching conditions. Fea-

tured one time with Mae West's nightclub show, he went on stage as the emcee announced, "There will be no ordering of food and beverages when Miss West appears. So order now." Waiters and patrons yelled frantic orders, banged chairs, and slammed trays, throughout— if not oblivious to—the monologue.

Then he married Dell Adams, had four children, and found other work, including cashiering in a club where he'd once performed: "You couldn't gypsy around in strip joints when you had kids and needed a steady paycheck." At one point, he turned his skills to cartographic and engineering drawings: "If some of the bridges in Washington, D.C., bulge, I'm responsible. I didn't know anything about engineering drawings."

In 1954, word came of his mother's death. He returned to New York for the funeral. Once there, and hearing that *Arthur Godfrey Talent Scouts* was holding auditions, he tried out. With the Godfrey auditions, the *Yarmy* changed to *Adams*. (Four years in the Marine Corps at the end of every alphabetical muster gave Donald James Yarmy reason enough to want to step to the head of the line.) Moreover, Adams clicked.

Engagements, and other successful auditions, followed. Herb Sanford, producer of the first Garry Moore show, in *Ladies and Gentlemen, The Garry Moore Show*, tells the story of Adams's try-out there.

Don took his place at the mike. 'Mr. Moore, Don Adams is not my real name. My father was a famous star in the theater. I don't want to trade on his

Don Adams in the early Sixties.

prime exposure on Perry Como's show, Ed Sullivan's, and Jack Paar's, he added comedy writing for *Moore* and other programs, meanwhile playing prestige nightclubs like New York's chick East Side boîte, the Ruban Bleu.

Among the impressions making up his act, his wily detective stood out. In it, the pompous sleuth assembles all the suspects in a room, summing up every last shred of fact related to the murder case, confusing them and himself. Adams based the voice on "the way William Powell talked in the old *Thin Man* movies. He sounded clever and sophisticated, but I exaggerated it a little and it came out funny."

One person who saw the act, Bill Dana, had just abandoned an act of his own: "My partner, Gene Wood and I, had been pages at NBC following that traditional route. Then we were a comedy team, but I hated the circuit so we very amicably split up. What I wanted to do was write. I went to see this young comic whom the people managing me were going to represent.

"I saw Don performing. The highlight of his act was this detective with that sort of 'There's your man, inspector. A liar, a cheat, a thief, and a homicidal maniac. But he's my son and I love him.' He was funny, and I said I thought I'd like to write for him.

"Remember Marjorie Morningstar's swank apartment in Wouk's novel, 300 Central Park West? Imogene Coca and her then husband Bob Burton had a posh duplex apartment there, on the twentieth and twenty-first floors. I had a back injury and was on unemployment, so

name—but if I were to tell you, a tear would come to your eye, there'd be a lump in your throat. You know him—I know you loved him—oh, well, I might as well tell you his name [long pause, blank look]. Funny, I was talking to him just the other day. His name is—[sneaking a look in the inside pocket of his jacket]. I know I had it here somewhere—it's . . .'

"At that point, Garry pressed the button and spoke into the talkback: 'That's all we need.' He then hastened into the studio.

"Don, looking distraught, said, 'But you haven't heard my act.'

"'We don't need to hear the rest right now,' replied Garry. 'With a start like that it's got to be great. You're hired.'"

Adams soon after, according to the *Saturday Evening Post*, "may have done more guest shots than any other performer of that period." To frequent

when Imogene went on tour, she asked me to be her apartment sitter, giving me the dignity of not putting me up. That's where I was staying when Don came to see me. After getting past the doormen, who accosted him, he took the elevator up to this glitzy, highly polished place, and I answered the door wearing Bob Burton's smoking jacket. Don's eyes came out on three-inch stems. It looked like wall-to-wall money, like I was some rich playboy wanting to dabble at comedy writing, so I went along with the gag.

"At one point, I had to find an address. When I pulled out my wallet, my unemployment check fell out. I just broke up, and Don saw the humor of it. I said, 'Hey, you're at least working.' "

They reached an agreement, one incredibly succulent fruit of which formed a new piece in Adams's act, a "British In India" riff. In this routine, a takeoff on movies such as *The Lives of the Bengal Lancers*, Lieutenant (pronounced Leftenant) Faversham confronted the Oxford-educated Mohammed Sidney Kahn. Adams did both voices:

"Not so fast, smarty Kahn. You think you've got me, but I have you surrounded by the entire mounted Seventeenth Bengal Lancers."

"I don't believe you."

"Ah, would you believe the First Bengal Lancers?"

"No."

"How about Gunga Din on a donkey?"

More historical than hysterical, it nonetheless sowed its seed. The formula echoed itself in "Defense Attorney,"

"The Football Coach," and other routines. Adams, hotter than ever, got on Steve Allen's show. Recalls Dana, "We had such *chutzpah*. Sometimes we'd leave the tier where the dressing rooms were, come down the metal staircases, and not have the punch line till Don was being introduced." Adams, once more, scored big. Dana, behind the scenes, attracted enough of Steve Allen's attention to find himself on the show's writing staff (eventually succeeding Leonard Stern as head writer).

"And," according to reviewer Cleveland Amory, "when Mr. Allen found that Mr. Dana got more laughs reading his own lines during rehearsals than the performers did saying them on the show, before you could say Hack Robinson, he got a chance as a performer."

In November of 1959, Bill Dana went out before the cameras as his own character, an endearing little guy named José Jiménez. Trusting innocent José spoke mangled English and embodied a blank slate on which the world, for all its efforts, could not leave its graffiti. Instead, the world took him to its collective heart. Stardom led to records, led to a part written in for José on *The Danny Thomas Show*. On *Thomas*, he played a lovesick elevator operator in Danny's apartment building. Afraid to approach the girl of his dreams, he asks Danny to write love letters for him. José can't—he writes in an accent too.

The *Thomas* show, which in 1960 had spun off *The Andy Griffith Show*, in 1963 spun off *The Bill Dana Show*. This series, written by Dana with felicitous contribu-

for British in India $25,635.10

Don Adams (as leftenant Faversham confronting Mohammed Selvey Kahn)

Adams (as Faversham) Not so fast, Smarty Kahn — you may think you've got me — but I've got you surrounded by the entire mounted 17th Bengal Lancers)

Adams (as Kahn) I don't believe that.

Adams (as Faversham) Would you believe the <u>First</u> Bengal Lancers?

Adams (as Kahn) No.

Adams (as Faversham) How about Gunga Din on a donkey?)

stay over for tonight show only?

"The original 'Would you believe. . . ?' Pencil on yellow paper, covered with lacquer, and 25+ years old" from the personal collection of Bill Dana.

tions from a young Garry Marshall, a young Jerry Belson, and the young director Jay Sandrich, presented José Jiménez as a bellhop at the Park Central Hotel.

In its first season, Dana teamed with Gary Crosby, who played another bellhop. When the chemistry didn't happen, Crosby left, and Don Adams, fresh from two years on *The Perry Como Show* (and notoriety with the gag line "You really know how to hurt a guy" which quickly passed into the vernacular) stepped in as nasal, self-important yet remarkably inept hotel detective Byron Glick.

Adams made the move because "I was doing a lot of variety shows in New York.* I was doing them because I wrote television material, and most nightclub comedians wrote nightclub material which in those days you couldn't do on television. And then Bill Dana called and asked if I wanted to do seven out of thirteen of his shows. I asked what the money was, and from that angle I'd have done much better signing with a variety show like Jimmy Dean or Como, so I had to make a choice—between taking one show that was situation comedy, a different type of comedy than I'd been doing, or continuing to do stand-up on variety shows for a good deal more money. I was recently married at the time [to his second wife, Dorothy Bracken, a former June Taylor Dancer on *The Jackie Gleason Show*] so the

*In the same years, he came out with a number of comedy albums featuring "the voice." He also provided the voice of Tennessee Tuxedo—the penguin who constantly sought advice from Mr. Whoopee—for the cartoon series of the same name.

money would have come in handy, but I decided that I wanted to do situation comedy, particularly since Bill Dana was a friend."

The chemistry between Adams and Dana fairly exploded. Scenes from their pairing remain classics today.

In the episode "What Elephant?", hotel manager Mr. Phillips (Jonathan Harris) has banished all pets from the premises. Glick, as hotel detective, must enforce the edict, which means insisting that José part with his rabbits. In dispatching them, José temporarily adopts a baby elephant in a frilly bonnet. Glick storms into José's room and, leaning his hand on the elephant, demands, "Well, José did you get rid of the rabbits?" Then, realizing he hasn't propped himself against a post, Glick does an amazed—and amazing—doubletake.

In the take, in the face, in the fool-in-charge attitude, one can hardly miss a germinal Maxwell Smart. Smartlike too, in several episodes, are Glick's references to Mr. Phillips as "Chief," along with variations on the "Would you believe?" gag—according to the original formula, or revised to give the punchline to José. For instance, in the episode "Blood For Two Turnips," Glick tries to convince José that they can ignore the company blood drive:

Glick: Don't you see what Phillips is trying to do? He wants us to give our blood, right?

José: That's right.

Glick: You know why?

José: Sure. So they would have it at the blood bank.

Adams as Glick on *The Bill Dana Show,* with Jonathan Harris (left) and Bill Dana (right). *Courtesy of Howard Frank Archives/Personality Photos, Inc.*

Glick: Fiddlesticks, José. Phillips is just trying to weaken us. He takes our blood. We're too anemic to do our work properly, and that gives him an excuse to cut our salaries.

José: Oh, I don't believe that.

Glick: You don't believe that?

José: No.

Glick: Well, how about this? His wife is a vampire.

José: Phillips's wife a vampire! No—Mrs. Phillips doesn't even like baseball.

Adams's Glick spoke with the distinctive, exaggerated William Powell rasp that would later crackle from the lips of Maxwell Smart. "But," says Adams, "the producers of the show, Danny Thomas and Sheldon Leonard—evidently they said this after the first *Dana* show, but it wasn't reported to me until long after it happened, and I forget which one of them said it to the other—one said, 'We've got to get rid of that guy,' and the other answered, 'Yeah, he talks funny.' And—this is what I was told—I almost got fired for using that voice."

Far from getting fired, as the *Dana* series went on, Glick's part got bigger. It occurred to Dana to pull back, perhaps eventually spinning things off to Adams entirely. But in January 1965, NBC cancelled the program and people went their separate ways.

As Adams reconstructs the chain of events, "I was under contract to NBC and had a year to choose a pilot. This happened when CBS wanted me to do something for them called *Lawyer,* so Sheldon Leonard countered with this offer of a contract if I would stay with his operation. Then NBC called and said they had a property, and I said, 'Well, I have a whole year to pick and choose, and I'm not going to rush into anything because it's now the end of the pilot season and it would have to be done right away, and I don't want to make the decision like that. We talked about it, and they told me it was a James Bond spoof, which seemed interesting, but I really didn't want to. Then I asked who wrote it, and they said Mel Brooks and Buck Henry, so I said, 'I'll do it.' All I had to hear were those two names."

Within months, NBC plugged Adams into *Get Smart*. His Byron Glick made for the perfect parody of a secret agent. When *Smart* aired in September, there were those who believed it a spinoff of *Dana* (in turn spunoff from *Thomas,* which by then had birthed not only *Dana* and *Griffith,* but *Gomer Pyle, U.S.M.C.*—by way of *Griffith*—as well. Since at the time *Thomas* had the lock on spinoff fever, it qualified as an educated guess).

But the concept and script, of course, existed long before. There remained only a matter of adjustment in minor details. As Leonard Stern remembers: "NBC wanted us to use Don Adams. Beyond that, Dick Dorso felt we had to make some changes in the script in order for it to appeal to NBC. He was very desirous of having a meeting at which we could hatch new directions. I read the script and felt it was excellent. What we lacked at the time was a signature, so I developed the door sequence, and discussed one or two other modest points. Dick also wanted to plan a strategy, an approach which would convince Grant Tinker. I, not having been present at the rejection, didn't feel a need for extensive rehearsal. But he was apprehensive, having apparently prepared himself for another rejection. I had no idea the degree to which this imbedded itself in his mind.

"We met with Grant Tinker, whom I didn't know other than by reputation, in Dick's hotel room. We were sitting in what amounted to an isosceles triangle, with me seated the farthest distance from both of them, about ten feet away. When we'd disposed of the amenities, Grant said to Dick that he liked the script very much and wanted to pursue it. Dick said, 'Don't worry. Leonard can fix it.'

"I thought that they must have been old friends, and that Dick was putting Grant on. It didn't register that this was a Pavlovian response to anticipated rejection. But the conversation progressed, and I finally realized Dick wasn't hearing Grant. He was assuring Grant that there were new ways to go, and not to worry."

Stern, a tall man at 6'3"—or, stretched out laterally, a long one—extended his leg and foot, hoping to unobtrusively signal Dick Dorso. "I continued to make myself longer and lower, without success insofar as reaching Dick, and I finally got into such an awkward position that when both men looked in my direction, they wondered why I had only my upper torso on the seat and my feet extended across the room."

Stern explained his contortions. Everyone laughed. Negotiations went smoothly therafter. *Get Smart* would happen after all.

Bill Dana once said, "Certainly some of the magic has to be that my show sank, but Don's unique and marvelous character was able to swim to a safe shore."

In a manner fully in keeping with the life and times of Maxwell Smart, the climactic scene of the first *Get Smart* in fact took place on the water, aboard a KAOS garbage scow.

Recently re-released by Raven Records of Australia and distributed throughout the U.S. *Courtesy of Raven Records, P.O. Box 92, Camberwell, Australia 3124.*

2

THE IMPORTANCE OF BEING SMART

"Smart: ME *smerten*, fr OE *smeortan*, akin to pain, hurt, Gk *smerdnos* terrible, fearful, Skt *mrdnati, mardati,* he pulverizes, crushes, destroys . . . and perhaps L *mort, mors,* death—more at murder."

— *Webster's Third New International Dictionary*

"Get smart: get fresh, brazen out, teach one's grandmother to suck eggs . . ."

— *Roget's Thesaurus, entry 885.7*

Across the country—as the Fifties gave way to the Sixties, as the baby boomers entered college, as the Eisenhower era yielded to Kennedy's Camelot—intellectual fervor vibrated like a tuning fork. Poi-ing! Aren't we smart! And aren't we smart to *be* so smart!

We may have celebrated the love generation, but above all, we reveled in our brains. After decades of putting the premium on getting smart—after hearing for years how smart would get us better jobs and better lives in a better world—we got smart, and wondered what to do with it. In retrospect, the smarts we acquired may largely have been misguided smarts. But our hearts were in the right place.

Maxwell Smart, the quintessential misguided Smart, wore *his* heart in the right place. He sported a phone in his shoe and a cigarette lighter in his telephone, but his heart remained on his sleeve. He cared about the battle of niceness versus rottenness. He even, astoundingly, managed to accomplish the things he'd been sent out to do. Bungling virtually every step of the way, but seizing the brass ring in the end. A good man, no doubt about it. Extremely qualified—anyhow, basically qualified—to be a hotel detective.

The quintessential misguided Smart. *Courtesy of Howard Frank Archives/Personality Photos, Inc.*

But a secret agent for the U.S. government?

The words *get smart* embody a direct command: wise up; learn before it's too late; get your act together; wake up and smell the coffee. *Get Smart,* at the same time, connotes the attitude of a smart aleck, as in "Don't get smart with me, young man." Either way, the title accosts the viewer. *Hey, we're talking to you!*

Leonard Stern wasn't convinced he liked it. "If you don't know what a program is about and you hear it's called *Get Smart,* you may expect a game show. We debated the title at great length. We considered the variation

Maxwell
GET ^ SMART

but it lost out. What's interesting is that it became the right title. I've always liked the example of *Green Grow The Lilacs,* which became *Away We Go,* which became *Oklahoma!* Logically, the least likely choice would be *Oklahoma!* It almost seems detrimental to designate one state to the exclusion of, then, forty-seven others. But it's the only right title now."

Call a show *Get (anything),* and whoever responds, responds in effect with the question, "What should I come back with?" On the surface, the answer here is "Maxwell Smart, Agent 86," but it might as well be, "Try coming back with reality. There's the myth of James Bond, the legend of Robin Hood, the fairy tale Cinderella. Now come down to earth, down to size. Get smart."

Graham Greene, in the wartime British Secret Intelligence Service before becoming a best-selling novelist, knew the stark reality of espionage (*The Confidential Agent*), the warped reality of espionage (*Our Man in Havana*), and the ludicrous reality of espionage (everywhere). His autobiography *Ways of Escape* describes the night he strolled the streets of Riga watching horses and prostitutes, oblivious to the revolution happening around him. On another occasion, "when I was going to stay at the embassy in Poland, a silly man had asked me to take in a tape recorder disguised as a wristwatch, and the ass produced some huge thing as big as a wireless."

Of those three realities, *Get Smart* focused on the ludicrously real. Satire generally does. A poke in the eye with a sharp stick has its impact, but not as an experience people seek out a second time for fun. Yet, deliver a whack on the head with a pillow—people generally come back for more.

Get Smart trafficked in metaphorical pillows, setting itself apart from, on the one hand, the bleakly disenchanted *Spy Who Came in From the Cold* (the movie came out the same year as *Get Smart*), and Milton Berle's ill-fated, merely silly, spy spoof pilot *Follow That Man* (1962) on the other.

James Bond, by the way, was hardly the only offending myth. To Mel Brooks, the standard family sitcoms spewed easily as much cotton candy: "In their supposedly true-to-life little episodes, they avoided anything approaching reality. For years I've always wanted to see an honest family TV series— maybe something called *Half of Father Knows Best*. The other half of him was paralyzed by a stroke in 1942 when he suspected we might lose the war . . . I was sick of looking at all those nice sensible situation comedies. They were such distortions of life. If a maid ever took over my house like Hazel, I'd set her hair on fire."

All things considered, the image of Brooks assaulting Hazel offers more giggles than did *Hazel*'s entire five years on the air. Just as humor makes the truth work, truth makes the humor work. "I wanted to do a crazy, unreal comic-strip

kind of thing about something besides a family. No one had ever done a show about an idiot before. I decided to be the first." Comedy, after all, is a "red ball. If you throw it against a soft, funny wall, it will not come back. But if you throw it against the hard wall of ultimate reality, it will bounce back and be very lively." In a nutshell, "the greatest comedy plays against the greatest tragedy." An example: "I maintain there is nothing you cannot deal with in comic terms and make a point. I proved that by spoofing Hitler in *The Producers*."

Maxwell Smart, in the first draft a simple yutz in the employ of what purported to be the most sophisticated espionage system in the world, fulfilled these needs. Maxwell Smart, played by Don Adams, fulfilled them and added one element more. He glicked. Did the Byron Glick (a.k.a. William Powell) voice. Did the Byron Glick (a.k.a. "British in India") type of catchphrases. "Would you believe. . . ?" passed from Don Adams's nightclub act to the *Dana* show to the revised *Get Smart* script.

"The point is," says Leonard Stern, "the script had been turned down, rejected, might not have been developed if Don Adams hadn't been under contract. We never had him in mind. Using him was Grant Tinker's proviso if we wanted NBC to buy *Get Smart*. But once you see Don in it, you say: 'What strange forces must have been at work!' Because he's the ideal person, had the perfect voice, delivery, and style."

At last, came the time to shoot the pilot. Mel Brooks urged that Howard

Morris, veteran comic actor of Broadway, *Your Show of Shows, Caesar's Hour,* and *The Andy Griffith Show,* and director of films and sitcoms (e.g. *The Andy Griffith Show*) be brought in to direct. Brooks and Morris had a friendship going back years, one based largely on Brooks's penchant for robbing Morris by threatening physical violence. (Once, in the *Caesar* days, just prior to Christmas, Brooks demanded Morris's wallet. When Morris resisted, Brooks gave signs of preparing to beat him up. Morris relinquished the wallet. Brooks returned it to him as a Christmas gift the next day. The following Yuletide, as the two rowed across a lake in Central Park, Brooks again confiscated the wallet and ordered Morris out of the boat. Morris tied his shoes around his neck and swam to shore. Morris got the wallet back for Christmas yet one more time.)

Morris recalls partaking of the *Get Smart* experience "with the insane cooperation of Mel and Buck and Don and other people who were involved. I think we shot for about eight days. And doing comedy isn't funny. It's hard, disciplined, demanding work.

"When you do a pilot, you're kind of digging to see what it is. You're not aware of doing anything great when you do it. You just do the best you can. What those guys had written was so right that doing it straight and honest—I use these words very loosely—was the answer to all the problems. The more reality we could get into it, the better. Whatever satire on current events we touched was already written in. The dopey CIA guys were all pretty well personified by this character. All we had to do was give it a basis of reality. There was a sense of revelation about it."

Revelation and careening disaster. Notes Don Adams, "Shooting the pilot was totally chaotic. Almost fistfights on the pilot, because there were so many top creative minds involved. You can't really analyze comedy, so you argue about these subjective questions, and have power struggles over which way of doing something is funnier. Everyone had a definite opinion."

Along with the heated opinions came imponderables and unpredictables in waves. One day Leonard Stern had a call: "They said, 'you'd better come down to the set. We seem to be drifting out to sea.' They were in San Pedro, shooting a fight on a barge, and the camera crew, in order to shoot it, was also at sea, on a flat-bottomed boat. They became aware of the two boats drifting apart, and had innumerable discussions as to who and how and why somebody must have started up the barge, the natural assumption being that the camera boat couldn't be moving because it was flat-bottomed and cumbersome, and we would have felt the vibrations.

"Ultimately, we learned that a fishing boat had come by, with its nets underwater, had caught our anchor, and hauled us along. We stopped shooting and sent for a diver to extricate us, but all the divers who lived in the nearby vicinity were working elsewhere that day. We finally found a retired diver, in his seventies, who volunteered to do the work.

We lost about six hours that day before we were unsnarled."

Yet a few minutes of the pilot—largely the opening teaser—sold the series to NBC's affiliates. The strategy proved entirely worthy of Maxwell Smart: the highlight reel the affiliates saw comprised the only minutes ready in time for the screening.

Adams continues: "We finished the pilot, and we were sitting around all depressed because it had weaknesses, and NBC called to say they were having affiliates down in New York, but they had so many pilots they couldn't show them all. They wanted to know if we had six minutes that we could show. We said, 'Hey, we've got thirty dynamite minutes we can show. It's going to be hard for us to pick out six minutes.' Hard. We had exactly six minutes that were hysterically funny, so we put on a big bluff. 'How soon do you need it?' They said right away. We said, 'Guys, come on, it's all funny. Cut it down to six minutes?' Then we rushed down and picked up the six minutes, edited them, and sent the reel to New York."

Adds Leonard Stern, "We had the distinct advantage at that time of being short and funny and not having any of our weak points exposed.* What we did not know, and I don't think NBC anticipated, was the presence at the dinner of a reviewer from the *New York Herald Tribune*. He wrote accolades, five months before it went on the air, before the network had really aligned all their affiliates and committed them. We came off looking very, very good by comparison."

Said the *Tribune* in part, "Some of the network's brass are so high on the show they can hardly contain their enthusiasm. 'I hate,' said one of them, 'to sound trite, but I think it could start a new trend in comedy.'"

In due course—more like overdue course—the ready-for-broadcast pilot episode came together. The black-and-white episode opens, even before the credits, with a view of the Capitol, and a serious voice extolling the importance of CONTROL, the top-secret government agency in Washington, D.C. The camera sweeps in on Washington's Symphony Hall, with a concert in progress. The voice continues: a man sits in this very hall, a key agent for CONTROL, one trained never to disclose the vital role he plays for his fellow citizens.

Wow. Sssshh. Secret . . .

His foot rings *Briiaaangggg*. Now everyone in the hall, hearing his foot, gapes in his direction.† He excuses himself, disappears into a closet, removes his shoe, then the sole of his shoe, and talks to it.

---

*Something else on the film that didn't get into the affiliates' reel: footage, taken on the set, of Don Adams getting word that his daughter Stacey Noel had just been born.

†For those disputing the scene's realism, the author of this book attests that she once attended a major orchestral concert in New York City during the water shortage. The man who escorted her, a prominent figure in the Save Water campaign, excused himself when his beeper sounded its alarm. As he left, he explained to the strangers around him, "Drought alert."

The shoe phone. *Courtesy of Howard Frank Archives/Personality Photos, Inc.*

Shoe phone (Mel Brooks's idea*)—inscrutably practical gadget. To use it, the agent has to bend over and take his shoe off. If he has to swing into action suddenly, he'll have one shoe to run with, and one in his hand. If people see him operating it, they're bound to stare relentlessly. Once on the foot, with every step the agent takes, the presumably complex instrument and its intricate circuitry slam onto the ground and rattle internally. When employing the shoe phone for speaking, the agent holds his face against the one part of his apparel

*Rumored to have occurred to Brooks when a phone rang in his office. Exaggerating his reaction to which phone to answer, he grabbed his shoe and answered *it.*

which unremittingly grinds into everywhere he has stepped. Who would want to use a shoe phone? A sane person? Aunt Rose? No—says *Get Smart*—not them. A government spy.

The agent in the closet talks to his shoe. His first words: "This is Smart." (Sure, brilliant. An idiot named Smart. What other series in the history of the medium ever revealed itself so succinctly, so fast?) "Maxwell Smart. Agent 86." His caller, we learn, is the Chief. Smart must leave right away, but can't. The closet door won't budge. Just as well. Max hasn't put his shoe back on yet.

After shooting the lock off the closet door—in this temple reserved for sweet sounds of symphonic music—Smart leaves for CONTROL headquarters. (In the highlight reel sent to the affiliates, Smart returns to his seat. Whatever plot is afoot, he has a ticket and plans to use it. But his shoe rings again, disrupting the concert again, blowing the secrecy of his identity again. Back to the closet, which he can't this time occupy, since another agent has beat him to it. So 86 heads for CONTROL.)

This tease—this setting up of situation prior to the opening credits and music—broke comedic precedent. TV comedies hadn't done it. TV dramas, cop shows, adventure series, had. Here *Smart* hit hard the notion of humor rooted in truth, by introducing itself in the idiom of a sort of *Naked City* of international intrigue, pitched slightly askew.

Get Smart's theme tune (written by Irving Szathmary, Bill Dana's innovative musicologist brother) swells. *Dumdadum! Dum! Dumdadum! Dum!*

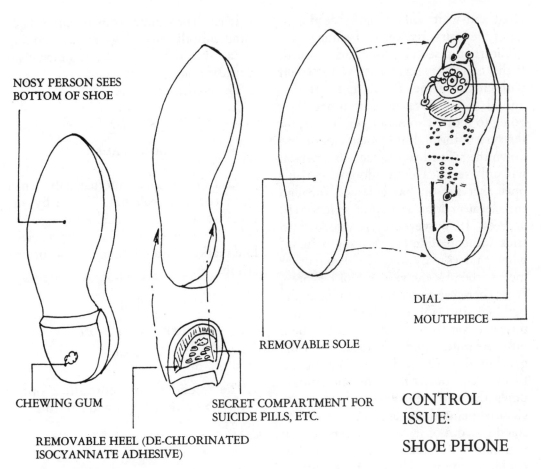

NOSY PERSON SEES
BOTTOM OF SHOE

REMOVABLE SOLE

DIAL
MOUTHPIECE

CHEWING GUM

SECRET COMPARTMENT FOR
SUICIDE PILLS, ETC.

REMOVABLE HEEL (DE-CHLORINATED
ISOCYANNATE ADHESIVE)

CONTROL
ISSUE:

SHOE PHONE

Courtesy of James B. Kruger.

Dumdadadada Dumdadadada Dadada Dum! As the vigorous cadences follow Maxwell from the symphony hall out to the street, out to his car, to the deep U-turn the car takes in order to park directly across the street at CONTROL's secret entrance, the Dada* as much as the dumb is unmistakably underscored.

*Dada: The international nihilistic movement stressing the role of the absurd, random, and unpredictable in artistic creation.

Across the screen flash two words:

GET

SMART

Opening credits accompany the signature "door sequence," created and shot by Leonard Stern. The camera tightens on an elevator door. The door opens, revealing that it conceals not an elevator car, but steps. Smart marches down the stairs. A heavy red stripe (black in the black-and-white pilot) marks dead-center of the stairs, red-carpet fashion.

Clearly top secret. No, clearly absurd. If the stairs are secret, they're better off without the stripe. If the stairs are disguised as an elevator, whom are they going to fool? If someone can only enter the system through the outside door and down the striped stairs, then that person will only see the elevator door subterfuge once that person has emerged through the elevator door and spun around 180 degrees. If, however, it is intended to trick someone like the cleaning woman, who wanders in by some accidental other means, then by the very fact of her presence, there are easier means to enter the building. But, for argument's sake, suppose she wants to use the elevator. She'll push the button and wait for it, until she gets bored, until she dies waiting, or until the door opens for someone coming down the stairs. By virtue of this sham elevator being there, she is persuaded to stand in front of it, waiting, expecting it will come. But the danger of this happening is remote. There is no button to push to summon the elevator.

There have got to be better ways to avoid calling attention to a secret staircase.

Commented Leonard Stern in 1986, "Over the years I've wondered if I might have been better off just starting with the elevator dial, and having the hand move from basement up, or from the higher floor down, to establish an elevator in the viewer's mind. Pull back, open the doors, and reveal there's a staircase. If we do it again, I'll do that."

Then the cleaning woman can lose her mind entirely, watching the dial, looking for a button that isn't there, hearing no elevator noises . . .

The credits continue.

Starring

DON ADAMS

Steel doors open automatically, on a short corridor sealed at the end by another set of doors. Smart strides to the second set of doors, along the straight line marked by a continuation of the red stripe.

And

BARBARA FELDON

as #"99"

The second set of doors slides open, revealing more corridor and a third set of doors.

Created by

MEL BROOKS

with

BUCK HENRY

Each set of credits diminishes in size to follow Smart deeper into the system, from door to door. The third set of doors opens, this time with the panel rising to let Smart through.

Produced by

JAY SANDRICH

Revealing more corridor and what look like iron bars.

Executive Producer

LEONARD STERN

The bars are not bars. They are bars painted on doors. Good plan. A cleaning woman who gets this far, seeing the bars, will lose interest and go home. She won't discern that her inability to see through them betrays that they can't be bars. She won't go over and touch them, and conclude it's another set of doors. She won't even be curious. Not when confronted by deception of such high caliber.

Smart passes through the last set of doors. No more corridor. No more doors. Just a phone booth. Lifting the receiver, he deposits his coin. The floor of the phone booth plummets swiftly. Smart vanishes. Naturally. If the elevator is a staircase with a red stripe, then something else—might as well be a phone booth, which he doesn't need for phoning as long as he has his shoe—has to be the elevator.

Besides, this way the government can collect a dime off every agent (and cleaning woman) needing to visit CONTROL.

"It's like a dream," observes Buck Henry. "Walking what might as well be a mile, to a phone booth. It's really irrational, surreal, and a very important part of the show."

Smart enters the Chief's (Ed Platt's) office, punches his card in the time clock, and learns that the fate of the na-

tion depends on him. Pleased and eager, he slaps the desk, flipping an ashtray and its contents onto the Chief. Impeccable timing. Nation, bend over, pick up your ashes, and kiss your fate good-bye.

Villains, it seems, have stolen the in-thermo ray and kidnapped its inventor, Professor Dante. Smart concludes that the evil KAOS (which he later in the episode defines as an international criminal organization founded circa 1957) must be back in action. The Chief says KAOS's unknown Mr. Big demands $100 million ransom not to use the ray. Smart demands—

The Cone of Silence (Buck Henry's idea). The Chief, plainly pained, accedes. A pair of connecting, transparent half bubbles descends from the ceiling, its appearance not unlike a gigantic plastic double-battery blister pack. One sphere encloses Max. One covers the Chief. They commence to yell at the tops of their lungs, because the Cone of Silence renders their exchange completely secure with regard to either of them hearing it, although the clerk outside the Chief's office, on the other side of the door, can make out every word. Not a moment too soon, the Cone is lifted.

Behind the Chief's desk, the viewer can't have failed to see a window framing an unconvincing painted skyline. The viewer concludes, perhaps, "cheap set." But no. It isn't supposed to be a window. It's another of CONTROL's devious blinds, a sliding panel to disguise CONTROL's weapons closet. Flawless logic. If an enemy agent pierces the elevator, corridor, and phone booth dodges and

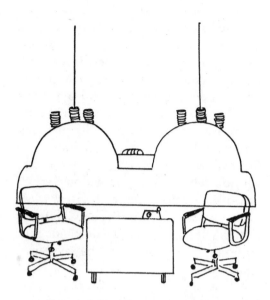

THE CONE OF SILENCE

Courtesy of Don Elmo.

enters the Chief's office, the painted street scene will confirm (1) that the government is too cheap to buy CONTROL a real view, or (2) that it's hiding something like a weapons closet, or (3) both.

Reminiscent of James Bond going to the lab, Max Smart, who apparently has a real affinity for closets, selects a few choice items—his bino-specs, a locker key, and a baretta. The Chief insists on Max taking the inflato-coat too.

Max's partner on the case will be agent K-13, Fang, a massive mass of hairy pooch who looks nothing like a Fang, and who punches the time clock strictly by the book.

The Chief dispatches Max and Fang to the airport, where an agent Max has never met—one named 99—will make contact by means of the password "New York Mets win double-header." Before Max leaves, the Chief warns him that he'll be in constant danger. Max, whose second language is cliché, replies with a snappy "And . . . loving it."

At the airport, Max accepts a six-and-a-half-year-old boy as an agent when the lad reads a newspaper headline out loud: "New York Mets win double-header." False start. Then a chauffeur gives the password—an extremely shapely uniformed chauffeur with a tiny waist, ample bosom, and short hair tucked under a chauffeur's cap. Max accepts her as an agent and, Max being Max, as a man.

They discuss the disappearance of Professor Dante and the involvement of his assistant, a curvaceous blonde named Zelinka (Buck Henry chose *Zelinka* as a tribute to Leonard Stern's former writing partner, Syd Zelinka), then elude a KAOS tail with maneuver Y-14. In Y-14, a CONTROL agent (in this case, agent 34) has already stationed himself inside an airport locker. The agent being followed walks past the locker. When the KAOS spy does likewise, the agent inside the locker opens its door into his face, knocks him out cold, then drags him by the feet into the bottom locker, from inside.

86, 99, and Fang find Zelinka, and a clue. A rubber banana peel. The peel leads them to the South Street Novelty Shop, where 86 misses demolition by the inthermo ray only because Fang senses danger and pushes him aside. In the fracas, 99 removes her cap. Smart notices. "Why, you're a girl." They poise for a kiss, but reality intervenes. An old garbage scow on the water tells its despicable tale when Max concludes that it hasn't attracted seagulls, hence carries rubber garbage, hence contains Professor Dante and the inthermo—"or I'm not Smart."

Max and 99 board the scow, fight the crew, and meet mastermind Mr. Big. "So you're Mr. Big," Smart acknowledges, as the camera pulls back to show Big is a dwarf (played by Michael Dunn). Big invites Smart to enjoy a cigarette, one from his personal collection, a premium blend. Smart smokes it all in one puff.

Big smells victory, but Smart dismisses the notion:

"At this moment seven Coast Guard cutters are converging on us. Would you believe it?"

"I find that pretty hard to believe," concedes Mr. Big.

"Hmm. Would you believe six?"

"I don't think so," Big allows.

"How about two cops in a rowboat?" Only Max Smart would attempt to plea bargain a bluff.

But no go. Big instructs his thugs to chain 86 and 99 down below, while he prepares to blast the Statue of Liberty out of the harbor. Fortunately 86, wearing his inflato-coat, inflates its false hands just in time for KAOS to chain *them* while his real hands dance freely inside the sleeves. Max releases himself and 99. Up on deck, they fight off Big's minions while Big, unaware that Professor Dante rewired the inthermo ray, self-destructs.

86, 99, and the professor swim to the safety of an emergency raft. 99, roughed up by the battle, looks like hell. 86, unmussed, laments the misspent life of the late Mr. Big, "If only he could have turned his evil genius into niceness." He calls the Chief on his shoe phone, expends tremendous pride on having overcome the vile forces bent on extinguishing Liberty's torch, and learn's that he's reached the wrong number.

Closing credits. *Dumdadum! Dum! Dumdadum! Dum! Dumdadadada Dumdadadada Dadada Dum!* Max retraces his steps from the phone booth down the corridor. Door after door slams behind him. Unflappable, confident, Max does not so much as look over his shoulder. Except once. Last door. Thinking of something, he turns on his heels to go back. Clunk. Right on the nose.

The pilot laid out the essence, the elements of *Get Smart*. Gadgets. Catchphrases. The Max-Chief relationship. The 86-99 relationship. An agent in a cramped and uncomfortable hiding place. A uniquely diabolical KAOS villain. Max, the clumsy, coming through.

Prior to broadcast, the completed pilot went to a testing outfit on Sunset Boulevard. It tested grimly. Among other things, worriers encouraged Leonard Stern to change Don Adams's strident delivery because it "grated on people." Fortunately, he refused.

The bad news about the tests couldn't have come at a worse time for Talent Associates. *East Side/West Side* (CBS) had gone off the air in September, 1964. Their *Mr. Broadway* (CBS), premiering in September 1964, had folded three months later. Other projects—*The Outsider* with Mike Connors, *Parker and Son* with Arthur Godfrey, and *Kelly* on Broadway—didn't even do as well.

Get Smart was TA's one network hope for the new season, and the tests offered little encouragement. Leonard Stern boosted Dan Melnick's flagging spirits with assurances that its detractors had had no point of reference, nothing to compare it with, therefore no way to know if they liked it, since nothing like it had been done before. Buck Henry pragmatically evaluated the basic concept of testing: "It gave me reason never to trust them again. All it can do is make you panic and go in the wrong direction."

3

THE YEAR OF
THE SPY

"May you be born in an important time."

—Confucian curse, circa 500 B.C.

There is such a thing as great—and would you believe, near great—minds running in the same channels. So it happens that ideas which no one had, suddenly everyone has had, and the fruition of each is witnessed in a synchronous burst. The phenomenon occurs particularly with entertainment, for obvious reasons. Success ties in with insight into what is, and what's about to be, popular—which explains how a single season can witness an explosion of similar novelties, all responding to the same momentarily universal tastes.

Cinema symptoms of the Year of the Spy: *Agent 8¾* starring Dirk Bogarde, *Where the Spies Are* starring David Niven, both 1965.

"WHERE THE SPIES ARE"

He's a special kind of spy...
he doesn't know enough to come in from the cold!

AGENT 8¾

DIRK BOGARDE · SYLVA KOSCINA · ROBERT MORLEY · LEO McKERN

Such bursts don't produce sitcoms about extra-literary aspects of nineteenth-century Madrid theater nor the cabaret licensing system in New York City, because the evidence out there thus far hasn't indicated overwhelming public enthusiasm for either genre. What the public might wake up clamoring for in stupendous numbers: evening soaps or miniseries, sports marathons or game shows. Mid-Sixties, the burst was Mr. Spy.

Though Bond creator Ian Fleming died in 1964, during the filming of *Goldfinger,* the craze continued to swell. Spy-related clothes, accessories, gimmicks, toys, and tie-ins spelled merchandiser heaven (007 aftershave gave "any man the license to kill . . . women"). Even the *Wall Street Journal* joined the parade, with photo-illustrated print ads linking "stocks and bonds and James Bond."

The Man from U.N.C.L.E., NBC's answer to Bond, hit the airwaves in 1964. NBC's *I Spy* (at the time deemed by *Newsweek* "by far the most adept of the attempts to capitalize on the James Bond mania") debuted in 1965. Those urbane imports, *The Avengers,* reached our shores on ABC in March of 1966 (the English had already been watching Jonathan Steed and Emma Peel for five years). ABC's *Burke's Law,* introduced in 1963 as a series about a Los Angeles chief of detectives, changed its name to *Amos Burke—Secret Agent* in September 1965, and became a series about the same man working a new beat, as a U.S. government spy. ABC's *Honey West,* featuring a female private detective who used Bond-like gadgets (tear gas earrings, garters

Diana Rigg and Patrick Macnee in *The Avengers.*

that convert to gas masks), spun off from *Burke* in 1965. CBS's *The Wild, Wild West,* premiering in September 1965, offered President Ulysses Grant's undercover agents West and Gordon, who wielded Bond-like gadgets (a customized railroad car equipped with a billiard table and detonating billard balls) in the century preceding James Bond's.

Straighter versions of the government agent game—*sans* radio-transmitter whoopee cushions—likewise began in September 1965: CBS's *Secret Agent,* acquired from British TV; and ABC's *The F.B.I.,* so sober it won the endorsement of FBI chief J. Edgar Hoover.

The movies-inspired Sixties Spies might have seemed more inventive had they not arrived all at once. Even so, they infused new dimensions and twists into a schedule otherwise inspired apparently only by itself.

Industry insiders widely viewed 1965–1966 as the "year of the retread." Never before had the three networks sprung all their new shows—fifteen on NBC, ten on ABC, and eight on CBS—in one Sunday-to-Sunday splurge.* NBC billed it "a week so big it lasts eight nights," yet *Newsweek* chided in August 1965, "Of the 33 new shows that will appear between September 12 and September 19, all but one or two are flagrant copies of past successes. Those 33 are children of chance, culled from 200-odd ideas, scripts and formats at a cost of around $20 million." Those two hundred sprang from upwards of twice as many that had been pitched but never reached the pilot stage. With pilot development running between $75,000 and several hundred thousand a throw and commitments to pay each aired show for a minimum of thirteen weeks, the gang with the checkbooks understandably hedged their bets. Strategy required the logically impossible—finding the "new" anchored by a proven track record.

The newness of the big new season derived largely from the network leap to color—catering to the five million color sets then in use, a figure gamely swelling by 1,400,000 a year. NBC led the pack, with 96 percent of its prime time in color (up from 70 percent the previous year).

Color could be counted on to add a ratings point or two, as well as to dress up sponsors' products.

The new season relied heavily on its old faithfuls: *The Jackie Gleason Show, The Ed Sullivan Show, The Red Skelton Show, The Lucy Show*, and *Gunsmoke* on CBS; *The Lawrence Welk Show* and *The Adventures of Ozzie and Harriet* on ABC; and nothing one could unreservedly label a long-term prime-time old faithful on NBC, a circumstance providing its own commentary on why NBC had fifteen debuts in its lineup. NBC had in fact dropped Jack Benny after fifteen years on television—the last year on NBC, the fourteen prior on CBS. (Had Benny kept his NBC slot of Friday 9:30–10:00 P.M., he'd have been the lead-in for *The Man from U.N.C.L.E.*).

Dr. Kildare, an NBC champ in the Thursday 8:30–9:30 P.M. spot since 1961, claimed two nights with the 1965–1966 season (Monday and Tuesday, 8:30–9:00). Though each half-hour ran complete in itself, the overall stories took on a more serial nature, while ABC's steamy *Peyton Place* jumped from two nights a week (Tuesday and Thursday, 9:30–10:00 P.M.) to three (Tuesday, Thursday, Friday, 9:30–10:00 P.M.). Prime-time soaps being *in*, ABC beefed up its hand with *The Long Hot Summer* (known by some as "Peyton Place South")—just as CBS folded its hand with *Our Private World*, a summer evening spinoff of *As the World Turns.*

Commented *Newsweek*, "No longer, it seems, are the networks content with imitation: rather than imitate, why not duplicate?"

*The previous year, ABC created a certain viewer allegiance to its new shows by airing them weeks before NBC and CBS unveiled their fall lines.

In search of the tried-but-new, NBC launched *My Mother the Car* and *I Dream of Jeannie*, two twists on the supernatural theme proved successful a year earlier by the debuts of *The Addams Family*, *Bewitched*, and *The Munsters*. Or, in the case of *My Mother the Car*—about a dead mother reincarnated as a 1928 Porter—the supernatural à la *Mr. Ed* (premiered 1961), about a talking horse. CBS toyed with merrily walking dead in a different form, that of *The Smothers Brothers Show*—a sitcom series concerning a publishing exec and his brother who died and came back as an angel.

McHale's Navy, four years old in 1965 (and at that, a variation on the service sitcoms pioneered 1955–1959 by *Bilko*) inspired NBC's *Mr. Roberts* and *The Wackiest Ship in the Army*, ABC's *F Troop*, and CBS's *Hogan's Heroes*. *Green Acres* spun off thematically from its sister ruralcoms *Petticoat Junction* (premiered 1963) and *The Beverly Hillbillies* (premiered 1962).

Responding to the widescreen success of the *Beach Blanket* (*Beach Party*, 1963; *Bikini Beach*, 1964), *Gidget* (*Gidget*, 1959; *Gidget Goes Hawaiian*, 1961; *Gidget Goes to Rome*, 1963), and *Tammy* (*Tammy and the Bachelor*, 1957; *Tammy Tell Me True*, 1961; *Tammy and the Doctor*, 1963) teen films, ABC offered *Gidget* starring Sally Field, and *Tammy* starring Debbie Watson.

Rounding out the menu, the number of Westerns rose from five in the 1964–1965 season to twelve during 1965–1966 (*Branded*, *Bonanza*, *The Virginian*,

Daniel Boone, and *Laredo* on NBC; *The Legend of Jesse James*, *A Man Called Shenandoah*, and *The Big Valley* on ABC; *Rawhide*, *Gunsmoke*, *The Loner*, and *The Wild, Wild West* on CBS). Barbara Stanwyck, star of *The Big Valley*, put the trend in perspective: "I'm just playing Lorne Greene in a Mother Hubbard."

A lone entry, inspired perhaps to some degree by the era of Bogart revival and the age of the antihero, starred Peter Falk as a rumpled criminal lawyer behind on his rent and alimony payments. *Trials of O'Brien*, witty, original, and popular with critics, would become one of the first casualties of the season.

Against a backdrop of unbridled cloning, an outcry for quality programs sparked ritual self-flagellation across the land. Educational channels hadn't quite been developed yet. For a nation of smarts, we looked—and hung our heads when we heard it—monumentally silly.

Such charges had been raised since the dawn of television, but they took on a second life when, in 1961, President Kennedy's newly appointed chairman of the Federal Communications Commission labeled it all "a vast wasteland." FCC Chairman Newton Minow announced to a national convention of broadcasters, "I invite you to sit down in front of your television set when your station goes on the air and stay there without a book, magazine, newspaper, profit and loss sheet, or rating book to distract you—and keep your eyes glued to that set until the station signs off. I can assure you that you will observe a vast wasteland. You will see a procession of game shows, violence, audience participation shows, formula comedies about totally unbelievable families, blood and thunder, mayhem, violence, sadism, murder, western bad men, western good men, private eyes, gangsters, more violence, and cartoons."

In early 1965, the prestigious Peabody Awards Committee declared itself unable to find a single entertainment offering of the 1964–1965 season good enough to receive a citation. The only awards it gave went to public affairs shows.

Serious drama, its death knell first heard with the cancellation of *Playhouse 90* in 1961, "hit an all-time low this season" according to *Good Housekeeping's* September 1965 appraisal of the new schedule. CBS dropped *East Side/West Side* in 1964, and the widely praised groundbreaker *The Defenders* in 1965.

On the other hand, TV world news availed itself of satellite capabilities to inform the public faster—and more thoroughly—than ever before. Reported the same *Good Housekeeping* article, "The tremendous impact on TV of such events as the funerals of President John F. Kennedy and Sir Winston Churchill, space flights and combat, civil rights demonstrations and controversial political issues has generated the medium's finest hours."

In May 1965, CBS pioneered a prime-time audience participation program acclaimed for its intelligence above and beyond most audience participation programs. *National Driver's Test* dramatized common road situations and polled stu-

dio and viewer responses, communicating valuable highway skills in the process. The same network followed up with a *National Health Test, National Income Tax Test,* and *National Citizenship Test* (41 percent of viewers could not name either of their state senators). NBC countered with *Testing: Is Anybody Honest?*

During the same season, Professor Henry Kissinger and two Harvard students debated British M.P. Michael Foot and two Oxford undergraduates on CBS's *Town Meeting of the World.* The former defended, not with resounding victory, the resolution that "the USA should carry out its commitment in Vietnam." On the CBS ninety-minute special *Vietnam Perspective: The Congress and the War,* Senator Morse faced the camera with a chilling plea to end secrecy, declaring that "we are an international outlaw in Vietnam." On each occasion, clearly, TV could have been accused of many things—for instance, of anti-administration vehemence—but not of settling for the mindlessly inoffensive fare of which the medium stood accused.

CBS even, in July 1965, mounted a candid vivisection of its own business. *CBS Reports: The Ratings Game* explored the relationship between ratings points, advertisers, and TV shows. *New York Times* critic Jack Gould completed the equation: "If just 1,130 families [the Nielsen families who represent 52.6 million viewers] keep their sets turned off from Sept. 13 to Sept. 19, the whole country can be spared the new TV season."

NBC's board chairman, Robert W. Sarnoff, had made a similar recommendation a few years earlier, with less menace: "The schedule offers something for everyone. If you disagree, I respectfully suggest that you employ the best little program regulator ever invented—the forefinger and thumb. Grasp the switch of your set firmly, snap it off, and your message will come through loud and clear. Sponsors, like nature, abhor a vacuum."

Rephrased: Hypocrites, cool your jets. In the final analysis, TV offered its smart alongside its silly. Much of its smart—for instance *National Driver's Test*—pulled such high ratings that the nation actually demonstrated a liking for quality, at least some of the time. If its smart inclined toward current events and practical applications, the trend belonged to its era, one of satellite broadcasts and spies fighting the cold war.

Which in no small way accounts for the year of the spy.

The spy fare—from *The Wild, Wild West* to *The Man from U.N.C.L.E.*—employed liberal doses of dry humor of the sort defined, then refined, by James Bond. Illya Kuryakin in *U.N.C.L.E.*, captured and chained to a wall, laments the appearance of his partner Napoleon Solo in similar straits. Quips Solo sardonically, without cracking a smile, "Wait till you hear my plan."

Their use of ironic banter proved in its way that TV had reached a certain level of maturity, that the audience could deal in subtleties, and that the industry paid the audience the extreme compliment of

acknowledging as much. Not surprisingly, some reviewers hadn't a clue what it meant. Confused, they dismissed the efforts as "semispoofs," or disparaged them for what they perceived as an unwillingness to decide whether to be comedies or dramas. *Get Smart* decided there's a fine line between urbanity and insanity, and that the real joke of the cosmos is to pretend there's not.

The publicity firm of Rogers & Cowan sent wax-sealed, "top-secret" envelopes to the desks of top TV critics. The messages purportedly came from Max. The first read: "Sssh!" The second included a pin, and instructions for deciphering the important revelation etched on its head. The third, an "invisible message," required the use of a "cigarette lighter or matches used judiciously." Then came "JE WAS LINKER OM IEMAND ANDERS TE NEMEN OM JE DIT VOOR TELATENLEZEN." Each message had the same translation: Get Smart. When a photo arrived—of Max, 99, and Fang—their eyes were blacked out and the caption confirmed: "A scene from ____ at ____ on ____."

Eager eyes watched to see if *Smart* would live up to its hype. Scheduled for Saturday nights between 8:30 and 9:00, sponsored by Lever Brothers and R.J. Reynolds Tobacco, the series premiered September 18, 1965. Its lead-in was *I Dream of Jeannie*, which made its debut the same night. *The Lawrence Welk Show* ran against it on ABC, *The Trials of O'Brien* on CBS. (O'Brien might have made a stronger showing had he not been forced to grapple with Maxwell Smart. In the world of TV programming, one

September 18, 1965   **Saturday**

TV
CLOSE-UP
GUIDE

8:30   **4**   GET SMART—Comedy

DEBUT This half-hour spoof of the current cloak-and-dagger trend stars Don Adams as Maxwell Smart, CONTROL's Secret Agent 86 Aiding the inept Smart (who needs all the help he can get) are Agent 99 (portrayed by tiger-cat Barbara Feldon), the Chief (Edward Platt) and Fang, an undercover canine.

Tonight The evil Mr. Big, leader of KAOS has kidnaped Prof. Dante and his Inthermo, an invention capable of melting anything in its path Mr. Big is willing to return both the professor and his machine—for 100 million dollars No one has that kind of money, so Smart is assigned to rescue Dante, wreck KAOS and get Mr. Big

Howard Morris directed this episode, written by comics Mel Brooks and Buck Henry, who developed the series

Guest Cast

Mr Big	Michael Dunn
Prof. Hugo Dante	Vito Scotti
Zelinka	Janine Gray
Garth	Kelton Garwood

'MR. BIG'

Barbara Feldon and Don Adams

TV Guide "close-up" of September 18, 1965, introducing the first *Get Smart* episode. *Reprinted by permission from* TV Guide® *Magazine. Copyright © 1965 by Triangle Publications, Inc. Radnor, Pennsylvania.*

T-154

MISSED IT BY THAT MUCH!

Can Max Smart find Dr. Livingstrom in darkest Africa, before KAOS steals his formula for world destruction?

BOOKS
60¢

GET
SMART
NO. 5

An original novel about NBC Television's most hilarious super-spy Maxwell Smart, Agent 86 for CONTROL

By WILLIAM JOHNSTON

An original novel about NBC television's hottest, most hilarious super-spy, MAXWELL SMART, Agent 86 for CONTROL.

BOOKS
60¢

By William Johnston

So popular was *Get Smart* that it inspired a series of paperbacks.

function of a good show is to knock other good shows off the air.)

Some of the new crop of agents fared badly. Jack Gould of *The New York Times* called *The F.B.I.* "the week's most depressing event." Dwight Newton wrote, in the *San Francisco Examiner,* "one suspected that by FBI they meant the Federal Bureau of Idiocy." Of *Honey West,* Bob Williams wrote in the *New York Post,* "she's pretty—pretty tough—and pretty repulsive, as well."

Get Smart, at the opposite extreme, shot to the top of the Nielsen surveys.* *Time* declared that "it dares to be healthily sick while the competition is all sickeningly healthy." Within a matter of weeks, Maxwell Smart's strident delivery became the most imitated voice in America, and even in space. When a urine bag broke aboard the Gemini 7 mission, NASA ground control commiserated with a "Sorry about that, Chief."

*On the night of its debut, Don Adams invited 150 friends to his house to watch TV. He rented enough additional TV sets to give everyone a ringside seat. But only one set worked—one with a five-inch screen, which everyone had to crowd into one room to watch.

4

EVERY MAN A GLICK

Maxwellmania hit, and hit hard. Soon it wasn't enough that everyone quoted 86. No, not by a long shot. Quicker than you could say "Would you believe?" much of the civilized world sounded like him too, as radio personality Bill Parkhurst recalls.

In the spring of 1966, I finally became a WTSN Playboy, a disc jockey on the hottest 5000 watt AM Top 40 station in the New Hampshire seacoast region. I was also a college junior, but who cared? Anyone could do that.

Being a Playboy meant that you ate free at half the restaurants, played miniature golf on the house, your money was no good at movie theaters, and, when you were doing holiday traffic reports in the Playboy van, you drew a convoy of pretty girls in the supercharged cars of

the day, most of whom let you know that if you weren't doing anything after work . . .

There was one hitch and it nearly cost me a summer of bliss. The program director asked me if I could do an impression of Don Adams. It was a must that spring. The sponsors all wanted Maxwell Smart sound-alikes on their recorded commercials, and they wanted them fast.

"Would you believe Helene's Furniture is offering Ethan Allen sofa beds for a dollar and a half, regularly priced at $695?"

"Would you believe a fabulously comfortable sofa bed with a Sealy Posturepedic mattress for only $495 while they last?"

The problem was that each sponsor who came up with a Don Adams commercial thought he invented the concept and the station owners, who were minting money from such vanity and the sudden madness surrounding a single television show, weren't about to tell their financial spigots they weren't original thinkers. And the sponsors got very proprietary about the announcers who voiced their spots. If you did Max for Brodhead Ford Village, doing him for Newcomb and Walsh, the Dodge Boys of Somersworth was something close to desecration of the flag.

We also had to be available to do variations of Max for station promotional fillers as in, "Hi, this is Maxwell and the Smart thing to do is tune in to the seacoast's powerpacked hit machine, where every night, Bob Prince will give away ten thousand dollars. Would you believe seven thousand five hundred dollars? Would you believe a salt and pepper shaker in the shape of an orange?"

My Don Adams was the worst in the history of broadcasting. The only impression I could do in 1966 was Bogart and any other came out sounding like Rick bemoaning Ingrid Bergman's arrival at his gin mill. When I said, "Would you believe . . ." it came off as Bogart trying to do Frankie Valli of the Four Seasons.

The competition for Playboy slots was as fierce as any national voice-over I ever got in New York years later. Word was out all through the radio grapevine. Parkhurst might be out on his ear because he just couldn't hack the commercials. I had to do something or plan on going back to WWNH in Rochester, where I'd spent the winter playing supermarket music.

Paul Leblanc, WTSN's program director let me write a spot that featured a very bad Don Adams impression, one that just couldn't make it. The guy couldn't even get "Sorry about that, Chief" out of his mouth. The spot ended with me saying that listeners should settle for no imitations, there was only one WTSN. The girls and I had a very good summer. I assume Adams did too.

—Bill Parkhurst,
WOR, New York

5

|||||||||||||||||||||||||||||||||||||||||||||||||||||||||||||||||||||||||||||||||||||||||||||||||||||||||||||||||

GOOD GUYS IN CONTROL

"Would you believe . . . ?"

—Maxwell Smart

Espionage comedy began long before *Get Smart.* In one banner year alone, 1942, Humphrey Bogart and his unlikely gang of shady New Yorkers overthrew a Nazi fifth column (*All Through the Night*), Jack Benny as an actor in Poland undermined Hitler (*To Be or Not To Be*), a female agent involved Bob Hope and his penguin in international intrigue (*My Favorite Blonde*), and Kay Kyser swung into action as a band leader with a secret mission (*My Favorite Spy*).

These films and others like them found humor in a *Confidential Agent* situation, yet in the process made propaganda fun. No one minded. The war was on. We enjoyed joking that any American with half a brain could accidentally become a spy and thwart the ludicrous caricatures who worked for the other side. When the war ended, comic quasi-spies continued along the same lines—from Bob Hope in *My Favorite Spy* (1951) to Wally Cox on TV's *The Adventures of Hiram Holiday* (1956–1957). We laughed with them and at them, never doubting for a minute that these accidental everyman heroes were happy flukes in an overall scheme of things that put smart good guys in control.

Then the cold war brought its new-era spy—its James Bond, its Napoleon Solo, its John Drake. Bob Hope as man with a penguin wouldn't suit as a spoof. But something had to. As soon as the Year of the Spy reached explosive proportions, some sensed it was doomed to fizzle out. *Newsweek* rated *Thunderball's* Bond (1965) as "a sea-borne Mighty

Mouse . . . a hero whose incompetence might still be engaging if it were not so patently authentic," while *The Spy Who Came In From the Cold* (1965) "had what it took to blow the whistle on the espionage cult that has all but engulfed the movie business this year."

By anticipating early enough the need for a new-era comic spy, Dan Melnick and company had *Get Smart* ready just months before the bubble burst. If Bond could do no wrong, even when he did wrong, then Smart would do no right. Right? No, wrong. Except for the fact that Smart fell off furniture, couldn't cut it with the ladies, and occasionally saved buildings from the enemy only to unintentionally blow them up himself—Bond and Smart got the same results.

MAX

"Missed it by that much . . ."

—**Maxwell Smart**

Like James Bond, Maxwell Smart grew up a mystery. As Sean Connery once described Bond, "He has no mother. He has no father. He doesn't come from anywhere and he hadn't been anywhere before he became 007. He was born—kerplump—thirty-three years old." In the same vein, Mel Brooks said of Max, "They wanted . . . Max to come home to his mother and explain everything. I hate

mothers on shows. Max has no mother. He never had one." Don Adams, asked about Max's early life, remembers that "it never came up, and I never gave it any thought. I only gave thought to the moment, the day, the hour, the minute. I never thought of past or future, only of present."

Five years of *Get Smart* episodes shed little more light than "kerplump." We hear Max was born as an infant when he reveals that a Dr. Linquist delivered him and saw the beauty mark which he had where he sits ("And Only Two Ninety-Nine"). We know Max became a toddler because he still has his baby shoes ("Witness for the Persecution"). He was raised in the city ("Snoopy Smart vs. the Red Baron"), apparently Washington, D.C. ("Pussycats Galore"). His mother, still alive according to "Diamonds Are a Spy's Best Friend" (Max sends her money regularly from his paycheck), never shows her face. Max's father never gave him anything but a pair of pants so that Max could go to work ("The Little Black Book," Part II). His brother, mentioned in "Rebecca of Funny-Folk Farm," apparently stays out of his life. Max's Uncle Abner and Aunt Bertha each think he's related to the other by blood ("My Nephew, the Spy"). Not his parents but rather Agent 4, Herbert Gaffer, provided his only discernible role model ("Dear Diary"). Max served as a corporal in Korea ("The Little Black Book," Part I). Max went to college destined for espionage—going straight after graduation into CONTROL as a bonus baby ("Maxwell Smart, Private Eye"). Maxwell Smart, instant spy. Living the role to the hilt. *And* loving it.

Like Bond, Max lives well. He earns $35,000 a year, which in the Sixties resembled money ("Don't Look Back"). For the most part, the outside world accepts his cover—that he works for a greeting card company. His obviously expensive duplex apartment has its own stocked bar. Max drinks and serves drinks, favoring for himself one Gibson before dinner: four parts gin, a touch of vermouth, a pearl onion ("Run, Robot, Run").

Like Bond, Max dresses stylishly, right up to the fashion minute: au courant high flap pockets, modish lapels, turtlenecks, and blazers. He's one of the ten best-dressed spies in the country ("Survival of the Fattest"). Even the men's fashion industry noticed. In 1966, the Men's and Boy's Apparel Club of California named Don Adams the best-dressed star on TV. (He accepted the award in a "cobalt blue shake mohair suit, bamboo sea island cotton shirt, and abstract print silk tie.")

Smart, like Bond, is a man of the world, speaking French ("Our Man in Leotards"), German ("Pussycats Galore"), Spanish ("The Only Way to Die" and "Anatomy of a Lover"), Chinese, and Swahili (including its declensions and conjugations, in "Our Man in Leotards"):

Chief: Mahanee gonga ghee.
Max: Gonga ghee? Don't you mean gonga gai?
Chief: No . . . gonga ghee.

Max: Really? I always thought it was gai after gonga except before goo.

Smart, like Bond, is a top agent. He won the 1965 and 1966 Spy of the Year Award ("Witness for the Persecution," "The Whole Tooth and . . ."), killed the founder of the American branch of KAOS ("Kiss of Death"), and creates sufficient menace for KAOS that they put a half-million-dollar price on his head, "dead or dead" ("Somebody Down Here Hates Me"). KAOS claims they've never found his weakness ("Kiss of Death").

Bond introduces himself: "The name is Bond. James Bond." Intones Smart: "This is Smart. Maxwell Smart. Agent 86"—even when he's phoning the Chief, to whom he needs no introduction.

Yet Bond and Smart are anything but twins. The surface distinction is that Bond, in short, is Bond—while Max is a lot of things Bond is not, including short. Max stands somewhere between 5'9" ("The Mummy") and 5'11" ("With Love and Twitches"), and tips the scale at 149 pounds ("The Mummy") making him, if not a shrimp, no incredible hulk either. But size, to Max, is no issue. What defines Maxwell Smart is his total, blissful ignorance of the distance between reality and the image he has of himself.

Max has eyes variously described as "squinty," "piggy," and "beady." (Buck Henry saw them as "deep-set raisins"). He has—observed "Little Joe" Torrenneva, Don Adams's hair stylist—"two different kinds of ears and an odd, triangular head." He speaks with the staccato whine of the no-nonsense private dick, his voice suggesting not espionage yarns but cheap detective sagas set in roller rinks and penny arcades, the sort that calls guns *roscoes,* and ladies, *skirts*—"like a thousand fingernails scraped over a blackboard," *Newsweek* wrote.

But Max pays no mind to his less than perfect traits. He'll use his flawed vocal instrument for the most grandiose rhetoric, and should he go somewhere with 99 and hear an awed "you're beautiful," he'll assume the compliment must be for him. He doesn't act like a short man because he doesn't see himself as short,* and having escaped notice of this quality in himself, is completely unprejudiced as to size in others. When he greets the diabolical 3'6" dwarf—"So you're Mr. Big"—he seems unaware of the irony. When he takes on brainless bullies of towering muscle, the odds of his losing rarely register, so he insults them, pummels them, flattens his fist on human concrete, then expects to recoup lost ground with a diplomatic "Listen, fella, I hope I wasn't out of line with that crack about . . ."

*According to Dr. David Rimon of the Short Stature Clinic of Cedars Sinai Medical Center in Los Angeles, "A man who's four feet two inches had to accept dwarfism as a kid. He gets used to it and goes on to make his life important. A man who is five feet two inches often blames all his problems on his height and believes that his problems would all disappear if he were just to get taller." Here, as in most things, Max goes against the norm.

Once in a rare while, he remembers his training in such matters—that the way to deal with monster brutes is to not antagonize them ("The Greatest Spy on Earth")—but even then, the memory fades fast, and he's in there swinging as though he stands a real chance. As a result, Max's fight scenes are wonders of nature. He's so earnest even when hopelessly outclassed, wears himself out, and wins—like Nelson Eddy duking it out with Victor McLaglen in *Let Freedom Ring* (1939). One can only respond to the sight with stunned disbelief. Yet Max, like Bond, thrives on conflict, sees his duty (against professionals, never amateurs), and does what must be done.

Interestingly, he doesn't just *try* to do it. He does, however impossibly, reach his goals. The experience confirms and inflates his view of himself. No wonder, then, that evidence notwithstanding, Max believes himself to be suave. Ronald Colman-like, he throws back his head to laugh at danger. He claims, totally inaccurately, to be impervious to pain. He invariably does hard things without apparent effort. It's the easy things he can't do right. Endowed with extraordinary powers of observation, he recognizes arch criminals by their walks and tics even when plastic surgery has altered them completely ("Someone Down Here Hates Me") and discerns that the agent shooting at him has an XK13074112082 Luger which only fires six shots ("Strike While the Agent Is Hot"). But he loses track of the number of shots, counting six when it's just been five; continues playing chess with a friend after the

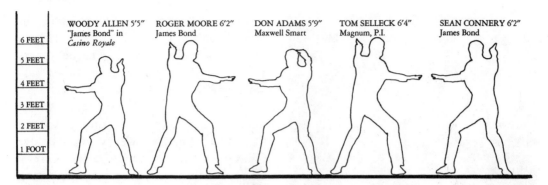

It's not how big you are, but what you do with what you've got. *Courtesy of Ilene Klinghoffer Goldfarb.*

friend has been killed (yet remembers the exact sequence of moves, in "Weekend Vampire"); explains that a ship's whistle has to be pulled three times to detonate a U.S. government building, loses track of the twice it's been pulled, and yanks it a third time ("The Only Way to Die"). Max habitually leans over dying agents to hear their last words, which are usually "Get your knee off my chest." Max swallows secret messages before finding time to read them. Under the influence of truth serum, he can't remember the product of seven times two ("The Decoy").

Accident prone, he loses out to inanimate objects at every turn, recovers, and doesn't bat an eye. He falls backward off chairs; can't operate a seat belt; can't lean against anything without knocking it down and keeling over with it; upsets ashtrays by pounding on them, aiming for the desks on which they rest; steps in spittoons and walks away wearing them. He pops a cigarette in his mouth, fingers his glass, lifts his glass to lips, submerg-

ing his cigarette—twice ("Casablanca"). He swashbuckles the tenderest part of his anatomy into tray tables (visiting 99's mother, in "Snoopy Smart vs. the Red Baron") and car doors (showing Amanda how to jump into a car, in "The Reluctant Redhead").

Psychiatric testing reveals him to be uncoordinated, lacking in perception, easily distracted, and childish ("All in the Mind"). In action, he is more: unflaggingly single-minded, uncoordinated, slow to perceive, and childish. It doesn't matter. Actually as well as metaphorically, Max always lands on his feet.

"The character never recognized that he'd done something stupid," explains Don Adams. "I'm smoking a cigarette, and I say something like 'Well, it's finally over. A matter of your wits over my wits,' and as I'm talking, I start down the stairs. I trip on the stairs, the gun falls out of my hand, and I fall down the stairs and roll over. In one motion as I roll over, I've got the gun in my hand, and I'm on my feet with my hand against the

Max strikes a characteristic pose. From the *Get Smart* **movie, the 1980** *The Nude Bomb.*

railing, and they're staring in incomprehension.

"Or I'm in a casino at Monte Carlo. I'm in a tuxedo, and I enter like royalty, with a glass of champagne in my hand. I casually glance at my watch. Of course, the champagne glass is in my hand, so I pour champagne down my tux, look down, and continue on my way.

"Henchmen were always getting the drop on Max, and you'd think the thing would be for them to kill him, and for the heavy to say 'We don't have to, he'll do it himself.' All they have to do is sit and wait and eventually he's going to kill himself.

"But he's always trying to be suave, and out of trying to be suave, he's a basket case."

Don Adams played it straight. An innocent shrug. Impeccable timing. Chevy Chase half-gainers, twenty years before Chevy Chase. In fact, better. Chevy Chase has been criticized for anticipating his falls and splattering without grace. Max Smart sprawled more in the Buster Keaton mode, with acrobatic artistry. As quickly and decisively as he fell, he'd be up again, a Johnny Carson of pratfalls with the best saves in the business. Wrote Jack Anderson in the *Miami Herald,* "he almost succeeds in being the straight man to himself."

Max is indelicate, as when he and the Chief have been prematurely aged by Dorian Gray paint ("Age Before Duty"). Max whines to the Chief about having been made a geezer. The Chief notes that he himself got the same deal. Max whines again, unsympathetic: "Yeah, but you were half there anyway." Max is unsubtle. He wears his secret agent number, 86, on his bathrobe (e.g. "The Day Smart Turned Chicken," "Expendable Agent," "The Decoy," "Bronzefinger"), his T-shirt ("Die, Spy"), his commando beret ("Satan Place," "Smart Fell on Alabama"), and ditty bag ("Rub-a-Dub-Dub . . . Three Spies in a Sub"). He has posed for *Popular Espionage* magazine and an ad for a decoding device sold through *True Impossible Spy Stories Monthly* ("The Mummy"). He has a favorite toy duck gun ("I'm Only

Human"). At least one of his neighbors, Mrs. Harriet Eulalie Dawson, gladly testifies in court that he hasn't a mental marble to his name ("The Day Smart Turned Chicken"). Max lacks musical acumen, having flunked out of spy music school ("Hubert's Unfinished Symphony"). Max's shoes squeak, and when he takes them off, his socks squeak too ("Perils in a Pet Shop").

Given Smart's drawbacks, it should follow that he's ill at ease with women. But given Smart's confidence, he's not. He fancies himself something of a womanizer, delivering kisses surprisingly brazen for Sixties TV. Though network program practices wouldn't permit Smart to open his mouth for kissing, he rose above the Bob Hope type of kiss where a face with pursed lips pushes forward into an opposite face. Like Bond in the movies, Max blazed a sitcom trail in the sensuous kissing department, putting as much of himself into each as network law would allow.

As a swinging bachelor, Max has few TV antecedents. Bob Collins (Bob Cummings) on *The Bob Cummings Show* (1955–1959) and Valentine Farrow (Tony Franciosa) on *Valentine's Day* (1964–1965) share some of his ground, but none of his scope. They get around, but Max's workplace is the globe.

Max briefly encounters a key club Pussycat, and can later describe her charms in mesmerized detail ("Pussycats Galore"). The Chief shows him a series of photos depicting attractive blondes. Max does his best to pocket a few ("Diplomat's Daughter"). An Arab prince sends him a dancing girl. He wants to keep her, despite CONTROL's rules against gifts ("Survival of the Fattest"). A beautiful woman collapses in his arms. Sighs Max, "I just never get tired of this business" ("The Girls From KAOS").

Max and 99 date (e.g. "Double Agent" and "My Nephew, the Spy"). He has her portrait in his bedroom ("The Day Smart Turned Chicken," "All in the Mind"). In early *Get Smart* moments of cloak-and-dagger stimulation, Max and 99 often stand poised to kiss, only to be intruded upon in keeping with the time-honored cliché. Max indulges with her in a very long kiss courtesy of the drug immobilo, which renders *both* of them motionless, giving rise to audience bemusement that only Max would cop a kiss he probably can't feel ("Our Man in Leotards").

With Tisha Sterling in "The Girls from KAOS." *Courtesy of Howard Frank Archives/Personality Photos, Inc.*

Just as Max believes himself to be equal to any fight, he figures himself to be equal to any loving. He may be maladjusted in that department (seeing men and women hugging in every ink blot of his ink blot test in "All in the Mind") yet mismatched in love as in battle, he wins. The lovely 99 has always adored him, and marries him in *Get Smart*'s 1968–1969 season. Adams: "In the first few years, there was never any thought of marriage because we wanted to have the kind of relationship we had, which was that she always wanted to and I was too dumb to know that she wanted to."

Suave nerd and imbecile hero, in his complexity of opposites, Max is all too human. Maybe people envy James Bond's sporty élan—surely more than they envy those wartime types forced into espionage by tragedy and duress—but as much as they love James, rationally, it's hard to buy Bond. With the advent of Max, they no longer had to. Explains Don Adams, "Maxwell Smart was James Bond as Everyman would be James Bond. James Bond as played by Sean Connery or Roger Moore is a kind of fantasy figure, over six feet, dresses beautifully, has all the chicks falling all over him, and he gets the bad guy in the end. He's Superman in that sense. The ordinary guy, the butcher, the baker, the candlestick maker, relate to him in a kind of fantasy way. Whereas if you were to take a cab driver and put him in a secret organization like the CIA or CONTROL, he'd be like Maxwell Smart."

In truth, Max falls somewhere between James Bond and that other phenomenon of the Sixties, Charlie Brown. If Charlie Brown were a spy, he'd be Maxwell Smart. What this implies about the espionage system comes out of the headlines, not the funny pages. Any time you portray a man in a position of responsibility as a fool—whether Maxwell Smart in *Get Smart*, Sergeant Ernie Bilko in *The Phil Silvers Show: You'll Never Get Rich*, or Captain Wilton Parmenter in *F Troop*—you point the finger of guilt upstairs. If the system hired an incompetent, the system is the fool.

The team behind *Get Smart* knew the rules of TV humor as well as anyone: Don't offend even small groups—small groups buy sponsors' products too; don't go too far afield for the critics—if they don't recognize what you're doing, they'll conclude you didn't fulfill their expectations; don't knock the hero—particularly if knocking him means knocking the government too.

Said Buck Henry in 1966, "The cardinal rule in television is, don't offend the audience morally, politically, or esthetically—just don't offend them. Primarily responsible is the sponsor, who must hope to have a nation of morons because only then can a commodity be packaged for the lowest common denominator and sold for extraneous, absurd reasons to the solid, untrammelled masses of people." He added that *Get Smart*'s tremendous success "is not because the show is so brilliant, but because TV has gotten so chicken." Above all, he rationalized, "If Bond is going to save the world, we should at least blow it up."

So radical was the thought of satirical TV in 1965 that to this day, when *Get Smart* is referred to as satire, Leonard Stern counters, "Not satire, spoof. You could sell a spoof to the networks, but the idea of satire made them uncomfortable. It was anathema, calling to mind George Kaufman's line, 'Satire is something that closes on Saturday night.' " Indeed, *That Was the Week That Was* was already off the air, and it would be another few years before *The Smothers Brothers Comedy Hour* (1967–1975) and *Rowan & Martin's Laugh-In* (1968–1973) took on the system:

Q. "Why does a chicken cross the border?"

A. "To avoid the draft."

—The Smothers Brothers
Comedy Hour, 1967

In *Get Smart,* CONTROL knows that Max bungles and blunders, so it doesn't always treat him well. He's the only one who doesn't get a three-week vacation ("Washington 4, Indians 3"); and when his death has to be faked to flush out the Blaster, he apparently only rates cheap flowers, a tacky headstone, and five guests at the funeral—the Chief, 99, Fang, and the two KAOS agents who killed him ("The Only Way to Die").

Yet CONTROL more than keeps him on the payroll. We hear time and again how he's one of CONTROL's best agents. They assign him to key opera-tions, and name him head of their medical security division ("Somebody Down Here Hates Me"). Then they compound his lunacy with gadgets only a loser could love. Max is conspicuous, attracts attention. Consults with an agent disguised as a sportswear mannequin by jamming his head into the mannequin's megaphone ("Our Man in Toyland"). Talks into a shoe phone, or a fire hydrant phone ("Stakeout at Blue Mist Mountain"). On occasion, his telephonic marvels require coin deposits. But Max didn't get these gimcracks from AT&T. CONTROL's top scientists devised them, and the fact is that *no one* squatting to speak into a fire hydrant looks suave. Moreover, keeping track of them demands major concentration, which Max apparently musters:

"Central, cancel my handkerchief, hold my glasses, cut off my shoe, and see if you can get that guy off my tie."

("Satan Place")

Max carries a business card—"Arnold Kipnis, furrier to the stars"—which reveals his real identity when held to the light ("The Day Smart Turned Chicken"). He listens to a tape that will self-destruct at the end of the message; the tape player destructs everything in the room but itself ("The Impossible Mission").

He spies for a network supposed to be secret, yet much of Washington can easily recite the address (variously 123 Main, the corner of W Street and 34th, etc.) and point out the top-security spy school located in a quiet suburban neighborhood. As often as CONTROL's phone number changes, the AT&T operators always learn about it first:

Max: Hello, operator. Now listen to me and listen carefully. I want you to get me a special Washington phone number. This is a top-secret number. Only a few people know it. I want you to forget it the minute that I tell it to you. The number is 628-3097.

Operator: Oh, you want CONTROL.

("All in the Mind")

Max has a furnished apartment ("Witness for the Persecution") which occasionally is refurbished. (The foremost behind-the-scenes refurbishment occurred when the kitchen was moved from an unseen screen-left area behind the bar in early episodes to an on-camera room, screen-right, later on.) Depending on the episode, Max's building is located either in a quiet suburban neighborhood or a densely populated urban jungle or, more likely, in the suburbs on either side, and in the big city outside his front window. His apartment, #86, seems to be on the second floor. He has told the landlord that he works for the IRS to explain the constant gun battles there ("Expendable Agent"). In some episodes, scads of locks secure the front door. In others not. But even fully bolted, the door swings open at a touch.

The apartment boasts the latest in CONTROL protections, yet they blast him more often than his enemies. CONTROL and Max, hand in hand, give new meaning to the words *booby traps*. Max could do better by himself at Abercrombie & Fitch. Furthermore, his building might as well be situated on the busiest street in Washington. The whole world can look into it, shoot into it, lob bombs into it.* The place across the street must do a thriving business in short-term rentals to KAOS assassins.

Get Smart portrays a Max and a CONTROL cut from the same cloth. Mel Brooks has said that if he were to teach screenwriting, he'd "teach one sentence. 'What do the leading characters *want?*' " Max wants what CONTROL wants—the triumph of niceness over rottenness. CONTROL hires people like Max to achieve the victory. They don't *have* to. They choose to. Uncle Sam wants him. He meets their needs.

Intellectually, Max is a straight arrow, naïve and ingenuous. Except for good versus evil, all propositions stand equal in his eyes. Everything is worth a try: "Would you believe that I can break eight boards with one karate chop? No? Would you believe three boards? Would you believe a loaf of bread?" Max doesn't would-you-believe to stall for time. He does it on the loony gamble that he'll be believed by his foe.

---

*Max's apartment foreshadows the building of the new Soviet embassy, set to be built sometime before 1990, high on a Washington, D.C. hill, with perfect sightlines to some of the most important windows in the capital.

His weakest suit may lie in the weighing of distinctions. Imprisoned in a Mexican jail in "Viva Smart," he nearly wrecks his chance to bribe the firing squad because he doesn't want to seem like a tourist and feels he has to haggle; then, standing before the readied squad with a senorita who loudly denounces their captor, he asks her to *sssh* so as not to get them in trouble.

Because he draws poor distinctions, oversimplifying everything, he can minimize everything to the level of a spilled crumb. "Sorry about that . . ." "Missed it by that much . . ." In the end, you'd trust Smart with a gun sooner than with a computer. If he slips with a gun, the worst he'll do is wing you. Give him a computer, he can foul up your credit rating for life. CONTROL responds by handing him the fate of mankind. Way to go, CONTROL.

In the words of Timothy Dalton, the movies' latest James Bond, "Bond is a lapsed idealist who is rediscovering what is right or wrong, what is the truth." Max's ideals, by contrast, never lapse. Out in the world in the Sixties, an unprecedented number of Americans found fault with national security agencies. Students demonstrated against CIA recruitment on campus. People questioned whether the FBI's J. Edgar Hoover—acclaimed as a hero from the days of the Lindbergh kidnapping through Prohibition and the spy-hunting roundups of World War II—was perhaps, in a state of cold-war frenzy, going too far to find commies in every haystack.

Not Max. As conservative columnist

What the well-dressed agent wore in 1965. *Courtesy of AP/Wide World Photos.*

Leon Wieseltier wrote of the White House in the wake of the Iran-contra scandal, in *The New York Times Magazine*, "since the Administration is always *already* right, since its confidence in its correctness is never shaken by events, it has become invulnerable to facts. The facts are there to be arranged, altered, and assembled into a picture of the world that will never challenge, but always confirm." When Max has misgivings, they're few and specific. At a conference of brilliant scientists, 99 advises him that each won the Nobel Prize, the Distinguished Service Medal, and is a special advisor to the U.S. President. Max thinks it all well and good, but asks if they can be trusted ("The Expendable Agent").

On the larger scale, Max won't judge.

Barbara Feldon. *Courtesy of LIFETIME Cabletelevision.*

CONTROL is already right. He's on orders, willingly working for goodness and doing as he's told:

99: Oh Max, how terrible.
86: He deserved it, 99. He was a KAOS killer.
99: Sometimes I wonder if we're any better, Max.
86: What are you talking about, 99? We have to shoot and kill and destroy. We represent everything that's wholesome and good in the world.

("Island of the Darned")

Remarked Mel Brooks to the *New York Herald Tribune* in 1965, "[*Get*

Smart] is a show in which you can comment, too. I don't mean we're in the broken-wing business. We're not social workers, but we can do some comment such as you can't inject in, say, *My Three Sons.*"

No amateur spy, 86 is a pro picked by inept bigshots, a schlemiel in the hire of schmendricks, and still we beat the enemy. *Get Smart* brought espionage comedy from the Forties into the Sixties. Wartime films made propaganda fun. *Get Smart* made fun of propaganda. Any number of comedies have poked fun at human beings. But Max, a parody of a human being, missed being James Bond . . . missed it by that much.

99

"It's even better when you help."

—Lauren Bacall after kissing Humphrey Bogart,
To Have and Have Not (1944)

Born in New York and raised in an upper-middle-class household in Pittsburgh, Pennsylvania, Barbara Hall studied ballet as a child, decided by first grade that she'd be an actress, was too tall for most boys she grew up with, and sometimes felt like a waif: "All kids are lonely. They want mail, like at camp." For the sake of getting mail, she made her first move as a future spy, sending away for her little Orphan Annie decoder ring.

After graduating from high school, she enrolled in the drama department at

86'S SIGN

In the episode "The Decoy," Max's zodiac sign is revealed to be Scorpio. According to Day-By-Day Zodiac International, Scorpio's traits include:

- Unswerving devotion to principles
- Speech that is plain, blunt, and sarcastic
- A strong chance of eyes that are deep-set and cold
- A love of fighting, from battles down to quarrels
- The ability to excel as a scientist, doctor, lawyer, detective, or investigator

- A successful marriage if your partner is docile and yielding
- And in the "lesser type of Scorpio . . . Often you think yourself victimized or undervalued and you may relieve your feelings through constant boasting. You may take secret pleasure in being tricky, subtle, and clever, and often disconcert others with blatant displays of knowledge."

Adds Jeremiah McAward, a private investigator who in the Sixties spied for the CIA, "Over the years, I have known seven assassins. Of them, five were born under the sign of Scorpio."

Pittsburgh's Carnegie Tech. She graduated in 1955, moved to New York, found acting jobs scarcer than expected, but landed a dancing part in Beatrice Lillie's Copacabana revival of "Ziegfeld Follies."

While appearing at the Copa, she heard that the game show *$64,000 Question* wanted contestants. She took the program's preliminary quiz, based largely on Shakespeare. A voracious reader who'd just finished reading *King Lear*, she aced the quiz and thrilled program management, who devoured the idea of a showgirl Shakespeare genius. They asked her to appear right away. She insisted on a three-month delay. For the next three months, "I memorized facts. I broke them down into categories—life, plots, characters, all the famous lines and soliloquies—just as I would for a college exam. I like things organized." In a few short months in 1957, Barbara Hall waltzed away with the $64,000 prize.

She invested her hefty winnings in blue-chip stocks and a pre-Pop Art gallery launched with New York photographer's representative Lucien Verdux Feldon. The two married in 1958. Then the 5'9" brunette, weighing a modish 107 pounds, commenced high fashion modeling for Pauline Trigère. Modeling led to TV commercials, the first for 5-Day Deodorant Pads. As her husband described the debut adventure, "Barbara stepped out of the shower with her hair piled up and a towel wrapped around her, not seeming in the least surprised to find you in the bathroom."

The spot brought stardom in the world of TV ads, along with an element of danger: "I did one with a leopard I will never forget. True to the tradition that the commercial must go on, we had started filming at seven in the morning and were still going at seven that night. But the leopard didn't care about tradition. He got mad and hungry and began munching on my ankle. When I protested to the director, he said, 'But it's just a baby leopard.' I went to the executive for the sponsor. His answer was, 'Don't worry, you're insured.'"

Feldon's greatest success in this phase of her life came with a campaign for Revlon's Top Brass hair cream. Stretched out and writhing on a tiger skin rug, she growled a sultry coast-to-coast, "I want a word with all you tigers . . . Grrr." It left a grateful male populace gasping for air. Characteristically, she later demythified the purr: "I taught myself when I was six years old, trying to sound like Pinocchio calling for help after being swallowed by the whale."

When Feldon first did commercials, friends warned her that once she schlepped products, she'd never be offered a serious acting role. "But it never stood in my way," she discovered. As she told reporters in 1966, fresh on the heels of her *Get Smart* celebrity, "Today, commercials are done in such a way that girls can come off as personalities. There used to be something tacky about doing commercials. Maybe we've grown up. Some commercials are the most sophisticated things on TV today."

When Feldon's enticements commanded the notice of Talent Associates,

she became the straight TV actress that friends swore a schlepper couldn't be. She appeared on *East Side/West Side* as a love interest for George C. Scott, and as an industrial spy on *Mr. Broadway*. As these shows went under, *Get Smart* emerged. But Feldon almost wasn't at liberty to join its cast. Talent Associates persevered, determined that no one but Feldon should play 99. States Buck Henry categorically, "We wrote Maxwell Smart so that any good comic actor could play him. But we wrote the part of 99 for Barbara."

Continues Henry, "You often write television scripts not knowing whether they will sell or whether you will get the people you want for them. As it happened, Barbara was not quite available because her commercial sponsors didn't want her appearing on a show for another product. It took a legal hassle to clear her."

It also took presenting her to Don Adams, who they felt might not appreciate her height. Efforts ensued to soften the shock. Recalls Adams, "One day they came to me and said, 'We have some film for you to see. Remember the girl who lies on the rug and says *Hey, tiger?*' I said, 'Yeah, that's a great commercial.' They said, 'Well, we have some film on her from *Mr. Broadway.*' So I went into the projection room, and in the scene she was sitting behind a desk, and Craig Stevens, the star of the show, stood near her. I watched the scene for a few minutes and said, 'She's terrific. She's perfect for the part.' 'Shall we hire her?' 'Sure, she's great.' Then I got up to walk out.

"They said, 'Don't you want to see

any more?' I said, 'No, that's enough. I'm sold.' Then I looked over my shoulder, and saw on the film that she stood up. I said, '*She's taller than Craig Stevens!*' Then I asked, 'How tall is that girl?' They said five-foot-six. I said, 'What are you telling me! I know Craig Stevens, he's over six feet. Are you trying to tell me that Craig Stevens is five-feet-five?' And they said, 'Well, she has high heels on, big, big heels.' So I said I didn't care."

At first, Feldon signed on to do the pilot plus three more episodes after it sold. Then she watched the pilot and liked what she saw: "I thought it would be a hit. I wouldn't have done it otherwise. After seeing the pilot, I called my agent and told him to notify the producers I had changed my mind and would do the series." She retained her Revlon ties, which netted her more money—though a smaller place in history—than she made on *Get Smart*.

Feldon brought to *Get Smart* all the traits innately hers: an arch innocence, a

Back when 99 wore her hair short. *Courtesy of Howard Frank Archives/Personality Photos, Inc.*

sensible worldliness, beauty, poise, the ability to radiate intelligence without having to say a word, and bedroom eyes which she attributed to myopia. Off-camera, she read haiku poetry and the *Wall Street Journal,* wore designer fashions which she made into pillows when she no longer wanted to wear them as clothes, did needlepoint, and painted pictures of friends with flowers blossoming from their ears. She had a very expensive camera and constantly took pictures. When producer Burt Nodella asked her, "Aren't you ever going to show me your pictures?" she replied, "I never use film. The picture is when I snap it. In that moment, it's in my eye, it's in my brain, and I keep the memory."

Feldon embodied the woman 99 had to be, a woman combining a tastefully ladylike version of such Bond-age she-devils as *Goldfinger's* Pussy Galore (Honor Blackman) and *Thunderball's* Domino Vitali (Claudine Auger) with the steadier comforts of the only lady who could ever really be good for Bond, his eternal co-worker Miss Moneypenny (Lois Maxwell). Teamed with Agent 86 and Fang (Agent K-13), long before she marries Max, 99 plus 86 echo the husband-wife chemistry of Nick and Nora Charles and their pooch Asta (*The Thin Man*) while foreshadowing Jennifer and Jonathan Hart and Freeway (*Hart to Hart*). As sometimes the only woman in a *Get Smart* episode, 99 has to cover all bases (except bimbo). Observed Leonard Stern appreciatively of Feldon's unique sexpot/helpmate appeal, "A man's wife

can be seated next to him while he's being enchanted with Barbara, yet the wife feels no resentment."

No less than Max, 99 keeps up with the fashion. They often donned safari garb, anticipating the *Out of Africa* craze of the Eighties. Early on, 99 had a strikingly sculpted style, which gradually softened. All told, it took a year for 99 to find her look. Producer Burt Nodella hated 99's original hairdo, while 99's costumes were at first selected by a woman who had worked with Loretta Young and favored velvets and chiffon. Because Feldon came to the show as a svelte fashion model, long sleeves were a must to cover her arms: "You'll never see me on that show with no sleeves, because I weighed about 110 pounds and I'm not a short woman. It's true that my weight fluctuated on *Get Smart.* You get bored sitting on the set, and people try to please you by bringing you coffee and pastry, and you don't resist. Sometimes you gain weight. But thin arms run in my family. On camera, I look healthier in long sleeves."

Burt Nodella recalls being "picky about the fact that her arms were so long, the cuffs wouldn't be long enough. Her long wrists would be hanging out. I'd ask them to add something, like a ruffle, or to get Barbara clothes that fit. Don't forget, though, she did lots of action things. We had to choose costumes she could move in. Pants or loose skirts. After a while, we had a tie-in with Capriotti, a great shop in Beverly Hills. At the time, I think the leading ladies in television, like Elizabeth Montgomery [*Bewitched*], Marlo Thomas [*That Girl*], and Barbara Bain [*Mission: Impossible*] tried to outdo each other in clothes." But Feldon, perhaps more *dernier cri* than any of them, didn't pay much heed to fashion trends. "Barbara did what we told her. The wardrobe lady gave her something to wear and if it fit, she was satisfied." And unlike any of the other ladies, she loved it when a particular scene called for her to wear a moustache.

Bright, attractive, stunningly attired, 99 fully lives up to her number. One percent short of perfection, since perfection in a woman can't help but scare men away. Mathematically inclined viewers might compute that 99 is the total of 86 and (K-) 13. Critics perceived her as being everything from an "efficient feminine sidekick" (*Christian Science Monitor*) to a "muddled Mata Hari" (Robert Musel, *UPI*) to "a little coy for our tastes" (Cleveland Amory, *TV Guide*).

Such was the price of being TV comedy's first Sixties woman.

A 1957 poll revealed that 80 percent of Americans declared any adult woman unmarried by choice to be "sick," "neurotic," or "immoral." But when Betty Friedan's groundbreaking *The Feminine Mystique* hit bookstands in 1963, it galvanized the contemporary women's movement as women began questioning foreordained goals. With the force of sudden revelation, they saw options to homemaking and childrearing. Increasingly, they demanded not just jobs but careers, applying special scrutiny to careers traditionally set aside for men. Agent 99 found such a position, one too tough for most women and likewise, for most males. Says Feldon, "On one level, it was easy to step out into the so-called man's world because the step I took was stylized and not real. On another level, many women have told me that they grew up watching *Get Smart* and were very influenced by 99."

99 was no halfway gal. Never mind that a woman and a dog (Fang) broke the professional spy barrier in the same year. It was a start. Moreover, she remained a career spy even after she married, and even after she had children. For a married woman with children and a well-paid husband to keep her job is a rarity on television today. For 99 to have done it when she did it constituted a miracle.

As an agent in her own right, 99 vamps the enemy, speaks foreign languages fluently (German in "I'm Only Human," French in "Casablanca," and Chinese in "Ship of Spies"), impresses people by using big words (*miniscule, diminutive, international parasitic sycophants* in "Kiss of Death"), sings, and dances. She won the Lamont Cranston Award for shadowing three years in a row ("A Tale of Two Tails"). Like Max, she relies on bizarre devices from the lab, from a lipstick which propels pool balls ("The Dead Spy Scrawls") to a razor ring ("Bronzefinger") to a radio transmitter in her portable hair dryer ("Ship of Spies"). Yet "American comedy's most sensuous spy" (*People*, March 1985), so frequently compared with that talented amateur Emma Peel (Diana Rigg) of *The Avengers,* seems in many regards her antithesis. Mrs. Peel fights like Bruce Lee. 99, who apparently mastered martial arts (she knocks the head off a practice dummy in "Bronzefinger"), is rarely seen using them. Mrs. Peel consistently asserts herself, center-stage; 99 just as gladly shadows suspects from an off-camera distance, or snoops discretely as a manicurist ("Maxwell Smart, Alias Jimmy Ballantine"), salesperson ("The Day They Raided the Knights," "Our Man in Toyland"), and the like.

But if 99 functions more in the manner of a John Steed than a Mrs. Peel—relinquishing center-stage to her partner—it's merely because if either she or Steed blew an iota of cool, the premise of their respective shows would collapse. 99 meets the challenge of fulfilling herself—as a woman and as a spy—largely by compensating for Max. 99 has known him since she was twenty-four (a writers' pun in "Closely Watched Planes," but once stated, also a fact). Without her presence of mind, Max is doomed. Considering mankind's dependence on him, she can do the world no higher service:

86 [aboard ship]: Ninety-nine, this ship is a freighter, right?
99: Right, Max.
86: And freighters run on fuel oil, right?
99: Right again, Max.
86: And wooden masts belong on sailboats, correct?

99: Exactly.
86: And this is a wooden mast.
99: Go on, Max.
86: 99 . . .
99: Yes?
86: I forgot where I started.
("Ship of Spies")

Max's best ideas, 99 provides, in ways that let him believe they came from his mouth:

99: "Oh, Max, there's too much light! They'll see us for sure!"
86: "You're right. We'll take care of that." [Shoots the light].
99: "Good shooting, 86. Look! There's one more!"
86: "I'm all out of bullets."
99: "Why don't you try the light switch?"
86: "Of course! The light switch!"
99: "Good thinking, Max!"
("Our Man in Toyland")

Gradually, Max takes for granted that 99 will fill in his blanks. He quotes the beginnings of proverbs, snatched from thin air and meaningless. Ten words into them, he's lost. No problem. "How does the rest of that go, 99?" Not that she knows or needs to. Max has already made his point: he's deep, having quoted profundities.

The Chief considers the pair to be his best-working team ("Appointment in Sahara"). For 99, this suffices. She asks for no credit; asks not what Maxwell can do for her, but what she can do for Maxwell. As Feldon told *TV Guide* in 1968,

99, looking as confused as 86. Appearances are deceiving. *Courtesy of Howard Frank Archives/Personality Photos, Inc.*

"Agent 99 is an ingredient in the oven; not the soup. She isn't the meat; she is the spice. She is a *character*, not a person . . . The show *is* Don Adams. Without him, nothing. My softness, sincerity, gullibility and loving him are simply a foil for his brittle wit."

We therefore never see 99 grandstanding, but rather, reacting. As a "character," she's "spoofy," "along the lines of a comic strip" (her descriptions). She doesn't have many punch lines, but on her are hung "typical female" gags: she drives badly ("I Shot 86 Today"), longs to use the honeymooner cover as a disguise ("Weekend Vampire"), and presses the Chief for contract terms for female agents—such as hairdos and bags for evening wear ("Strike While the Agent Is Hot").

Writers occasionally tried to give her the punch lines, but the formula didn't stick. There's something intrinsically gratuitous about 99 making Max look silly when he's fully qualified to do it himself.

When we see 99 in "action," it's subtle. Said *Get Smart* director Richard Donner: "86 is that little boy everybody wants to mother. If I need a bit of business to fill a hole, I say, 'Hey, Barbie Doll, mother him up a little.' Barbie's perfect. Even standing around, she's working." Added Burt Nodella: "If we had no ending for a scene, we'd have Barbara do her eye thing. She used to drop one lid, one eye would close, and it was a great get-out on a scene." Raved TV critic Michael McWilliams, "She'd lean against a desk while Don Adams did his shtik. But would you believe Feldon was a delicious comedienne? The more dialogue Adams had, the more Feldon animated different parts of her body: bobbing her head, rolling her eyes, wetting her lips. She did more silent comedy than anybody since Mabel Normand."

For one of *Get Smart's* strongest running gags, she merely had to exist: that exquisite, desirable 99 wanted 86 as her fella. The difference in their heights might have made the joke broader still, had Feldon been less accommodating. No doubt about her being tall. Recalls Bernie Kopell, "She was tall, had long legs, and took giant strides. Whenever you walked with her, it was hard keeping up." But on purpose, she stood short. She'd turn her ankles and spread her feet, or she'd slouch, or she'd lean, or she'd sit. Burt Nodella would chide, "That's part of the thing that's funny. That this tall, beautiful girl is in love with this dummy." Feldon would kid, "I'm the only actress in town with callouses on my ankles." Then she'd obligingly shrink.

Don Adams concedes that "if you ever watch any of the *Get Smarts,* if you see us enter a room, she's about two inches taller than I am. When we get in a two-shot, I'm about two inches taller than she is. I'm standing on a half apple box. She's in bare feet. She went through all those years in her stocking feet, or in slippers, except when we entered the room in a very long shot. Then you could see it. Otherwise, I was always standing on an apple box or something."

A very few facts emerge from 99's private life. Unlike Max who grew up in the city, 99 is a country girl ("Snoopy Smart vs. the Red Baron"). Max has relatives but no visible parents; 99 has a mother ("Snoopy Smart vs. the Red Baron," "Absorb the Greek," "The Worst Best Man") and though 99 didn't realize it during his lifetime, her father spied for a living ("Snoopy Smart vs. the Red Baron").

Max has a name; 99 just has a number. In the episode "99 Loses Control," she admits to being Susan Hilton, but later rescinds the admission, explaining it was a cover. When trivia fans dive on the Susan Hilton "revelation," Buck Henry sees blood: "I always thought that 99 should have no name. I fought in the first or second year—I fought a battle with someone somewhere to keep her nameless. She stayed that way all through, even when they were married. And no, Susan Hilton was definitely never her

name." The most revealing thing about 99's name is that Max never bothers to inform himself of it. In "99 Loses Control," believing Susan Hilton to be 99's name, Max pouts that she never told him. When he later learns that the name is a fiction, it doesn't occur to him to ask, "Then what is it really?" After Max marries her, and even after she has his children, he continues to call her 99. This may or may not betray shallowness on his part, but it certainly underscores 99's willingness to be tolerant and probably a little mysterious.

According to "Kisses for KAOS," 99's apartment is smaller than Max's. We don't see her apartment; we just hear that it's smaller—a simple verbal device introduced to avoid the behind-the-scenes production expense of building a set for 99's apartment. Her apartment's being smaller creates the opportunity to use Max's (a standing set).

99 dates eligible bachelors, but generally in the line of duty ("Kisses for KAOS," "The Only Way to Die"). In "The Little Black Book," she breaks habit by warming up to Max's obnoxious army buddy Sid (Don Rickles), but through all the *Get Smart* years, the man she really wants is Max. In discerning something to love in him, she gives him credibility in the eyes of others. Though the choice is a hoot, consider her options. Who else does she meet? Handsome enemy agents, forlorn CONTROL operatives huddled in washing machines and lockers, a CONTROL agent formerly a KAOS robot (Hymie), a CONTROL agent formerly an ape (Chuck in

"The Apes of Rath"), a schlub played by Don Rickles, the Chief, Larabee, and Max.

A popular commercial of 99's day congratulated women on having come a long way, baby, and offered as evidence the fact that women suddenly had their own cigarette. At least 99's had ballistics devices inside. After all, not just any woman deserved the name Mrs. 99 Smart.

THE CHIEF

"Sorry about that, Chief."

—Maxwell Smart

Born in Staten Island, New York, Ed Platt could have been a stockbroker, as his father wanted, or an opera singer, as his mother hoped. Partial to his mother's notion, he progressed from Northwood School in Lake Placid, New York, to Princeton University, then entering the Conservatory of Music in Cincinnati. After eighteen months there, he enrolled in New York's Juilliard School of Music, cultivated his pipes, and embraced the unmonied life of a serious bass.

Platt made his professional debut in 1937 with Happy Felton's Band. The year 1939 found him in the musical revue *All in Fun,* which closed the day after it opened. He served for four years with the Army Air Corps, still longer with the

Mozart Opera Company, and for years paid the rent by performing in Gilbert and Sullivan operettas. His appearance in *The Mikado* may have been the least welcome in the history of lively arts, opening as it did the day after the Japanese bombed Pearl Harbor.

When Platt joined Paul Whiteman's prestigious band—the band for which Irving Szathmary was once an arranger and musician—Platt's luck began to change. From two years with Whiteman, he segued into a ten-month Broadway run in Rogers and Hammerstein's musical about institutional corruption, *Allegro.* Following *Allegro,* he played on Broadway in *The Silver Whistle, Texas Li'l Darlin', Twentieth Century, Stalag 17,* and as José Ferrer's brother in *The Shrike.* In 1954, he decided to relocate near his brother who was in the Texas oil business.

Once in Texas, he signed aboard with a local TV station, as host of *Uncle Eddie's Birthday Party.* Hosting entailed major responsibilities: "Every day we had a birthday party. I'd order the cake, buy the paper plates and napkins, get the favors for the birthday child who was permitted to invite nine of his friends, placate the mothers whose children's birthdays couldn't get on television—it was first-come, first-invited. Then clean up the mess after the half-hour party on air for organized pinning-tails-on-donkeys and all that." In the next half hour, Platt did the local news program, reporting on activities of garden clubs and residents visiting with family out of town.

When Platt married—and wondered

Ed Platt before the Chief—in *The Rebel Set* (1959).

how far his $65-a-week salary would go with a wife to support—a call came from friend José Ferrer. It led to a part in the movie version of *The Shrike,* and a weekly paycheck in the hundreds range. Platt's impressively active movie career had begun, and would soon include roles in films ranging from *House of Numbers, The Lieutenant Wore Skirts, Storm Center, The Loves of Omar Khayyam, Written on the Wind, The Tattered Dress, North by Northwest, Cape Fear* to, most memorably, the role of James Dean's sympathetic juvenile officer in *Rebel Without a Cause.* TV parts transpired too, from *Playhouse 90* to *Mr. Novak.*

Moviegoers and TV watchers came to recognize the brown-haired (then), 5'9" Platt as a character actor of grave bearing

and concerned, often paternal, authority.

Though Platt was only eleven years older than Don Adams, he offered precisely this sort of steady, reliable, gray and balding (by 1965) maturity figure to Agent 86, beginning with the pilot episode of *Get Smart.* Leonard Stern liked the idea that Platt could sing, which gave him a singer's sense of timing. Within weeks of the pilot, fans recognized Platt on the street as they never had done during all his years in the movies. Some would lightly bump him or stomp across his shoes to be able to chuckle, "Sorry about that, Chief." Toward the end of *Get Smart's* first season, Platt went to the Kentucky Derby. A whole section of the grandstand rose to shout the famous refrain.

In the first *Get Smart* episodes, Platt's role seems more substantial than his screen credit: his name follows the program, as a featured performer in the cast of characters list. But in very short order, his billing precedes the program. Once it does, a new element is necessarily added to the door sequence since another name has to be accompanied by a scenic movement. This element is the listing of the executive producer's name not over the last door, but over the phone booth. For one season, Leonard Stern's name disappears into the bowels of the earth along with Max as the floor of the phone booth descends—after which season, it appeared and disappeared without sinking. Such are the vicissitudes in the life of a Chief.

Max's Chief, above all—and in many an odd way, just like a TV producer—is the human voice of his organization. He translates CONTROL's political and bureaucratic decisions into manpower, assignments, and action. He's the interface between orders and their executions, between word and deed. In early episodes, there's a timeclock in his office. Agents punch in and punch out. After a while, it's removed. Timeclocks are accusatory. But the Chief, by being a nice, regular guy, humanizes the frightening monolith designated CONTROL.

His last name, highly classified information, is never revealed. His first name, Thaddeus, Max badgers out of him when the Chief takes the witness stand in "The Day Smart Turned Chicken." Par for the course with Max, the Chief's name is irrelevant to the testimony, but gives Max an opportunity to smirk at the Chief's expense.

As a lonely child, Thaddeus had recurring dreams of being Secretary of the Army when word came that all his men had been captured—which caused him to realize in a blinding flash that he was out of a job ("All in the Mind"). As a young agent in CONTROL's totem pole, Thaddeus romanced Mary "Jack" Armstrong, the world's strongest female spy. They drifted apart when he had no other address for her than c/o KAOS ("Survival of the Fattest"). His marital status is generally given as "never married," except in "Too Many Chiefs" to set up a joke. He suffers from fear of heights ("Temporarily Out of Control"). His favorite dessert is chocolate mousse ("The Farkas Fracas"). He developed the comb phone because he hasn't enough hair to make other use of a comb ("A Tale of Two Tails").

He earned his promotions, finally becoming Chief of Washington's branch of CONTROL. However, he's not CONTROL's number one man, whose identity is unknown to Maxwell Smart ("Cutback at CONTROL") nor, as several episodes indicate, is he CONTROL's only chief. He is simply the one in Washington. According to "The Spy Who Met Himself," CONTROL has secret branches in Washington, New York, Baltimore, Los Angeles, Cleveland, and Phoenix. They had one in Las Vegas, but lost it. (For the awards ceremonies in "How to Succeed in the Spy Business Without Really Trying," there are "so many chiefs, the only thing missing is a wigwam.") Presumably he's CONTROL's chief Chief. In this capacity, he sends Max on missions, eternally warning him not to be an idiot—though fully aware that Maxwell's eternal state is to be an idiot. Sometimes he barely tolerates Max. Sometimes he wants to bash him. According to revelations in "Cutback at CONTROL," Max has only taken six or seven suicide pills in his career, and these only to please the Chief. Yet on other occasions, the Chief praises Max and seems to love him like a son. Explained Platt of his character, "I'm a foil, a frustration symbol, a wall of stone off which Max can bounce his humor." Max gives the Chief migranes trying his patience. The Chief has an ulcer. The Chief and his patience get what they deserve.

The same pained patience the Chief extends to CONTROL, while forever falling prey to devices which make him look no less silly than Max. 99 calls him on a martini phone. Reception is fuzzy.

The Chief, answering on a sandwich phone with a potato chip mouthpiece, must discard some meat and cheese to improve the quality of the transmission ("Closely Watched Planes"). Contract negotiations compel him and Max to take opposites sides of the dealings. Max, representing the agents, consults with the Chief in a room in which other agents are present—says Max—but not obvious, since they're in disguise. The Chief proceeds to take up his debate with pieces of furniture: "You there. Have you ever been shot on Grellman's* birthday?" Max, with disdain, informs the Chief that he's talking to a sofa ("Strike While the Agent Is Hot").

Most often, the two men differ on the use of faulty CONTROL security measures. The Chief would as soon bend the rules and dispense with them. Yet Max inflicts them on the Chief, every time. In "Dear Diary," Max demands that they light the Magna Lamp to read small details in a document. The Chief hesitates. Max holds his ground. The light goes on, so bright that no one can see anything, and so hot, it incinerates the paper. The Chief could have left the Magna Lamp off; Max gave him the choice—it, or the Cone of Silence.† The Magna Lamp won. The Chief will agree to any number of horrors to avoid the Cone of Silence. Max can't understand the Chief's resis-

tance. Max has a short memory. He never remembers that the Cone never works.

The Chief remembers, and constantly reminds Max. This object, invented by Professor Cone, started out as inferior goods. CONTROL, tight of funds, didn't buy it from the government. They bought it from a discount house. But Max doesn't listen, so the Cone crashes through the Chief's desk in the pilot episode; a bee gets loose inside the Cone, threatening to sting both men to death in "I'm Only Human"; the portable Cone won't come off the Chief's head in "Hubert's Unfinished Symphony"; and people outside the Cone or in the next room can hear you better than the person you're inside the Cone with—except in "The Whole Tooth and . . ." Here, the Cone jams with both men under it. Max can squirm out but the Chief can't. Max runs off on an emergency, forgetting the Chief is inside. The Chief bellows for help, but for once, the Cone of Silence works. No one can hear his screams.

During yet another budget cut, CONTROL has to lease the Cone to the CIA (Congress can't cut the CIA's budget because they don't know what it is). In lieu of Cone, Max insists on the Closet of Silence. The Closet, a nuisance packed with clothes, drives the Chief to the breaking point. He wants out. Can't get out. Closet's locked. Max shoots off the lock, wounding the agent attempting to open the door from the outside ("Maxwell Smart, Private Eye"). In "The Mummy," Max and the Chief resort to the coughing code when the Cone is broken. CONTROL itself has abandoned

*Grellman: CONTROL code for Washington.

†Not to be confused with the Cube of Safety, a clear bulletproof box that descends from Max's ceiling, and one of the few devices installed in Max's apartment that actually does what it ought to, when it ought to ("Witness for the Persecution").

the code because too many agents were giving each other colds, but Max is a stickler.

Unable to employ the Cone due to a security leak, Max and the Chief exchange their vital data in a jet 30,000 feet off the ground. This adds up to considerable flying time, since Max forgets everything he heard the minute the plane hits the landing strip ("The Impossible Mission"). One wonders how Max and the Chief would fare were they stationed in London, where the Umbrella of Safety is the norm ("That Old Gang of Mine"). Chances are they'd be wearing eye patches most of their lives.

Possibly Max is aware that these things are mechanized equivalents of David Letterman's Stupid Pet Tricks. But possibly, for his purposes, it doesn't matter. Max is like a little boy running over to Daddy with something astounding to holler—"Daddy, Daddy, wait till you hear this!"—and Daddy dismisses him, "Come back later, Son. Can't you see I'm busy?" If Max has a revelation which

the Chief demotes out of hand, groaning that it's not worth bothering with the Cone of Silence, then by ultimately getting the Cone of Silence, Max confirms his importance.

Observed Platt of his role as the Chief, "Naturally, I'm bordering on psychosis—I would have to be, with a guy like Max around all the time. While Agent 99 serves as a mother image, I guess, I am the forgiving father, always willing to turn the other cheek and give my 'son' just one more chance."

Amazingly, Max isn't always the bane of the Chief's existence. In "Anatomy of a Lover," he saves the Chief's life. Hymie is strangling the Chief. Max stops Hymie, AC, by plugging him into a DC socket and short-circuiting him. In "Spy for a Spy," Max saves the Chief and most of CONTROL. KAOS's Siegfried kidnaps the Chief. Only Max, by masterminding a wave of spy snatching between CONTROL and KAOS, manages to secure the Chief's and the other agents' freedom. In "Satan Place," Max once more

The Chief, waxing paternal with Max. *Courtesy of Howard Frank Archives/Personality Photos, Inc.*

springs the Chief from a ransom situation, after running an auction of the Chief's property to raise funds for the trade. Max asks no greater reward than the Chief's happiness—and the Chief's car, which he wins in a free-the-Chief raffle for a few dollars.

The Chief, for the record, is not the brightest man in the world. Max tells him as much, under the influence of truth serum in "The Mummy." The Chief proceeds to prove it by unintentionally dropping 86 repeatedly on his face while 86, bandaged head to toe, is powerless to break the fall. Then the Chief instructs Max to take time off without pay, because Max can't work but is technically not sick—only stiff as a board—so doesn't qualify for sick leave. Max offers to stand around CONTROL headquarters as a security guard, and if he has to sound an alarm, to fall loudly. The Chief hadn't thought of this; Max had to.

Before leaving, the Chief drops Max again, then makes it all up to him by saying, "Sorry about that." In addition to being Max's father figure and boss, he's Hardy to Max's Laurel, Kramden to Max's Norton, and Flintstone to Max's Rubble. When it comes to plying the old insult upon injury trick, Max could learn a few things from the Chief.

SELECTED TOP-SECRET PHONE EXCHANGES

117: When 117 is dialed on Max's living-room phone after pressing the trigger, the phone fires a shot in "Too Many Chiefs."

555–3743: CONTROL's number in "Bronzefinger"

555–6213: CONTROL's new top-secret number, in "Smart, the Assassin." Smart gets it from the operator.

555–9417: CONTROL's number, disconnected for nonpayment, in "Cutback at Control."

Klondike 5–9365: The Chief's number in the Emergency Telephone Plan ("Our Man in Toyland"). Note that Klondike is a 555 number.

XVB: Exchange of the CONTROL phone hidden in Max's bedpost in "The Day Smart Turned Chicken."

(The publisher advises that CONTROL numbers not 555 exchanges are strictly classified, as they are potentially "live" numbers.)

FROM CONTROL'S CATALOGUE OF ESPIONAGE DEVICES

Balloon Phone: You have to blow it up before you can use it ("Rebecca of Funny-Folk Farm").

Comb Phone: Invented by the Chief because, being bald, he has nothing else to do with a comb ("A Tale of Two Tales").

Inflato-girl: Inflatable female dummy used by Max as a prop on lovers' lane ("Kisses for KAOS").

Magic Ear: Amplifying device that looks like a big lead ear ("KAOS in Control").

New Shoe Phone: This model offers steel enforced toes for kicking. Inside the heels are secret compartments with the latest emergency pellets. Inside the left heel, the smaller of two pellets is the concussion pellet; the larger brings instant, painless death when swallowed. The right heel conceals a pellet which produces a smoke screen. Shoe comes in black only ("Diplomat's Daughter").

Pen Gun: An ordinary looking writing implement equipped with cartridge of high potency sleeping gas ("I Am Curiously Yellow").

The Professor Peter Peckinpah Mini Mauser: A.k.a. the Professor Peter Peckinpah all-purpose antipersonnel Peckinpah pocket pistol ("Smartacus"). (Director Sam Peckinpah sometimes shot movies on the same lot as *Get Smart*.)

Steering Wheel Phone: The wheel is the actual dial, rotates for dialing, and has the numbers placed clockwise around its circumference. ("Kisses for KAOS").

PERSONNEL SPOTTED IN THE CONTROL LAB

Dr. Arrick (Roger Price in "Weekend Vampire"): Works the detecto-tune.

Dr. Bascomb (George Ives in "Witness for the Persecution"): Head of CONTROL crime lab.

Professor Bush (Byron Foulger in "Dear Diary"): Retired CONTROL scientist, creator of invisible dust.

Professor Carleton (Frank de Vol):

Ongoing lab scientist, in "Diplomat's Daughter," "I'm Only Human," etc.

Professor Carlson (Stacy Keach, Sr.): Creator of the umbrella rifle with a high-speed camera in the handle ("Girls from KAOS"), edible buttons ("Appointment in Sahara"), bazooka butts which, ignited and puffed, become a grenade ("Island of the Darned"), etc. (This Stacy Keach is not to be confused with his son, who is TV's Mike Hammer. This Stacy Keach, in addition to a distinguished career as an actor, has been head of an industrial film company since 1948. The senior Keach gave up his *Get Smart* duties after one too many clients asked him, "Where have you been? I couldn't reach you."—and he had to respond, "I've been working in the CONTROL labs.")

Dr. Drago (Martin Kosleck in "Weekend Vampire"): The former CONTROL scientist was dismissed by CONTROL when he dabbled in unauthorized experiments, then swore a vendetta against all agents who had testified against him. He is the inventor of the twin-channeled flute which, at high C, fires two poison pellets.

Dr. Minelli (Del Close in "Aboard the Orient Express"): When you yank down on the brim of his bowler, it converts to a gas mask. When you knock together the heels of his strato shoes, a jet stream lifts the wearer off the ground. He also invented a rigged electric briefcase.

Professor Parker (Milton Selzer): Max is always wrecking Parker's inventions during their demonstrations. Parker's devices include the ice cube transmitter, the remote control cue ball and shotgun cue stick ("The Dead Spy Scrawls"), and a dinner service and foods that can tape, photograph, and fingerprint their users ("Kisses for KAOS"). He also developed the transmitter, receiver, and radar-tracking fly, which took two and a half years to perfect and a second for Max to swat to bits ("Double Agent"). But you can't blame Max. Why would anyone invest so much effort in creating something that *anyone's* first reaction to would be to swat?

Dr. Simon (Ann Elder in "The Impossible Mission"): Exotic dancer scientist who gives Max a computer trumpet ("The Impossible Mission").

Dr. Steele (Ellen Weston in "Classification: Dead," "The Groovy Guru," and "Operation Ridiculous"): CONTROL's head toxicologist. Nine out of ten doctors who get poisoned go to Dr. Steele. She graduated from Stanford, studied for six years at Johns Hopkins, spent four years at the Winthrop Institute of Research, and toured for two years with *Hello,*

Dolly. Dr. Steele works backstage at the Follies, uses dancing in a chorus line as her cover, and has a telephone in the handle of the crook that goes with her Little Bo Peep costume.

Windish (Robert Cornthwaite in "KAOS in Control"): Invents world's first electro retrogressor gun, which causes even the most brilliant mind to regress to the age of eight.

THE ADMIRAL

"You always know when you've got a character well, because you think of things you wouldn't think of if you were being yourself."

—William Schallert (The Admiral)

The Admiral is what the Chief can look forward to being if he stays long enough with CONTROL.

Admiral Harold Harmon Hargrade, the former chief, has the President's ear, a glowing record, is called in to replace the Chief when events require a heavy-weight, and can't hold a thought for a second, nor even remain standing up. He enters the Chief's office via a secret tunnel under the desk. He thinks Herbert Hoover is still President. He danced with Louisa May Alcott in 1886. He attributes his good health to prunes. With a lampshade on his head, the Admiral can be mistaken for a lamp. In "A Man Called Smart," he observes how odd it is to imagine the country in the hands of an actor—many years before the country in fact took such a step.

Apparently recruited in the dear dead days when the service sought operatives surreptitiously, through blind college newspaper ads and the Ivy League old boy network, the Admiral is the past imposed on the present. With him in CONTROL, bye-bye future.

He is a benign and probably perfect old man, except in that position. Ac-

William Schallert as himself, today.

cording to William Schallert, who portrayed him, "The Admiral echoes the glory days, when it was a kind of amateur profession played a lot like lawn tennis; a band of old cowboys, Spanish American War vets, and World War I flyers who, after they shot the enemy down, drank a toast to him. After a point, if those old boys stay around, they can do an awful lot of damage and cause an awful lot of trouble with their cockamamie ideas." The Admiral is the snail-paced car on the speedway who causes accidents by forcing others to move precipitously past him.

Schallert came to the role as a young man, with decades of experience being old: "When I first began acting, during World War II, it was at UCLA, just before I went in the army. A friend suggested I read for the part of the old man, Corbaccio, in *Volpone*. It wasn't anything I ever thought about doing, but I saw someone else read for it, and like the song in *Chorus Line*, I felt, 'I can do that.' I got the part. About three days after I opened, I got a call from 20th Century Fox, and they asked me to come down to the studio. I spoke to a few people, and one asked, 'By the way, what's your draft status?' I answered, 'I'm in the ROTC. I have two or three months.' The interviewer said, 'Oh, be sure to look us up after the war.' What this told me is that they'd just been looking for warm bodies, male. Then, right after the war, I was playing an old guy again. I did a character called Sam Ego in the world premiere of Saroyan's *Sam*

Ego's House at the Circle Theatre [the prestigious Hollywood theater of which Schallert is a co-founder]. So I seemed to have an instinctive flair for this ancient type."

A Fulbright fellow at the British Repetory Theatre from 1952–1953, Schallert pursued his acting career on stage, on screen, and on television. There wasn't much call for his old guy until, as Patty Duke's father on *The Patty Duke Show*, he played his uncle from New England in one of those double-role stories which was *Duke*'s stock in trade. The uncle didn't dodder, and wasn't as old as the Admiral. "But he was much, much older than I."

It was during the years of making *The Patty Duke Show* (1963–1966) that Schallert would wander across the lot to visit the *Get Smart* set. Impressed at once by a sense of the "unusual and very funny," as well as by the sight of Barbara Feldon in a tutu, he thought he'd really enjoy working in the show. When open readings were held for the role of the Admiral, Schallert interviewed with producer Arnie Rosen:

"They had given me the script in the outer lobby, and I took one quick look at it and saw what the guy was like, and I didn't even bother to read it. I knew what I was going to do. It's just one of those kind of made-to-order roles, so I did my shtik, this old guy I had.

"While sitting in the office, I came up with something and suggested it to Arnie. I said, 'He might find it hard to get out of a chair. But here's a funnier idea.

Suppose he has a hard time getting into a chair?' It developed into a running bit for the Admiral. The Admiral would try to sit down: 'Could you give me a little shove?' Then someone would push him lightly, and he'd keel into the chair with a 'Thank you' in his very frail voice. Or he'd say, 'I have a plan' or something along those lines, then keel backward by mistake and say 'Thank you' in that same voice. I suggested these things to Arnie on the first day.

"And the other thing when he falls, instead of being frightened, he just says 'Oh dear,' or 'Oh heck.' Though I wasn't conscious of it at the time, what I did was take the curse off the fall. The guy is used to it. He's survived plenty of falls. He's not hurt, making him a less pathetic character. It wasn't damaging, just funny."

The Admiral wears a perpetually puzzled countenance. The man is startled by life. He hasn't a clue what to make of anything. Someone accosts him with an important message. "What is it?" people ask anxiously. "An important message," he intones, oblivious to his having answered nothing. You might hesitate to give Maxwell Smart a submachine gun; you wouldn't trust the Admiral with soap on a rope.

Yet there's method to the madness of putting him in charge. The Admiral isn't a parody of senior citizens, but of a system that puts superannuated geezers in command. Such antediluvian souls, so used to life's traumas, can't be traumatized. Placed in key strategic posi-

William Schallert as the Admiral in the Sixties. *Courtesy of William Schallert.*

tions, they behave as people who can't be traumatized. Their unflappability is labeled *objectivity* until they make a bad guess. Then everyone asks, "What's the matter with the old bird?"

Since *Get Smart*, Schallert became an authority figure in his own right as president of the Screen Actors Guild, and has appeared as his old guy on *The Carol Burnett Show*, *Ironside*, *The New Gidget* (as "The Commodore"), and as a running character on *The Wild, Wild West*.

Since *Smart*, The Admiral, by other names than Harold Harman Hargrade, has made his presence felt around the world.

HYMIE

"At a party, you'd ask, 'Why is that guy moving that way?' But in the world of TV, he passes for normal."

—Dick Gautier (Hymie)

The most perfect agent at CONTROL is Hymie, a robot. Not only is he their most perfect agent specimen, but he's also one of their few machines that work. Not surprisingly, CONTROL didn't create him, nor did they buy him in a bargain basement. Rather, civilization's foremost evil genius, Dr. Ratton, invented him, naming him after his father. Ratton sold him to KAOS for one million dollars. KAOS sent Hymie to kidnap a lunar scientist and to destroy Maxwell Smart if need be. Back then, Hymie was a fiend. But Smart befriended him, rewired him, programmed him for goodness, and brought him into CONTROL ("Back to the Old Drawing Board").

Hymie's features are chiseled, à la Fred MacMurray or Captain Midnight. His every hair is in place, his attire immaculate. He's attractive to women (and women robots) and dances beautifully. He's programmed for neatness, and wallops those who don't respect the spotlessness of his floor ("Anatomy of a Lover"). Hymie is the strongest, most intelligent machine in the world, with an IQ of over 200 ("Back to the Old Drawing Board"). He's sturdy, weighing in at 982 pounds ("It Takes One to Know One"). His delicate circuitry can detect and analyze poison with a taste. Hymie can mentally compute the height of a window, and he has a built-in computer, yet he runs on simple rechargeable batteries. ("Anatomy of a Lover" and "Run, Robot, Run"). He is easily serviced, having the constitution of a shark or a billy goat. He smokes only when he drinks cheap oil, and enjoys a good glass of kerosene and oil now and then ("When Good Fellows Get Together"), or a hot dog in one swallow, complete with its cellophane wrapper ("Run, Robot, Run").

Hymie, lacking the insights of a human brain, takes everything literally. Max asks for a hand. Hymie twists off his hand to give it to Max. Max says, "Hop to it, Hymie." Hymie hops away. Max reminds Hymie to "kill the light." Hymie shoots the bulb. Max pays Hymie a compliment: "You knock me out." Hymie knocks him out cold ("Back to the Old Drawing Board"). Max asks him to grab a waiter, and to get a grip on himself; Hymie picks up and carries the waiter and grips himself. Max says "You tickle me," and Hymie tickles Max ("Anatomy of a Lover"). Hymie thinks nothing of conversing with the door. His friends, after all, include Ethel the PBX board, Frances the coffee machine, and Bruce the elevator ("When Good Fellows Get Together").

At once his greatest failing and greatest asset is his squishy-soft sentimentality. Even before Max rewires him, Hymie responds to Max's treating him as something more than an invention. He falls for a female robot ("It Takes One to

86 and 99 examine Hymie (Dick Gautier). *Courtesy of Dick Gautier.*

Know One") and enchants the Chief's niece Phoebe ("Anatomy of a Lover"). He broods over personal slights, for instance when the Admiral rather than Hymie becomes best man when Max weds 99 ("The Worst Best Man"), or when he's been cooped up at home all day and Max won't take him to dinner ("Anatomy of a Lover"). "It's the same old story," Hymie pouts. "Nobody cares about a robot. Just wind him up, turn him loose, and grease him every thousand miles" ("Run, Robot, Run"). On

the other hand, placed in charge of Max, he's a martinet issuing demerits. He is, all in all, awfully human.

Says Dick Gautier, who portrayed Hymie, "People have pointed out a combination of sinister threat and power, but at the same time, a niceness about the character, a sweetness coming from this thing. I think one of the reasons the character worked is that 86 and I had a warm relationship, almost a male-female relationship, especially in the 'Odd Couple' scene of 'Anatomy of a Lover.' 86 had a sort of adversarial relationship with the Chief, even though there was also a little affection. Between 99 and Max there was affection on her side but not on his. He was almost oblivious to her. But between Hymie and 86, there was a shared warmth. I was an outrageous character being a robot and having some sort of a soul, and Smart wasn't afraid to express affection for me. To Smart's way of thinking, I was safe."

Gautier—born on Halloween to an MGM grip and a studio wardrobe mistress—won the state prize for Humorous Declamation in the Forensic League while in high school. But he "unceremoniously" left school just prior to graduation, reportedly for choosing the wrong time to be humorous. With opportunities to go into both art and drama, Gautier turned to comedy, beginning at a nightclub in San Diego for $42 a week. By age eighteen, he was writing material for Buster Keaton's TV show. Within a few years, San Francisco's legendary "hungry i" signed him to replace Mort Sahl. After a year at the "i," Gautier decided to conquer New York. He instantly found work there, waiting tables, designing greeting cards, and demonstrating pogo sticks at Macy's. Then came the top clubs—the Blue Angel, the Village Vanguard, the Bonsoir— along with tours, frequent TV guest spots, and in 1960, originating the role of Conrad Birdie in the Broadway smash *Bye Bye Birdie.*

Then came Hymie. A close friend of *The Man from U.N.C.L.E.*'s Robert Vaughn—ever since Vaughn and Gau-

tier's wife Barbara starred together in the national tour of *Under the Yum Yum Tree*—Dick Gautier thought nothing of enlisting with a rival espionage network: "By socializing with Robert Vaughn, I was peripherally in the spy business anyway."

Gautier got the Hymie part through an open cast call. King Moody, who later became Shtarker, also turned up for the role. As part of the audition, Gautier was asked how he imagined Hymie to be. He drew on childhood memories of a man in a store window who did mime-like movements, and whose gimmick was that he'd give $100 to anyone able to make him laugh. No one could make the man laugh, and Gautier remembered. Later, in his nightclub act, Gautier did strange voices and noises—slow motion, backwards, and the like. He also had a knack for oddly flexing his head and face muscles. Gautier's Hymie incorporated these various mannerisms with the idea that a robot would hone in on sound, but would be slower and less subtle than people are in turning to it.

He already knew Don Adams from the days when they both played nightclubs and, beginning with the episode "Back to the Old Drawing Board," welcomed the challenge of faking robotics:

"I wore a wetsuit under my clothing. The wetsuit looked like a second skin. The box that contained Hymie's gears and components fit flat up against my chest, under the wetsuit, and the wetsuit was cut in such a way that, when I opened my shirt, I seemed to have this gear and computer chamber behind a panel inside my chest. This is how they got the illusion of opening a panel in his chest to reveal his inner parts.

"There was an electrical wire running down my clothing, down my leg, out of frame and into a socket, which is how they got the wheels to spin in my chest. Wearing the suit was hot. Very, very hot.

"For my first episode, the special effects man said, 'I'm going to put some squibs in your chest.' I didn't want to admit that I didn't know what squibs were. I'd never had squibs. He said, 'They're just half loads,' or quarter loads, or whatever he said, so I answered, 'That's great,' which seemed more professional than something like 'What the hell are squibs?' Then they told me that the other actor would fire a gun at me, and since I was an invulnerable robot, I couldn't blink. I said, 'Hey, you got it,' because anyone can control a blink.

"They said, 'Roll 'em, ready to go,' and the squibs, which of course are small explosive devices, erupted all over my chest. When I finished blinking every which way, I looked down at my fake chest and it was shattered, blown apart. It looked like the eating scene from *Alien*. They said, 'You blinked.' I said, 'What the hell happened?' They said, 'Those are squibs.' And I replied, 'Oh yes, sure, squibs, right.' Then I had to get out of the clothes, take off the wet-suit, get into clothes that weren't blown up yet, get new squibs, which took maybe two hours. We must have had to do this four times and finally gave up

because it's an involuntary response. You just cannot help it. When your chest is erupting underneath your nose, it's very hard not to blink a little. So on film, I'm still fighting the blink.

"Then, in the Olympics episode ('Run, Robot, Run'), I had to run track in a suit, tie, and shoes. I ran around that track about fifteen times before we had it, and it drove me out of my mind. It got hotter and hotter, and they kept telling me to go around again."

Frequently, after a good take, Don Adams would congratulate Gautier: "That performance was wooden, mechanical, absolutely one-dimensional. . . ."

Gautier briefly had his own series while doing *Get Smart* (*Mr. Terrific*, 1967–1967), and at about the same time discovered the theoretically flawless Hymie's one imperfection: "On the one hand, you can't get stereotyped playing a white-collar robot because you can't play it enough to do yourself in. On the other hand, it doesn't lead to other roles because they're never written. How many normal robots are in fact seen on prime-time TV?"

It is not entirely uncommon for casting people to take an actor's last role as literally as Hymie responds to "give me a hand." When Gautier starred as a mono-syllabic rock 'n' roll idol in *Bye Bye Birdie*, some radio interviewers assumed that he had Birdie's bad habits and vocabulary, and shied away from booking him on their programs—despite his having won a Tony nomination and the title of "Broadway's Most Promising New-comer" for the role, and in spite of the successful seven-year nightclub career which preceded it.

Fortunately, Gautier avoided the label of specializing in robot parts. His credits following *Get Smart* include movies of the week, feature films, and stage appearances—besides which, he directs, sings, cartoons, and impersonates everyone from Christopher Lloyd to Maria Ouspenskaya (" . . . beware my son when de foooll moon rises . . .").

Meanwhile, men and boys throughout the country have earned the nickname "Hymie" because they happen to look like him. Mostly, they take it as a compliment.

the first to admit it. Before *Get Smart*, he wasn't an actor at all. He'd been a football player in school, then a Marine, deriving fame from the physical prowess and striking similarity he shared with his twin brother. The two were golden gloves boxing champs in the Marines, and their antics as look-alikes were detailed in several pages in John Monks's book *A Ribbon and A Star*, about the Third Marines at Bougainville. (Not long ago, the Brothers Karvelas appeared on *Good Morning America* with another famous pair of brothers, the Smothers Brothers.)

When he returned to civilian life, Robert Karvelas went into the brokerage

---

Max: Hymie, answer the door.
Hymie: Hello, door, what was the
          question again?
                    ("Run, Robot, Run")

LARABEE

"Max couldn't laugh at himself. Larabee was his Maxwell Smart."

—Don Adams

Larabee (or sometimes, Larrabee) works for CONTROL because he's related to the boss: Robert Karvelas, who portrays him, is—as noted earlier—Don Adams's cousin and boyhood chum. Karvelas is

The Chief and Larabee, disguised for "The Day They Raided the Knights." *Courtesy of Robert Karvelas.*

business: "After some years of living in New York and working on Wall Street, I kept hearing from my friends in the business who had moved West, and kept telling me to go out there. New York was getting pretty bad, so I wrote three or four letters to brokerage firms, got all positive answers, and had my choice of jobs. We relocated, but my wife didn't like California. It's a real adjustment in life-styles from New York to California. I still wasn't able to adjust after five or six months. I was already ready to go back to New York. Kept telling my wife, 'Pack your things. We're leaving.'

"Then Don called me, I think from Florida, and asked how I liked California. I told him I didn't like it much. 'People die in the sun here. They dry up. I'm going home.' He said, 'Don't do that. I think I'm going to do a TV show in Los Angeles.' I asked, 'What's the name of it?' He said, *Get Smart.* I didn't know how I'd fit into a quiz show, but he said it was a sitcom and maybe he'd find something for me to do. So that's how it happened. I got a line, maybe 'Right, Chief,' then when I proved I could handle it, they trusted me with two lines, and in the fourth year, I got fan letters."

In fact, in his first appearances, whether Karvelas is Larabee is anybody's guess. He rushes into a room with a gun; or hands someone a note; or stands on a ladder taking pictures of a corpse in Dr. Sontag's lab in "Weekend Vampire" (1965). The episodes give him no character name, nor does his own name

flash with the closing credits. He finally steps into the slot of a sort of secretary to the Chief, stationed in an outer office, occasionally backing him up with a gun.

As the Chief's assistant, he assumes a function first performed by Hodgkins (Bryan O'Byrne) and briefly by Hobson (Gordon Jump). He has more personality and fewer wits than his two predecessors combined. His flair was a long time in coming: "When I first got the part, with those two-word lines, I couldn't louse up. That's what they were counting on. I was supposed to play a straight part, sitting at the outer desk. But then I started to develop the character, and the writers started to give me my own lines, funny lines. The funny lines they gave me, I played straight. That's what made them funny. I would play this hopelessly incompetent person straight. Next to me, Smart looked Smart." After a while, when the *Smart* gang would go to the dailies, Larabee would execute one of his blank maneuvers on screen, and Adams would quip, "Karvelas stole the show again."

What Karvelas stole in the last analysis were the jokes too stupid for Smart to utter. Remarks Adams, "In the last years, he was dumber than I was. The writers had all these really dumb jokes that were so stupid, Smart couldn't say them. So Larabee said them, and became a great foil for me. Then I could play off his stupidness. So to me, he became one of the funniest characters we had on the show."

Larabee is the sort of man who can be

leaning against the door of a car, but when told "Follow that man," takes off on foot. He slyly observes the combination of the Chief's office safe—a combination known only to the Chief and the Vice President—in order to be able to stash his lunch there ("Do I hear A Vaults?") (Max had the combination, but locked it inside for safe keeping before commiting it to memory in "Perils in a Pet Shop.") Larabee and Max, cornering the Chief, can drive him insane, then stare at each other innocently and ask, "Got another headache, Chief?"

In the final episode of *Get Smart*, CONTROL captures the heinous Whip in his lair ("I Am Curiously Yellow"). This pillar of infamy has a gong which puts those gazing at it in the power of whoever strikes it. The Chief casts a glance at the gong. Larabee strikes. *Kaboonnng*. The Chief falls under his spell. Larabee seizes the reins of CONTROL. It's a dirty job, but somebody's got to do it.

FANG: AGENT K-13

"We fought the urge to call him Agent K-9."

—Buck Henry

Fang, essentially incompetent, is CONTROL's top canine spy. He and Max graduated from the same class at spy school ("The Only Way to Die"). Other than the Chief and 99, he's the only CONTROL agent grieving for Max at Max's feigned funeral ("The Only Way to Die"). Fang supports Max's contract demands for CONTROL agents until Max gets too gung-ho about Fang's future spine-tingling, horrible cases—whereupon Fang leaves the room, leading Max to comment that he's almost human ("Strike While the Agent Is Hot"). Fond of Max and sharp enough to walk away from most danger, he represents that rare coincidence in show business—an actor whose role consists in playing himself.

Remembers Leonard Stern, "He typified the show. We hired a dog who couldn't do anything. We unwisely chose him because of his personality rather than his ability to respond to commands. In his first scene in the pilot, Max puts a card in the time clock and punches in, then the dog does the same. My memory is of spending many hours on that shot, and I imagine I must have had to apologize profusely to everyone who made up the budget.

"It slowed up the days considerably with the trainer yelling 'Here, Fang! Here, Fang!' very authoritatively while Fang failed to respond. We even tried having the actors not speak until the dog crossed. We tried to synchronize it. But nothing worked. He was a highly independent dog. He had wealth in his own right and didn't need the job."

For the pilot episode, Fang had to untie the ropes around 99's wrists. But Fang, a Method dog, couldn't be both-

Striking terror in the hearts of villains everywhere. Maxwell Smart and Agent K–13, Fang. *Courtesy of Howard Frank Archives/Personality Photos, Inc.*

ered without the proper motivation. Explains Barbara Feldon, "I was in a rowboat, and he had to untie my bonds. At first, he wouldn't jump into the boat, and he wouldn't do what he was supposed to do with the ropes. Finally, someone had to stand off camera and throw Fang into the boat But he still wouldn't go for my wrists, not until we put meat between them. This time we couldn't keep Fang off camera long enough. And then, he didn't stop at nibbling the meat from my wrists. He began searching me. He was thinking, 'You never know where else there might be meat.' So I had to fend off Fang."

Concludes Leonard Stern, "This dog who occupied maybe a minute or two in the early episodes routinely took up several hours on the set, and people were hoarse from screaming at him. Ultimately we wrote him out, deciding he was irreplaceable. We didn't want to go through that again."

CONTROL'S NUMBERED AGENTS

Some CONTROL agents have names on the job—among them, Maxwell Smart; Larabee; Charlie Watkins, the male agent who works as a curvaceous and buxom key club hostess; Porter, disguised as a railroad porter ("Smart Fell on Alabama"); Rosa La Costa, CONTROL's singing agent ("Pheasant Under Glass"); Webster, posted for surveillance purposes in a furnished steamer trunk on Pier 8 ("The Apes of Rath"); Armstrong (Agent 77), a.k.a. Chucko the ape ("The Apes of Rath"); Sam (Agent 72), who while moonlighting in his laundry truck during the CONTROL cutback, rescues Max and 99 ("Maxwell Smart,

Private Eye"); Joe Froebus (Agent 63), whom Max doesn't recognize (because Max hasn't heard about his train accident and the plastic surgeon who remade his face), and beats up ("Someone Down Here Hates Me").

Others have gone down in CONTROL history identified only by numbers—the lower the number, the earlier they joined CONTROL. On *The Prisoner* (1968–1969), Number 6 (Patrick McGoohan) used to loudly insist that he wasn't a number; he had a name. No doubt he struck a sympathetic chord with CONTROL agents everywhere.

Agent 4: Herbert Gaffer, one of CONTROL's oldest agents and in fact the twit Max patterned himself after, according to "Dear Diary."

Agent 8: The old spy hiding behind the dart board at Spy City in "Dear Diary."

Agent 8½: Hid inside the ball return at the bowling alley in "Diamonds Are a Spy's Best Friend."

Agent 12: Disguised himself as Santa Claus at Bower's Department Store in "Our Man in Toyland."

Agent 13: (See *Special Mention* on page 90–91.)

Agent 17: The CONTROL agent who helps get Max out of jail in "The

Little Black Book," Part II.

Agent 17: An organ grinder's monkey in "KAOS in Control."

Agent 18: Like Agent 42, was found dead and toothless after attempting to transport microfilm in his teeth, according to "The Whole Tooth and . . ."

Agent 21: CONTROL's lawyer who handles divorces, according to "The Little Black Book," Part II.

Agent 23: One of Dr. Drago's previous victims in "Weekend Vampire."

Agent 24: Snatched while speaking back-to-back with Max in "The Mummy."

Agents 24, 25, and 26: Hiding in the hall closet (24), outside the window as window washer (25), and as the maid (26) of the prince's room in "The Man from YENTA." Max, thinking they're from KAOS, neutralizes all three.

Agent 25: Poses as a mannequin in the sporting department in "Our Man in Toyland."

Agent 27: Hunted down by Hans Hunter and shipped to CONTROL in a box, in "The Island of the Darned."

Agent 34: Hides inside the restaurant serving cart in "Our Man in Toyland."

Agent 34: Moonlights as a cab driver during CONTROL's budget cut, in which capacity he rescues Max and Trinka, in "Maxwell Smart, Private Eye."

Agent 38: CONTROL courier replaced at the airport by a look-alike operative from KAOS's League of Impostors, in "The Spy Who Met Himself."

Agent 39: Successfully employed the Oriental houseboy disguise to crack the Hong Kong Smuggling Case, according to "Casablanca." The disguise seems to have been convincing primarily because 39 was an Oriental houseboy.

Agent 41: The chambermaid in "Too Many Chiefs."

Agent 42: Like Agent 18, was found dead and toothless after attempting to transport microfilm in his teeth, according to "The Whole Tooth and . . ."

Agent 43: Passenger on the bus attacked by Indians in "Washington 4, Indians 3." According to 99, 86 is worth two of him.

Agent 44: (See *Special Mention* on page 90–91).

Agent 46: Left the Dead Spy Scrawls in wet cement at the bus station after being shot by Leonard Nimoy in "The Dead Spy Scrawls."

Agent 47: Head negotiator for the new labor contract between agents and CONTROL, he's shot and killed in a phone booth by KAOS. While dying, he swears Max in as his successor, in "Strike While the Agent is Hot."

Agent 48: The elevator operator in "Too Many Chiefs."

Agent 49: A previous victim of Dr. Drago in "Weekend Vampire."

Agent 49: Cosmetician/agent at Brigette Beauty Salon in "A Tale of Two Tails."

Agent 51: The spy in the gorilla suit at the circus in "The Greatest Spy on Earth."

Agent 52: Dr. Drago zaps him in the neck in Professor Sontag's lab, in "Weekend Vampire."

Agent 53: Disguised as a mirror in Bower's menswear department in "Our Man in Toyland."

Agent 54: Painted blue to death in "Bronzefinger."

Agent 73: Destroyed by his German shepherd after sending him to KAOS's Washington Animal Spa Kennel in "I'm Only Human."

Agent 74: Shot down helping Max in "How To Succeed in the Spy Business Without Really Trying." Max questions whether this constitutes help.

Agent 77: Couldn't find the Choker at the airport in "Casablanca."

Agent 85: Fourth CONTROL courier to leave Paris with a briefcase chained to his wrist. Like the three before him, he doesn't reach his destination, but instead, is gassed to death "Aboard the Orient Express."

Agent 91: First CONTROL agent subdued by Hymie in "Back to the Old Drawing Board."

Agent 95: Kidnapped and tortured by KAOS for thirty days, he emerged ranting and unintelligible, and went into politics, according to "The Expendable Agent."

Agents 198 and 199: Rookie CONTROL agents Lundy and Caruso in "A Tale of Two Tails."

Agent B17: A parrot expert at imitating voices and repeating what he hears in "I'm Only Human."

Special Mention

For the special assignment of hiding out in cramped, uncomfortable places, CONTROL seemingly set aside two

Agent 13 (Dave Ketchum) refamiliarizes himself with daylight. *Courtesy of Dave Ketchum.*

numbers, 13 and 44. Agent 44 (Victor French) came first, to be found inside a clock ("Back to the Old Drawing Board"); outside a ship, contacting Max through the porthole ("Ship of Spies"); upside-down in a cello case ("Hubert's Unfinished Symphony"); in a medicine cabinet, charging Max for messages because he hasn't been paid in so long ("Aboard the Orient Express"); and elsewhere. 44 does not enjoy his work, and shows it. In "Ship of Spies," Part II, the Chief and Max agree that he'd be a good agent if he broke the crying habit.

With the departure of Agent 44, Agent 13 (Dave Ketchum) came on the scene, griping all the way, generally with good reason. He was once stationed in a washing machine for three days, and in a litterbox ("The Decoy"); also inside a penny scale ("Perils in a Pet Shop"); in an ice cube vending machine ("Somebody Down Here Hates Me"); behind the panel in a hotel wall ("The Man from YENTA"); inside a couch ("Kiss of Death"); inside the Rembrandt painting "Man in the Golden Helmet," and in the Chief's wall safe ("Bronzefinger"); in an airport cigarette machine ("The Expendable Agent"); in a mail box, then arrested by a cop for being in a mail box ("The Only Way to Die"); in a potted plant in the Metropolitan Museum ("The Mummy"); in the towel steamer in a barbershop ("Maxwell Smart, Alias Jimmy Ballantine"); in a washing machine at Three Brothers Omniwash ("A Man Called Smart," Part III); and in an airport locker, with his KAOS double, a perfect look-alike, occupying the adjacent locker ("The Spy Who Met Himself").

13's mother is a spy, but won't tell his family her name or her side ("The Mummy").

When 13 moved on, a new Agent 44 (Al Molinaro) filled his shoes, enjoying his task whether dressed in a baby bonnet and hidden inside a baby buggy ("Ironhand") or wearing Bermuda shorts to deal with the heat engendered by standing inside a lit pot-bellied stove ("Ice Station Siegfried"). His good humor served him in excellent stead, which is just as well. With that attitude, 44 may not have lived long enough to see his pension.

6

||||||||||||||||||||||||||||||||||||||||||||||||||||||||||||||||||||||||||||||||||||||||||||||||||||||||||||||||||||||||||||||||

KAOS IN CONTROL

"While we are sleeping, two-thirds of the world is plotting to do us in."

—Dean Rusk,
former U.S. Secretary of State

"If KAOS goes out of business, what happens to us?"

—Agent 86 ("Maxwell Smart, Alias Jimmy Ballantine")

Even before the Chicago riots (1968) and Woodstock (1969), the conventional concepts of *good* and *evil* were subsumed by the operative words of the Sixties: *control* and *chaos*. *Chaos*, by definition, had always been undesirable. *Control* had been the ideal. Harnessing the random power of nature provided electricity, irrigation, and farmlands. Controlling savage civi-

lizations made for progress and culture. The Bible begins with God controlling chaos, creating everything, and designating all things good or evil—making God the first agent of control, the first control agent.

If you went by the Bible, history, or technology, control was good. Then came mind-control drugs . . . the control of revolutionaries . . . best-sellers about "subliminal seduction" with which advertisers by-pass consumer awareness with ads commandeering the subconscious brain . . . and one school of thought read *control* as another word for repression. This school of iconoclasts marched to protest moral chaos. Law enforcers called them anarchists and controlled them.

Enter *Get Smart*'s CONTROL and KAOS, representing nothing so simple as mind-control subjugation on the one hand and anarchistic moral chaos on the other—but reflecting, instead, how confusing old-fashioned *good* and *evil* had become. Does control bring safety, or a police state? Does chaos mean lawless rampage, or the freedom to wear cut-off jeans? You could go on believing one side purely good and one totally evil, or merely accept that whatever your side bungled, the other guys were worse.

During the planning stages of *Get Smart,* considerable time and worry were devoted to whether CONTROL should be terrorized by unrelated villains or by disparate members of one organization. In the end, KAOS won out—with the result that, just as Bond has his SMERSH and S.P.E.C.T.R.E. (Special Executive for Terrorism, Revolution, and Espionage), and Napoleon Solo's U.N.C.L.E. has its THRUSH, Maxwell Smart has his work cut out for him by a menacing brotherhood of foes known as KAOS (which, like CONTROL, is not now and has never been an acronym).

Early *Smart* episodes, beginning with the pilot, carefully identify KAOS as an international organization of evil formed to dominate the world. In "Hoo Done It" (1966), further details surface when spy Omar Shurok responds to the question of whether he's heard of KAOS: "The international organization of evil formed in 1904 in Bucharest, designed to foment unrest and revolution throughout the world? I never heard of it." This contradicts Max's statement in the pilot that KAOS began in the Fifties, which only serves to confirm the success of KAOS security.

In the remaining *Smart* years, little more is said about the historical KAOS.

In fact, after the series' initial need to define KAOS for its audience, even the basic tag-line is dropped. Viewers watching the endless parade of scoundrels, listening to their assorted take-over plots, and perceiving that their schemes won't win friends among the readers of *Readers Digest,* get the picture. It's simple. In the war of good guys versus bad guys, KAOS guys are bad guys.

They are also terrorist assassins, but to Maxwell Smart, *bad guys* says it all. In this sense, *Smart* satirizes the entire tradition of spy shows, detective shows, cop shows, and Western shows before it. By lampooning the most basic, unchallenged values of previous decades, *Smart* marks the shift from the old order toward the new, while recording the transmogrification of buzz words that the Sixties was all about.

KAOS, Inc., is a Delaware corporation for tax purposes ("A Man Called Smart," Part II). Its symbol is a dour vulture, perched atop an egg-shaped version of the globe, set against a squared-off shield. South America is its glorious fatherland ("The Not-So-Great Escape," Part I). KAOS henchmen frequently wear black suits, black turtlenecks, and black fedoras. KAOS has CAD, a Contrived Accident Division ("Run, Robot, Run"). KAOS gives productions of *The Killing of the Shrew* because KAOS doesn't stop at taming. KAOS won't permit its defectors to live ("The Spirit Is Willing"). No informer has ever lived long enough to testify against KAOS ("Witness for the Execution"). At KAOS training school, if you don't graduate,

you're shot ("Cutback at CONTROL").
KAOS is the first private organization to
own a nuclear bomb ("Appointment in
Sahara"). KAOS even perverts parades,
transmitting instructions by the color of
the confetti ("Hurray for Hollywood").
KAOS pays its agents more than CON-
TROL, and has a great health and wel-
fare plan ("The Not-So-Great Escape,"
Part II). Never mind that their agents all
love opera ("Pheasant Under Glass") and
would rather attend the annual KAOS
dance than be bribed for $10,000 ("Rub a
Dub Dub . . . Three Spies in a Sub")—
they're up to serious mischief. You know
they're rotten, explains Siegfried, because they're all former quiz masters,
disc jockeys, used car salesmen, TV re-
pairmen, and politicians ("Cutback at
CONTROL").

Like the KGB, KAOS starts with a *K*.
Like the CIA, CONTROL starts with a
C. This was unintended by a team that
took pains not to single out the U.S.S.R.
as the enemy, and to give KAOS a multi-
national flavor. Dan Melnick remembers
having "very strong feelings about that,
not to make KAOS a national but an
international terror organization. I certainly didn't want to contribute to the
cold war."

SIEGFRIED (A.K.A. SEIGFRIED)

**"If you're so smart, how come you lost
two wars?"**

—Max to Siegfried ("A Spy for a Spy")

Bernie Kopell as Siegfried of KAOS. *Courtesy of Bernie Kopell.*

The thing about international societies of
evil is that in reality, as much as they
enjoy evil, they don't exist to do evil.
They exist to take over the planet. They
hope to accomplish this by evil means,
but are greedy enough to settle for polite
means when left with no other choice.

In early TV drama, bad guys wrought
evil to control far less than the globe. In
contemporary TV offerings, they aim for
the universe and are hard to tell from the
good guys for weeks at a time. Leaping
this chasm—from Fifties stick figures to
the J. R. Ewings (*Dallas*) and Alexis
Colbys (*Dynasty*) of the late Seventies
and early Eighties—shtik figure Conrad
Siegfried led the pack.

James Bond did battle with Dr. No, Odd Job, Auric Goldfinger, and their ilk. Max took on Dr. Yes, the Claw, and Bronzefinger, but his archnemesis—the Moriarty to his Holmes, the Boris to his Rocky—was the infamous Conrad Siegfried, KAOS's Vice President in charge of Public Relations and Terror ("Spy, Spy, Birdie"). Portraying Siegfried (sometimes spelled S*ei*gfried) was an actor much younger than the man he played—an actor who did his first character part out of spite—Bernie Kopell.

As Kopell reconstructs the progression, "When I began acting, I did character work exclusively for my first eighteen months, at a time when character work meant a moustache and an accent rather than the connotation it seems to have today, of a Charles Durning type. What happened is that I'd go to casting people, and they'd always say the same thing: 'What are we going to *do* with you? You're not handsome enough to be a leading man, and you're not ugly enough to be a heavy.' I was as confounded as they were. I thought to myself that here I'd gone to NYU, had my classical training, carried my spear for two years, and learned to speak as precisely as possible without a trace of my Brooklyn accent, and I asked myself, 'What now? What am I going to do with me?' And I had no idea.

"Overwhelmingly frustrated anyway, I compounded my anxiety by meeting an agent who would constantly send me up for things that had already been cast. I was supporting myself by driving a taxi, and my bad luck was really getting to me, to the point that I probably created my own bad luck by having a certain mental fix about things. So this agent sent me to CBS, and once more, the part had been cast. But the very nice lady there, I think trying to pacify me in some way, said, 'As long as you're here, they're reading for a soap opera in the adjoining office. Maybe you'd like to read for *A Brighter Day.*' I knew she was just doing a tap dance, being sweet and sympathetic. I said, 'What part will I be reading for?' She said, 'For Pablo.'

"It hit me in such a strange way that I felt, 'Okay, fine. That's the way it's going. I'll go and read for Pablo.' It was a revenge reading. I had no beginning of a notion how to do it, but I thought, 'I'm going to go in there, and stand in this producer's office, read his script, and take up his valuable time. *Waste* his valuable time. Read his stupid script until he throws me out.' Then I went to wait, and saw other guys out there, with moustaches and dark hair. Great. Wonderful. They *were* Latinos. What could I come up with? I thought of José Melis, Jack Paar's piano player. I went in angry, did José Melis, got the part, and played Latinos for about four months.

"Suddenly, this was supposed to be my niche. This is the extraordinary phenomenon called casting. Casting is what you have established, not what you can do. Right off the bat, I did Jack Benny's show, Danny Kaye's, and Steve Allen's, each time doing a Latino accent. I developed other accents figuring, okay, this is what I do. I developed an Oriental accent based on an Oriental actor in town who had a thick Chinese accent but was obsessed with playing Hamlet." (In the years following *Get Smart*, Kopell appeared in accent roles on *The Flying Nun* and *Bewitched*. "I played a German submarine commander and a hundred-year-old apothecary on *Bewitched*. Then the producer, Bill Asher, asked if I could play myself. That threw me. How to do me took a lot of thought. It's a strange world out there.")

Leonard Stern first met Bernie Kopell, along with future *Get Smart* actor Harold Gould, on the set of *I'm Dickens, He's Fenster*. The initial impression evoked wrath mixed with pity: "Since I began working with Bernie, I haven't made a pilot without him, or had a series on the air in which he didn't appear. But the day we met, he and Harold were represented by an agent who was impossibly audacious. You might also say insensitive. I was directing a sequence, and this man tapped me on the shoulder and asked if I had a moment to meet two actors. I was so incensed, I wanted to have him banished, then I looked over and saw these two unfortunate souls standing there, recognizing that their agent had performed a horrendous act. So, out of concern for them, I went over and we established instant rapport. They were both very bright, and I promised myself then to work with both of them. We had Bernie in the pilot of *Run Buddy Run* before he became a regular on *Get Smart*, and Harold, a former college professor, became a semi-regular in *He & She*.

Says Kopell, "The agent had unor-thodox methods, but I was about twenty-four or twenty-five and very interested in working, and I figured that if they threw me out, so what, I wasn't working anyway.

"At the time, I'd been getting work in dribs and drabs. I was doing things at the Players Ring Theatre. The first time I worked there, they had great motivation in hiring me because I wasn't with Actors Equity and they didn't have to pay me anything. Equity minimum for Hollywood area theaters in those days was $40.00 gross, $33.35 after taxes, which I didn't get. Then something very important happened for me. They had a play called *The Forty-Ninth Cousin*, and I got the title role as a very shy Russian immigrant peddlar with some wonderful scenes, and some wonderful comedy. The play ran for nine months, during which I had the experience of laughs and recognition and being paid.

"Leonard Stern came to see the play. He loved it, came backstage to see me, and to hear him tell about it subsequently—though I don't remember this happening—he says I was so in character that I still used the accent. After it, he wrote me a letter saying we would work together. But I never believed anybody who said that.

"Then in 1966, a call came from Mike Marmer, one of the *Get Smart* writers. I knew him and his partner, Stan Burns, from our working together on Steve Allen's show where I'd done so many accent routines. Mike asked if I could do a German accent. I said yes, then found out what he was calling about—the chance to play Siegfried, a guy fifteen years older than I was. We changed my hair, my look, and gave me a Heidelberg dueling scar made with collodion, a makeup material that shrinks your skin, and when it's taken off, you stay red and indented for days."

Kopell borrowed his Siegfried accent from a Viennese psychiatrist he'd met: "Anybody who has the ear will recognize that it's not the kind of hammy German that's not German at all. Generally, an English-speaking European with an education will speak English with a bit of a British accent because he learned his English from an Englishman. And Siegfried's had a haughtiness in it, a contempt, and anger. Siegfried is always angry about something."

Perhaps Siegfried's anger stems from his being the only fully uniformed Third Reich Nazi too stupid to head for South America. Instead—an anachronism and a cartoon—he stalks his entirely fitting match, Maxwell Smart.

Siegfried's role evolves with each new foray. In his first appearance, he pretends to be a magician in order to kidnap the Chief ("A Spy For a Spy"). Having kidnapped his rugged victim, he phones Max to convey his ransom demands. Max asks to speak to the Chief. The Chief tells Max not to give in, no matter what Siegfried threatens. Siegfried has the Chief silenced with a knock on the head. Max, offended by the violence, suggests that Siegfried could have gotten the same results by shushing him. Siegfried disdainfully retorts, "Vee don't shussh here!"

The response, which became a key to Siegfried's character, sprang not from the script but from the floor. Leonard Stern suggested it as he watched the scene in rehearsal. "From that line," recalls director Bruce Bilson, "it sort of led to who Siegfried was. That explosive, angry stance of superiority."

Traits gradually accrued, all nasty. In "Rub a Dub Dub . . . Three Spies in a Sub" he modifies his own rule: "You don't shussh here. I shussh here. *Shussh!*" In "How to Succeed in the Spy Business Without Really Trying," Siegfried defects to CONTROL, winning the Defector of the Year Award, only to turn on CONTROL as a double agent. In "Ice Station Siegfried," he joins the Mounties, bewailing how KAOS has dumped him, then goes about reversing the world's climates with a giant electric fan. Escaping from prison after Max subdues him, he sends Max a death threat. By telegram. Collect ("Rub a Dub Dub . . . Three Spies in a Sub").

Siegfried's actions are an open book but his background, like Max's, reeks of mystery. Either could have been birthed by a Cracker Jack box. We learn little more of his origins than that his mother refused young Siegfried a sled (shades of *Citizen Kane*), probably because they lived in Florida. Consequently, he joined the underworld, starting out as a KAOS office boy and part-time killer ("How To Succeed in the Spy Business Without Really Trying"). KAOS gave him a code name, Ludwig, ("Spy, Spy Birdie"). He has been with KAOS for twenty years ("How to Succeed in the Spy Business Without Really Trying").

Where Max relies for surveillance on various agents stashed in sofas, lockers, and portholes, Siegfried has a sister who works in a decoding machine disguised as an airport insurance vendor ("How to Succeed . . ."). Max enjoys the affectionate companionship of 99, the Chief, and Hymie. Siegfried just has Shtarker (also Starker)—Yiddish for big, strapping dolt—who smirks at Siegfried's enemies while blissfully accepting Siegfried's abuse. Shtarker claims to have been the all-time track star of the Third Reich and the second man out of El Alamein—Siegfried having been first ("The Not-So-Great Escape," Part II).

When the Shtarker role came up, Kopell suggested King Moody, a close friend ("I was divorced in 1962. I was depressed at the time, and said to King and his wife, 'Can I stay here overnight?' They harbored me, sheltered me, for a year"). Moody had already appeared in *Get Smart* as KAOS stooge George Markovich, a Russian ("All in the Mind"). Someone felt it might confuse viewers if Moody returned as a German. Kopell pressed his point, ultimately securing for Moody the loftier position of Siegfried's stooge.

Shtarker has the mind of a child. At the mention of an outboard motor, he assumes an infantile grin and makes brmppprfff noises. Siegfried scolds him, "Vee don't brmppprfff here." ("Schwartz's Island"). When really furious, Siegfried gives him both barrels: "You zissy!" ("Spy, Spy Birdie").

At first glance, it appears that cold, calculating Siegfried commits fewer boners than Smart; and that Shtarker, the *dummkopf*, must make mistakes Siegfried will pay for (whereas 99 saves Max from Max's mistakes). But the truth is that Shtarker's inanities are harmless. Strutting his proud proto-Prussian supremacy, Siegfried trips himself up.

Besides, if Siegfried's so smart, how come Max always ultimately outwits him?

7

S, WRITERS
HERE

"Earn your laughter and hire top writers."

—Leonard Stern

When *Get Smart* introduced its opening credits, with its prominently featured names of creators Mel Brooks and Buck Henry directly following the stars, viewers took notice without entirely knowing why they wanted to. But *Get Smart,* topheavy from stem to Stern with top writers, let the secret out of the bag: The stars don't just walk into camera range and think of clever things to say. Somebody actually gives them words, written down, already. These somebodies, variously referred to as the guys, the boys, the kids, and nobodies, sometimes enjoyed less esteem than Higgins accords "the lads" on *Magnum P.I.*, and might as well have lived in caves.

In darker days, not many years earlier, the industry hadn't so much as formed the practice of asking writers to the Emmy award ceremonies. When Leonard Stern and Sydney Zelinka finally attended, they gained admittance not as authors of *The Jackie Gleason Show,* but because Audrey Meadows and Art Carney invited them, and as guests, they couldn't be turned away.

On another occasion, Stern's affable, outgoing father gained the team's access behind closed doors. Stern senior made friends with everyone, including at the theater where the Gleason show took place. One night, caught in a miserable downpour, Leonard Stern and Sydney Zelinka attempted to enter the building

Gene Wilder (left), Zero Mostel (right), and Kenneth Mars (seated) in Mel Brooks's *The Producers* (1968).

through the front door. The doorman barred their way, ordering them to the stage door despite the pounding rain: "What makes you writers think you're coming through the main door?" Then Max Stern arrived, greeting them. The doorman immediately beckoned them in: "Why didn't you say you know Max?"

To the TV audience at large in the Fifties and even the early Sixties, the concept of comedy writers came as a shock. Major TV comics rarely acknowledged their writers, feeling it reflected an inability on their own parts to crack jokes without help. A rule-of-thumb prevailed that the better the writer, the higher his wages to maintain his anonymity.

Comedy writers' credits may or may

not have crawled by on the screen when a program closed, but viewers made no mental notes. A writer's name meant considerably less than "Daytime dresses by Pat Perkins," or "Makeup by Max Factor." Before *Get Smart*, the name *Mel Brooks* would have registered as a talk-show personality or as the 2,000- (and 2,500-) Year-Old Man, but not as a man who wrote comedy. The name *Buck Henry*, outside select circles, would have pretty much drawn a blank.

After endless, nameless years as a boy, fella, kid, and guy—yet notable success under his belt—Mel Brooks deserved his due in recognition. Buck Henry, with fewer years in comedy writing, deserved the same but hadn't been deprived as long. Hence *Get Smart*'s "Created by Mel Brooks *with* Buck Henry."

In addition to co-developing *Get Smart* and co-authoring the pilot, Mel Brooks had committed for several more scripts, which he wrote bicoastally. Maintaining his home on West 11th Street in New York, he commuted west once a month, meanwhile pursuing other projects. In January, 1966 *The New York Times* reported that he'd finished two screenplays, *Marriage Is a Dirty, Rotten Fraud* and *Springtime for Hitler*. After many months of writing scripts and providing ideas to meet *Get Smart* commitments, and feeling he could "run dry very soon," Brooks left *Get Smart*. His *Springtime for Hitler* became *The Producers*, which would launch him on one of the most successful careers in movie comedy history.

When Dan Melnick phoned to bring Buck Henry to the West Coast, Henry agreed with one proviso: "I'll do it if you give me an office overlooking a girl's gym." Though the job left him little time to peer through his window, Henry remained very involved with the show for two years as its story editor. He provided ideas, salvaged ideas, rewrote scripts, came up with characters, and worked with writers on every level—as did Leonard Stern, of whom Henry observes, "It's nice to have writer-producers around. I'd have Lennie to run down the hall to, or enabling me to say to a writer, 'Go see Lennie, I can't stand you any longer.' And I assume vice versa. I've never done it since."

Emulating the moving finger which having writ, moves on, Buck Henry departed *Get Smart* for the sadly short-lived *Captain Nice* (1967–1967). Created by Henry and starring William Daniels as the "nut in pajamas" who embarrassed himself while thwarting crime, it spoofed superheroes the way Maxwell Smart debunked espionage. "It was about a highly reluctant superhero with a harridan mother," Henry has said. "One of the major critics accused it of being a homosexual plot to take over America."

Yet the same year *Captain Nice* folded, *The Graduate*—screenplay by Buck Henry—scored phenomenal box-office and critical acclaim. The picture won stardom for its then unknown Dustin Hoffman, the Best Director Oscar for Mike Nichols, and accolades as America's hottest screenwriter for Buck Henry—not to mention a part for him in the film, as the desk clerk at the hotel.

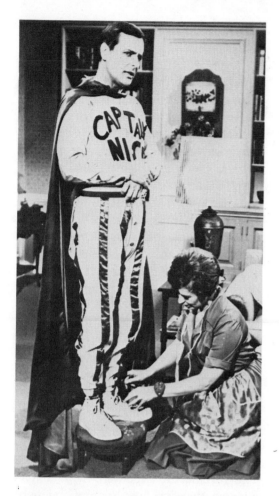

William Daniels and Alice Ghostley in Buck Henry's *Captain Nice* (1967). *Courtesy of Howard Frank Archives/Personality Photos, Inc.*

As executive producer of *Get Smart*, and as a tall man among short ones, Leonard Stern exerted a power akin to Olympus. "I apologize only for thunder," he would advise, and word got around that he thanked people when they noted conversationally, "It's a nice day." For a

while, he used to pass Dick Van Dyke every morning. Every morning, Van Dyke would smile and say "Nice day, isn't it?" and Stern would return the sentiment in kind, till eventually Stern remarked to his wife that the Van Dyke guy wasn't as clever or original as his reputation implied. Mrs. Stern said, "Maybe he's heard about the thank you." When next Stern passed Van Dyke, Van Dyke said, "Nice day," which Stern accepted with the nobility of a gracious Zeus: "Thank you." Van Dyke laughed, and they finally moved on to more varied amenities.

After the first *Get Smart* year, and producing several different Talent Associates series, Stern became less present on the physical scene without ever being uninvolved: "When you function as executive producer, and you're a good executive producer—to my way of thinking—your involvement should be minimal. You should have picked gifted people for all of the jobs, who seldom need to confer. I think, by the end of the first year, I had established a staff which remained constantly in place throughout the subsequent years. The only change was in the producer,* and there were accommodations made there to hold on to certain key writers, such as Arnie Rosen and Arne Sultan. Buck and I were more involved the first year than we were in subsequent years, although I wrote many episodes after the first year myself.

*A producer who left often didn't go far away, but simply moved over to another series in the Talent Associates family.

Whenever we felt we were getting into script trouble, I would revert to being a writer." *

Constantly busily preoccupied, Stern occasionally couldn't avoid behaving like Max. One time, he grew agitated looking for an important piece of paper. He asked around, "What happened to it? What could have happened to it?" His secretary told him, "You ate it with your sandwich." Another time, with both hands broken and in casts, he attempted to light a cigarette while sitting in his office chair, propelling himself backwards onto the floor.

Despite occasional outward signs of euphoria in the writers' quarters—Henry running through the halls in his underwear, Brooks springing into office windows from the ledges outside, and Stern creating nice weather—writing *Get Smart* very much resembled work. Buck Henry, like Stern having tremendous input in the series, paid the price in missed merriment: "My fantasy was that I spent hours on the set, laughing and talking, flirting with beautiful girls, and throwing lines in. But I couldn't get out of the damned office, ever."

Both while Brooks and Henry were with *Get Smart*, and all the years after they left, a bevy of brilliant writers filled the weekly demand for scripts. "Those days are gone," observes Don Adams. "Today you don't get guys like those to work for that kind of money for televi-

sion, unless they're young and just getting established. That kind of writer is not available for television writing any more. They do movies, and pieces of movies, and points of movies."

But in the late Sixties, *Get Smart* had no trouble attracting the best in the business. Writers knew, first off, that instead of being veiled in anonymity, they would be surrounded by peers, by people who could discuss their work in their own language, by people who had vested interest in treating writers with respect.

Not only did writers write *Get Smart*, but they also executive produced, produced, and in some cases directed and acted in it. This engendered a certain inevitability of every script's being rewritten—Buck Henry, Leonard Stern, and Arne Sultan embellished constantly—but scripts are always rewritten anyway. On *Get Smart*, writers had the satisfaction of knowing they were being reshaped by masters of the form.

Get Smart writer Elroy Schwartz, for example, wrote for a number of other series as well, "and in those days, it depended what show you were writing for. With shows like *My Three Sons* and *Family Affair*, sometimes 100 percent of what you wrote would appear on the screen. On these shows, writers were not necessarily in control of being script supervisors or producers. As writers became more involved in production, and as executive story consultants, the rewrites started becoming more frequent, because it's hard to second guess another writer. . . ."

Beyond actual working conditions,

*Buck Henry and Leonard Stern won the 1966–1967 Emmy for comedy writing with their "Ship of Fools."

Get Smart writers could anticipate a freedom to experiment with dialogue and situation. Explained Brooks, "We are the only restaurant in town for the gourmet comedy writer. Here he has a chance to swing, to go as crazy as he wants."

Buck Henry particularly requested Stan Burns, a friend and previous co-worker: "Stan was the first person I'd been with in television, the first serious job I ever had, when I was writing for Steve Allen and they put me with Stan Burns. It was one of the nicest accidents of my life, because he probably is the greatest natural joke writer I ever met in my life, or can imagine there being."

Stan Burns, who played an early, major role in shaping the *Tonight* show, credits much of his comedic training to Abe Burrows. From the first, Burns thrived on spoofery: "That's the only way I can function. I have to have a little fun off something."

With Stan Burns came partner Mike Marmer, of the Allen crowd, and before that, of *The Ernie Kovacs Show*. Marmer attributes much of *Get Smart*'s flavor to the training of writers on those landmark variety programs:

"One reason, I think, is that we had the opportunity in variety to play around with more characters and to expand to larger-than-life characters. We didn't have to write the same thing every day. Steve Allen was the greatest outlet for his writers. If you gave Steve a pun, he'd come back with a pun, because that was his natural sense of humor. He is basically intellectual, and appreciated whatever his writers gave him. A lot of us were spoiled by that. That's why we were able, in *Get Smart*, not to pay attention to conventions or what people did. We just did what we did, because that was what we wanted to do.

"Then too, in those days of live television, we learned to actually be writing while the show was on the air. It honed our reflexes. I would walk in sometimes, working with Ernie Kovacs, and maybe he felt tired and didn't want to rehearse. So he'd say, 'That's a terrible sketch. Give me something else before the end of the show.' I'd sit down, write a new sketch, put it on the teleprompter, and he'd see it for the first time before the show was over. Or you'd write it five minutes before the show started. Variety writers learned to do that. Whatever later writing we did, we brought this ability with us."

Along with Stan Burns and Mike Marmer, Buck Henry brought the team of Gerald Gardner and Dee Caruso, formerly of *That Was the Week That Was* (and soon to be co-writing *The Monkees*, 1966–1968). These two teams contributed most heavily in the initial years of *Get Smart*, Burns and Marmer bringing a decided topical edge, Gardner and Caruso adding a notable craziness.

Of the other writers, writer/producers, and story minds who followed, Arnie Rosen, a *Jackie Gleason Show* writer, became a producer on *Get Smart*. (His *Gleason* partner, Coleman Jacoby, was immortalized as the two characters, Kohlman and Jacoby, in "With Love and Twitches.") Marvin Worth and Arne Sultan hailed from Steve Allen's show. Sultan, a former comedian turned writer, had additionally written for *The Martha Raye Show* and *The Colgate Comedy*

Hour. Sultan eventually became producer, then executive producer, of *Get Smart.* Arne Sultan could invent jokes as fast as he was funny. Years after he and director Reza Badiyi were no longer working together on *Get Smart,* Badiyi phoned from Hawaii in a panic: "I was doing a movie of the week and I needed three jokes in a hurry. I called Arne in his office, and he was having a bad day, with big problems coming one after another. He said, 'Reza, you're calling at the worst time in the world. Where are you calling from?' I said, 'Hawaii, and I need three jokes.' He said, 'Okay, write these down.' Then boom, boom, boom, he gave me three great jokes in a row, as easily as if he were talking. His mind worked that way."

Chris Hayward, another future *Get Smart* producer, had written for *Crusader Rabbit* and *Bullwinkle.* With partner and former *Bullwinkle* writer Alan Burns, he then progressed to "the Smothers Brothers show that didn't work, the one about the angels," followed by *He & She.* Notes Burns, "*Bullwinkle* was a very satirical show. Doing it probably primed us for the sort of things we would be doing on *Get Smart.* Parenthetically, I hear there's a rumor that *Bullwinkle* did Boris and Natasha at the behest of the CIA, to make the Russians look silly." (The ludicrous rumor could be a *Get Smart* plot.)

Another writer from the *Bullwinkle* family, Lloyd Turner contributed heavily in the later *Get Smart* years. Among writers who remained memorable though they may have penned less: Don Adams and his sister, Gloria Burton.

Personalities ranged from that of the

The source of many a *Get Smart* writer as well as performer—*He & She* (1967–1970), starring Paula Prentiss and Richard Benjamin. *Courtesy of Howard Frank Archives/ Personality Photos, Inc.*

quiet, laid back, philosophical Arnie Rosen to fast-talking nightclub types such as Arne Sultan, who shared Don Adams's sort of comedy background, and could at once be funny and tough.

All together, all professionals versed in the shorthand of their trade, they paid homage to the higher laws of humor while ignoring assorted lesser rules along the way. Scripts ran the gamut from a moral and political irreverence à la Buck Henry to a Mel Brooks sort of omnivore zaniness. To Don Adams, "Some people will tell you it was like a great Keystone Kops comedy, sight gags, broad way-out farce, then others will describe it as pure satire. This is probably one big reason for the success of the show. It had such a wide range of appeal to so many different people."

It further enlarged its scope by going places physically. It offered, according to Mel Brooks, "a man's show, the first in a long time. . . . Women and kids, they rule TV. It's a matriarchal society. But *Get Smart* is for men." Because it spoofed James Bond, a spy adventure, it reached beyond the usual sitcom kitchens and malt shops. It provided locations, variations, reasons for Max to duel in a remote European monarchy, and for 99 to become a cabaret singer.

As a spoof of James Bond, *Get Smart* lambasted Bond's distinctive opening titles, catchy theme music, wild fights and violence, spine-tingling chases and escapes, bizarre characters, exotic sets, stupefying gadgetry, and flawless hero. Such, satirized, afforded the elements of *Get Smart* scripts—all subjected to the exigencies of a small budget and the need to compress movielike scenarios into a half-hour minus time for commercials. Remarked Mel Brooks, "It's hard to capture one's vision and dream in 24½ minutes."

As a sitcom, *Get Smart* whenever possible ignored the strictures of sitcoms.

For Buck Henry, "I think the advantage we had was that I'd not only never tried to write a sitcom, but—and I know no one will believe this—I'd never seen one. I still to this day don't think I've seen more than six. I simply can't concentrate on them. The form doesn't interest me at all."

As "camp," a phenomenon first identified in the Sixties and most ardently mined by *Batman* (1966–1968), it accentuated the potentially silly while, unlike *Batman*, aimed for trappings of the real. *Batman* doesn't so much spoof law enforcement as it parodies comic strips about crimefighting—whereas *Get Smart* becomes a comic strip version of real-life espionage.

As satire, *Get Smart* operated like a holograph, interweaving pointed commentary with shtik so goofy that you could stare right at it yet overlook the aggression by choosing to hold it at a different angle. As "fresh" material in both senses of the word—(1) inventive, and (2) smart-mouthed—it managed volumes by wielding its bayonets under whoopee cushions.

Of "Our Man in Toyland," *Get Smart*'s second episode, critic Bob Williams wrote, "*Get Smart* got smart Saturday night with a sardonic war-toy battle. It might, ironically, have been the strongest dramatic statement of the TV season." Yet to those not looking for lessons, the same battle easily provided a broadly farcical scene. Buck Henry remembers "specifically, or at least I think I remember specifically, Lennie and I running into each other holding the same newspaper, a story about the CIA or FBI having pension hassles, and the agents threatening a strike. It gave birth to an episode." The same episode, viewed without benefit of headline, can give the impression of being bizarre, it-can't-happen-here, good fun.

Granted, media censorship had come a long way since the Thirties, when only a pitched battle enabled Rhett Butler to utter *Gone With the Wind*'s immortal "Frankly my dear, I don't give a damn"; when, in England, the BBFC (British Board of Film Censors) banned Germaine Dulac's *The Seashell and the Clergyman* on the grounds that "This film is apparently meaningless. If there is any meaning it is doubtless objectionable"; and when, responding to the script for *Zaza* with the heroine's outburst of "Pig! Pig! Pig! Pig! Pig!" the censor's office instructed, "Delete two pigs."

Twenty years later, a utility company sponsoring a major TV drama about the holocaust forbade the writers to mention gas as a means of execution. By the early Sixties, Reginald Rose's controversial *The Defenders* (1961–1965) bucked censors with the serious treatment of such issues as abortion and blacklisting. By the mid-Sixties, drama had crossed any number of lines, and comedy—from *The Dick Van Dyke Show* (1961–1966) to *That Was the Week That Was* (1964–1965)—had begun to.

With *Get Smart*, says Mike Marmer, "believe it or not, we concerned ourselves with what was going on. We hated government boondoggling. We hated being lied to. How are we going to get

back? We did it in a script." From 1965–1970, *Get Smart*, a comedy, regularly raided enemy terrain despite network Broadcast Standards Department memos, often signed by a person named Messerschmidt (same name as the German twin-jet Messerschmitt that bombed and shot down Allies in World War II). The memos specified concerns ranging from a caution against using brand names to:

"Please delete Smart's use of the term 'nut.' Substitute some other term, such as 'weirdo,' 'kook,' etc;

"Take care that Dietrich's scream, as he falls to his death, is not morbid or shocking;

"Please avoid anything morbid or grotesque in the display of the dead midget lying under the table;

"I assume Potlow's scarred fingers will not be made up or shown in such a way that they would sicken anybody but Max;

"Caution on the actions of the young couple so their kissing and fondling is within the limits of television propriety; avoid the open-mouth kiss or any other familiarity which might be embarrassing;

"Please elminate the underlined from the Chief's speech, implying Jewish tightness, 'They [YENTA] work on a limited budget, Max. *They had to wait until 6:00 for the long distance rates to change.*'"

The network took exception to the

title of "Survival of the Fattest," slated to air on Christmas day. Fat seemed too harsh a concept. They advanced "Survival of the Stoutest" as an alternative, but "Fattest" stayed. In the pilot episode, Standards and Practices objected to the idea of rubber garbage in a scow: "People are eating dinner, and you expect to do jokes about rubber garbage?" Brooks and Henry defended themselves by carefully noting "that the rubber garbage was really lovely things like fruit."

The network scrutiny of small details never ended. Yet no sooner did *Get Smart* hit the top of the ratings than the writers found themselves able to get away with more on their own show, while liberalizing the possibilities of TV comedy across the board. In "The Not-So-Great Escape," Max lands in a KAOS prisoner of war camp. Plotting his break with fellow captured agents, he suggests climbing over a wire fence. They tell him not to—it's electrified. He asks if anyone ever tried before. They point out the man who did, a black man. Max comments that he doesn't look any the worse for wear. Then they tell him the guy used to be white.

In "Appointment in Sahara" (1966), one KAOS Bedouin gloats to another:

First Arab: "We'll destroy New York, London, Paris, Rome, Tel Aviv.
Second Arab: No, not Tel Aviv.
First Arab: Why not Tel Aviv?
Second Arab: [Whispers in First Arab's ear]
First Arab: Really. You don't look it.

These jabs—ridiculing the inane clichés of racial humor—involved the creation of characters as well as scenes. Along with Siegfried, the unregenerate Nazi, *Get Smart* offered the Charlie Chanlike Harry Hoo, the diabolical Chinaman the Claw ("Not Craw. Craw.") and the two other equally fiendish Orientals, the Whip and Dr. Yes.

In "The Greatest Spy on Earth" (1966), Gertrude/Gerald—drawn from sexual rather than racial stereotypes—may have been TV's first "half man/half-woman." He hates diamonds. She loves them. He enjoys weightlifting. She prefers embroidery. Her half wears a dress. His wears half a suit. Smart is unsure how Gerty-Gerry should be frisked. (Standards and Practices advised, in a note to producer Arnie Rosen, "Will he/she—or is it she/he—be half stacked, and if so, a half caution on her/his costuming.")

"Island of the Darned" (1966) plays with sexual connotation at Max's expense, when Hans Hunter refers to him as a *homo sapiens* and Max in a huff protests that he's perfectly normal.

Get Smart, in spoofing everything else, took a swipe at TV violence which, once a major bone of contention on action shows, seldom presented any problems for *Get Smart*. The big battles had been fought several years earlier, in the era of TV Westerns and cop series led by *The Untouchables* (1959–1963). On *Get Smart,* any level of violence might be implied provided no one displayed it graphically: a man falling down an elevator shaft ("Cutback at CONTROL"), a man falling from high atop a construction site ("Smart Fit the Battle of Jericho"), Smart blowing a man to kingdom come with an explosive cigarette ("Island of the Darned").

In one of the earliest episodes, "Too Many Chiefs," CONTROL attempts to check a KAOS informer into a hotel. The desk clerk, a KAOS agent, pulls a gun on them. The cashier, a CONTROL agent, pulls a gun on him. The bellboy, with KAOS, takes aim at the cashier. The chambermaid, with CONTROL, draws a bead on the bellboy. The elevator operator, also with CONTROL, covers the chambermaid, because CONTROL isn't too sure about her loyalties. Because this creates a stalemate, Max, 99, the Chief, and the woman they're protecting, are able to leave. As they depart, several gunblasts are heard. They look back, and every one of the agents is slumped over, wounded or dead.

In "The King Lives?," recalls Don Adams, "I had to sword-fight my way through at least a dozen guys. I kill off about four or five of them. I'm fighting on the stairway, and knock some guys down there, and then I go inside, and there's bad Basil. I've come to rescue 99, who's in with him. She says, 'Don't fight him, Max. He's one of the greatest swordsmen in Europe.' And he says, 'Maybe in all the world,' and slashes his sword through the candles on the table. Nothing happens, so I laugh, 'Haw, haw, haw,' and Basil taps over each one, showing he's sliced right through the candles.

"Then he says something like, 'Yes, I am the greatest swordsman in all the world, and I shall now proceed to show you. First I shall cut your forehead, then I shall nip your eye, your nose, your mouth. I shall rip your shirt from your back, and then the pants from your skinny little legs.'

"I hear this and say, 'Hey—' and motion my arm, and just accidentally run my sword through him. He falls. 99 says, 'Oh, Max, how terrible.' And I justify it with, 'Well, he shouldn't have said that about my legs.'"

Beyond an unwillingness to present grisly deaths, some writers went a few steps further. For Alan Burns, "the business of bloodletting weighed very heavily on my mind, and on many of our minds. There were a lot of liberals doing the show. I'd always try to figure out a funny way of eliminating people that did not necessarily imply they were dead."

In "Appointment in Sahara," they spoke out against the worst kind of violence—the nuclear bomb. The exchange that takes place in the episode, as Max and 99 watch a mushroom cloud rise to the skies, represents what is probably the strongest antibomb statement made by situation comedy up to that time:

99: Oh, Max, what a terrible weapon of destruction.

86: Yes. You know, China, Russia, and France should outlaw all nuclear weapons. We should insist upon it.

99: What if they won't, Max?

86: Then we may have to blast them. That's the only way to keep peace in the world.

Scripts began when writers brought story ideas to producers and story editors, or vice versa, and Don Adams would have suggestions. Considerations included establishing the week's jeopardy as early as possible—enabling writers to move on to the business of being funny—and a grounding in reality. For "Weekend Vampire," Buck Henry insisted "that the villain can't be a vampire. He's either a guy pretending to be a vampire, or using the vampire method, but he can't be a real vampire, and he can't be a satire of movie vampires. He has got to be in the real world, lunatic though the real world is." The resulting episode begins when an agent dies mysteriously, with an apparently vampire-inflicted wound on his neck. The culprit, however, emerges as a deranged scientist seeking to get back at CONTROL.

For Henry, "The wonderful moments of being a script editor, or being in a position where writers come and talk to you, is that beginning flush of enthusiasm where you really think that they don't do it just as a job, but because they're genuinely happy with some lunatic idea they have.

"When Dee and Gerry would come in and say, 'What do you think about a guy who. . .?' you'd start laughing, or Stan Burns, who would and can make me laugh whenever he wants to, would start one. 'The cement is fresh. The guy has been shot. He's making notations in the fresh cement. We call them 'The Dead Spy Scrawls.' I'm on the floor. So The Dead Spy Scrawls gets a writer an assignment on the spot. How can it not?"

At the opposite end of the spectrum, Burt Nodella recalls the many times when "Writers would come in and sit there with their clipboards and say 'okay,' expectantly, and we'd work on a story together. And after a while you'd say, 'This is silly. It's easier to write them yourself.'" By the final *Get Smart* season, outside writers contributed very little, while the bulk of scripts flowed from the in-house pens of Alan Burns, Chris Hayward, Leonard Stern, and Arne Sultan.

As Alan Burns describes this process, "It was one I had not been familiar with until then, but one I have largely adhered to since. And it was that the ideas came out of a kind of brainstorming session. Arne Sultan was very big on that. So was Leonard Stern. He loved the camaraderie of writers. You could see him glow.

"These two loved getting a bunch of writers in a room and just pitching. We would then begin to develop an idea, and it was like, 'Okay, you're going to do this one' to one team, and 'You're going to do this one' to another team, and you'd go and think about it for a while, then you'd come back with ideas and you'd work with Leonard and Arne and the story would gradually evolve. There would be a secretary in the room, furiously taking down notes, or sometimes it would be on tape, and then you'd get notes back. They would be very, very fleshed out. It's a wonderful way of working because the writer has so much material, and it's protection against a script coming back and the producer saying 'That's not it at all.' It takes time, but I find that the time spent at this end saves you triple time at the other end."

With story editor Norman Paul, Burt Nodella wrote "I Shot 86 Today." The concept began when Nodella took a ride: "I was driving by a golf course one day, and saw a guy hitting the ball, and the idea came up about doing a show involving a missile golf ball. I came in and Norman and I talked about it, sat down, and we both wrote it maybe a week later."

Anything might have inspired the writers to devise a joke, script, or character. Several of Don Adams's club routines worked their way into scenes, and the pantomimed gun-disarming sequence from "A Tale of Two Tails" began with the club act of the two men who did it, Fred Willard and Vic Grecco. Split-screen work and the novelty of double roles led to premises ranging from "Too Many Chiefs," "The Return of the Ancient Mariner," and "The Spy Who Met Himself," to several variations on *The Prisoner of Zenda*. The premise of "The Day Smart Turned Chicken," script by Pat McCormick and Ron Clark, had its basis in McCormick's own life, a life punctuated by McCormick's penchant for dressing like a chicken. In a courtroom scene from the same episode, the Chief reveals his first name to be Thaddeus. The exchange, written by Buck Henry, "was probably inspired by the scene not working."

Henry guesses that his personal fascination with the grotesque provided the germ of Gertrude/Gerald: "Albert/Alberta was a creature I had seen all my life on 42nd Street, and I used to have a poster in my house, or maybe in my office, of Daisy and Violet Hilton, of whom I know too much. Daisy and Violet Hilton, as you undoubtedly know, are the Siamese twins who were in *Freaks*, and made a living on the vaudeville stage, about whom there are legendary tales that have nothing to do with *Get Smart*, and about whom I can speak for hours, and probably did. Whether I told Gerald Gardner and Dee Caruso about it, I have no idea. Their imaginations are certainly fertile enough to have come up with all those creatures."

Running characters, a significant ingredient through most of the years of *Get Smart*, generally began as one-shots who took on a life of their own. According to Leonard Stern, "Though you recognize and discuss the need to have them, it's interesting that when you try to sit down and write a unique running character, you're usually not too successful. They evolve and surprise you." The notion of Hymie the robot came from outside the circle entirely, from writer/actor C. F. L'Amoreaux.

Sometimes, bad luck demanded a script direction. When Ed Platt suffered from a bad back and had to miss a month, his lines were rewritten for Barbara Feldon. When Don Adams called in sick during the final *Get Smart* season, his part was recast with Bill Dana as a CIA agent assigned to work with 99 ("Ice Station Siegfried").

One evening, Adams said his good nights along with a few words about dental surgery. The portent didn't register until he'd gone. Then Jay Sandrich looked at Leonard Stern and the two gasped simultaneously, in horror, "Dental surgery!" They phoned all over town, but could find neither Adams nor his dentist. The next day, Adams arrived—just as they'd feared—with his jaw too swollen to film. In desperation, they swathed him in head bandages and redid "Maxwell Smart, Alias Jimmy Ballantine" to give Max a reason for bandaging his head.*

The movies gave rise to a whole genre of *Get Smart* episodes that played on the popular taste for nostalgia which in the Sixties reached its all-time high. Stan Burns and Mike Marmer, responsible for so many on *Get Smart*, pursued this particular art form when, in later years, they took their talents to *The Carol Burnett Show*.

Get Smart's film spoofs stopped short of literal parody, and instead found their fun in riffs on a theme, relationship, or memorable role. Don Adams, with a flair for voice impressions and a fondness for film classics, relished and often suggested them. His Bogart came to the fore in "Casablanca" *(Casablanca)*, "The Treasure of C. Errol Madre," *(The Treasure of the Sierra Madre)*, and "Maxwell Smart, Private Eye" *(The Maltese Falcon)*, and his Ronald Colman in "To Sire With Love" and "The King Lives?"

(The Prisoner of Zenda)—though while Buck Henry served as story editor, Henry preferred other types of material: "I saw no reason to believe that Smart could do any of those things."

Other riffs had little to do with impressions, and focused on story points ranging from the cinema—"Greer Window" *(Rear Window)*, "The Mess of Adrian Listenger" *(The List of Adrian Messenger)*, and "The Mild Ones" *(The Wild One)*—to television's *I Spy* ("Die, Spy") and *The Fugitive* ("Don't Look Back"). "Don't Look Back" became Don

Maxwell Smart goes Bogart in "The Treasure of C. Errol Madre." *Courtesy of AP/ Wide World Photos.*

---

*That evening, Don Adams attended a party for the series. Unable to talk, he turned his emcee duties over to Leonard Stern. When Stern finished a very funny stint at the mike, he introduced Adams, who scrawled on a blackboard in self-defense: "Who was that guy?"

Smart in a scene from "Die, Spy," parody of *I Spy*, here with Poupee Bocar.

Adams's favorite episode, because it worked so well, because he directed it, and because it shared a common theme with his favorite novel, *Les Miserables.* Some episodes simply kidded a single scene—as when "Tequila Mockingbird" takes off on the shootout from *The Good, the Bad, and the Ugly*—or a title: "Tequila Mockingbird" *(To Kill a Mockingbird)*, "Widow Often Annie" *(Little Orphan Annie)*, "Absorb the Greek" *(Zorba the Greek)*, "Satan Place" *(Peyton Place)*, to name a few. In the early seasons, titles had no function beyond what went on scripts to facilitate tracking them. Only much later did they actually appear on the screen. The spelling of proper names had no function what-soever other than for people reading the printed script and to identify performers in the screen credits, hence closing credits vary between Siegfried/Seigfried, Larabee/Larrabee, Who/Hoo, and Starker/Shtarker.

In addition to ribbing familiar movies and TV programs, the writers took potshots at well-known commercials. Greyhound's celebrated slogan, spoken by a driver leaning out of a bus window, urged watchers of Steve Allen's show to "take the bus and leave the driving to us." In *Get Smart*'s "A Spy for A Spy," KAOS and CONTROL exchange prisoners and prepare to depart in their respective vehicles—but Siegfried nabs CONTROL's bus. As he pulls out of the lot, he strikes the Greyhound pose from the window, boasting "Next time, leave the schpying to us."

Another Steve Allen commercial featured John Cameron Swayze subjecting Timex watches to various forms of unnatural abuse. Drowned them. Strapped them to surf boards. Wrapped them around boat propellers. After the watch survived each punishment, Swayze strode toward the camera holding it up and enthusing, "The watch took a licking, but it kept on ticking." In the *Get Smart* episode "Schwartz's Island," a giant magnet yanks the watch from a passing sailor's wrist. Max and 99 appear dumbstruck. Shtarker confirms the source of their amazement, marching the timepiece toward the camera: "Yes! The watch took a licking, but it kept on ticking."

Jokes of this sort, known to comedy writers as "club names" and "street ad-

The permanent residents of "Schwartz's Island"—the cast of *Gilligan's Island,* created by Sherwood Schwartz. *Courtesy of AP/ Wide World Photos.*

dresses," cash in on familiarity and work best when most unexpected, and when used in the most incongruous circumstances.

Some club names go unobserved by viewers because they're really in-jokes. "Schwartz's Island" drew its name from the set on which it took place—the *Gilligan's Island* set on the Paramount lot. Sherwood Schwartz produced *Gilligan's Island.* Inside jokes also inspired the names of the character Melnick Archer ("Put a Red in your bed Melnick") in "And Only Two Ninety-Nine," Melnick Uranium Mines in "With Love and Twitches," and Melnick the Smiling Killer ("Perils in a Pet Shop")—Dan Melnick being a partner of Talent Associates. The leggy burlesque dancer/CONTROL scientist Doc Simon

("I Shot 86 Today") took the name of TV-comedy-writer-turned-playwright Neil "Doc" Simon. Bacon Cab Company picked up the name of the series' art director, Art Bacon. The independent judging organization in "How to Succeed in the Spy Business Without Really Trying," "Price Sloan Stern," combined an allusion to the real judging group Price Waterhouse with one to Leonard Stern's publishing operation, Price-Stern-Sloan.

Chris Hayward particularly appreciated "the classic in-joke, which we owe to Arne Sultan. He really spiffed things up, and some of the great lines that were in scripts that we get credit for were Arne's. Before Alan Burns and I came to *Get Smart,* when we were trying to break into sitcoms, we gave birth to what has become known as the worst sitcom idea ever. It started out as 'My Wife the Car,' because we had in mind a satire of *Blythe Spirit,* in which the wife got killed by the car and came back as a ghost. The switch would be that here, she would come back as a car. But the people at United Artists and NBC felt that it amounted to necrophilia, to loving of the dead, so they insisted that we change the wife to the mother. It was a condition of getting it on the air.

"It didn't last long on the air. Then, after a while, Alan and I found ourselves with *Get Smart.* In one episode, 'The Secret of Sam Vittorio,' there is a scene in which the gangland leader is dying. He says it will be okay if they tell him, just before he goes, that *My Mother the Car* is returning to television. Max and 99 ask why. He says that if they say this, he won't mind dying. The joke is Arne, typical Arne."

The catchphrases and running gags, which contributed so greatly to the immediacy of *Get Smart*'s success, and became "club names" and "street addresses" on an international scale derived from several sources, though their inclusion was something insisted upon by Don Adams when he did the pilot. His personal record with two lines—"Would you believe . . .?" from his club routine, and "You really know how to hurt a guy" from his Perry Como tenure—convinced him that he was on the right track. Buck Henry initially doubted the value of "Would you believe?" until he "saw how the repetition of it underscored the asininity of Maxwell Smart, the dumbest secret agent of all time. I'm glad to say that the sponsors got the point a lot faster."

"Sorry about that, Chief" soon joined "Would you believe . . .?" in Maxwell Smart's vocabulary. Adams attributed the line to Joe Mikalos, former song lyricist and "Ernie Kovacs' right-hand man. He applied [it] to such incongruous situations that he convulsed old pros in the business. I figured if they were funny enough to get laughs in a hip crowd, they would strike a responsive chord with all types of audiences." Reported *Newsweek* in early 1966, "Mikolas himself took the phrase over from the Vietnam GI's, whose phrase 'Sorry about that' is applied to everything from a short round to warm beer."

Like "Sorry about that," Smart's

"Missed it by that much," accompanied by his holding up two fingers to show an itty bitty distance, attempts to reduce every massive gaffe to the trivial in cases where distance is everything. It's a horse-player's phrase, and as every handicapper can attest—and Adams could readily confirm from the time and wagers invested in his favorite hobby—to fail by a nose is still to finish out of the money. Smart applies the phrase when enemy agents leap from windows to their death, when bullets go fatally off course, or when the Chief informs him in "Maxwell Smart, Alias Jimmy Ballantine" that Barry Goldwater lost the 1964 Presidential election by a seventeen million vote landslide.

Just as *Get Smart* went after clichés in attitude and situation, it nailed the verbal variety. Agent 86 savored any chance to assert "And . . . loving it," his kneejerk rejoinder to the Chief's recitation of the dangers a new assignment would bring.

When the Chief tells Max, "Listen carefully," then expounds on details of elaborate intricacy, Max is likely to respond that he got everything but the last part. What last part? The part after "Listen carefully." Yet Max can totally recall—or more probably, purports to recall—every finesse ever discharged in the name of espionage. These he reels off the way James Bond knows champagne. He also seems to keep a mental record of how many times he's fallen for each in the past month, week, and year.

The more preposterous they are, the greater his familiarity with them. The more ordinary, the more intense his surprise. When Max's friend Sid (Don Rickles) finally believes that Max is a spy in "The Little Black Book," Sid masters the litany exhibiting quicker response time than Max, combining subtle observation and keen common sense with his intuitive awareness of the absurd. *Get Smart* kidded the nonplussed sophistication of superspies who have witnessed everything, and already experienced every situation, with "That's the second biggest _(arrow) (cannon) (etc.)_ I've ever seen" in response to an impossibly large object, as well as with "ah, yes, the old _(gun in the rabbit) (lighter in the gun in the rabbit) (etc.)_ trick," implying that the most improbably lunatic combinations of events are as routine as carrying a hidden weapon.

The writers underscored Max's personal oafishness with "Get your knee off my chest," "I hope I wasn't out of line with that crack about ___," and "I asked you not to tell me that." The latter would follow his saying, for instance, "Don't tell me the gun isn't loaded," and 99 informing him that it's empty.

Because everyone conceived of *Get Smart* as a series of little movies rather than so many little plays, because *Get Smart* was filmed as opposed to videotaped, and because it was shot as movies are shot—in pieces, out of sequence, with no live studio audience watching—scripts could accommodate changes long after the written words were approved.

When handed a script that he felt

FALSE CIGARETTE LIGHTER PISTOL

FLAME

STUFFED RABBIT

THE OLD LIGHTER IN THE GUN IN THE RABBIT TRICK

Courtesy of James B. Kruger.

Angelique as Charlie Watkins. *Courtesy of Angelique Pettyjohn.*

didn't work, Don Adams might himself ask for changes, or make them. When Angelique Pettyjohn (Charlie Watkins) reported for her *Get Smart* debut, "I am compulsive. I really study a script. So I went in, having learned this one, and was just finishing in makeup when Don Adams arrived. He sat down next to me, said hello, and started going through the script with a pencil. 'No. No. Not this.' Rewriting the script. Then they dashed it off to be typed. My mouth dropped open.

"I'd had a few pages of dialogue. It came back with changes and additions, nothing like the original. It worked just right. And I did manage to learn it.

"And Don used to kid me on the set. I'd be wearing this revealing Charlie Watkins costume, and he'd stare at my cleavage and joke during rehearsals. 'Find me someplace else to look. Any place but there.' Some of this turned up in the story, as Maxwell Smart's reaction to Charlie Watkins, a male spy assigned to be a sort of Playboy bunny."

SIGNS AND COUNTERSIGNS

An Alphabetical Selection of Passwords and Responses from the Top-Secret Files of CONTROL

- "Bismark" and its response, "Salt Lake City," in "Bronzefinger."

- "The blue sun melts the red snow" and its response, "And the purple water runs uphill," in "Back to the Old Drawing Board."

- "The geese fly high" and its response "The frost is on the grass," in "Dougle Agent."

- "I lost my dinghy" and its response, "Why don't you try the Brooklyn Navy Yard?" in "Age Before Duty."

- "Pussycat, pussycat, where have you been?" and its response, "I've been to London to visit the Queen," in "Ironhand" and "One of Our Olives Is Missing."

- "Ricardo Montalban hates tortillas" and "Herb Alpert takes trumpet lessons from Guy Lombardo" in "Viva Smart."

- "Tanganyika" in "Aboard the Orient Express."

- "A warped barrel is a fool's frustration" gets a KAOS kewpie doll from a shooting gallery in "The Wax Max."

- "Who wrote *Little Women?*" in "The Return of the Ancient Mariner."

**More Complicated Sign/
Countersign Sequences**

To enter Agent 86's apartment (Apt #
86):

Password: "Knock, knock."
Response: "Who's there?"
Response: "Me."
Response: "Me who?"
Response: "Me the Chief."
  ("And Baby Makes Four," Part I)

To make contact with Scotland Yard in
England:

Password: "There'll be bluebirds
  over the white cliffs of
  Dover." (no response)
Password: "A nightingale sang in
  Berkeley Square." (no
  response)
Password: "Johnny Doughboy
  found a rose in Ireland."
Password: "To each his own."
  ("House of Max," Part I)

To establish contact in certain mu-
seums:

Password: "Camptown ladies sing
  this song."
Response: Doodah doodah."
Response: Camptown racetrack five
  miles long."
Response: Oh dee doo dah day."
  ("The Mummy")

All-purpose, to be replaced as soon as
it's mastered:

Password: "Migrating birds fly low
  over the sea."
Response: "Shadeless windows ad-
  mit no light."
Response: "The wingless dove pro-
  tects its nest."
Response: "The toothless tiger rules
  the restless jungle." Su-
  perseded by:
Password: "Apples."
Response: "McIntosh."
  ("Too Many Chiefs")

To contact Siegfried in the frozen
wastelands:

Password: "When I'm calling you."
Response: "Ooo-ooo-ooo ooo-ooo-
  ooo."
  ("Ice Station Siegfried")

THE OLD
LABELING-IT-AN-OLD-
TRICK TRICK

Given the strictly classified nature of
these revelations, certain tricks must
be withheld from publication at this
time.

- "The old airplane in the haystack
  trick" ("Snoopy Smart vs. the Red
  Baron")

- "The old back door to the alley

trick—what will they think of next?" ("Pussycats Galore")

- "The old beeping button trick" ("Appointment in Sahara")

- "The old bomb in the bonbon box trick" ("Witness for the Execution")

- "The old bomb in the snack truck trick" ("Where-What-How-Who Am I?")

- "The old bullet-proof cummerbund in the tuxedo trick" ("99 Loses Control")

- "The old check the baggage, take out the insurance, page him to the phone, spin the booth trick" ("The Not-So-Great Escape," Part I)

- "The old Chief in the brown beard and wig trick" ("Die, Spy")

- "The old communications equipment in the French bread trick" ("The Hot Line")

- "The old double agent with the two faces in the twin locker trick" ("The Spy Who Met Himself")

- "The old double door deception trick" ("The Impossible Mission")

- "The old drug his prunes, fake the fight, ransack the apartment, and switch places with the Admiral trick" ("The Return of the Ancient Mariner")

- "The old fake fingertips on the fire escape trick" ("The Apes of Rath")

- "The old false hands in the chain trick" ("The Little Black Book," Part II)

- "The old false neck trick" ("Casablanca")

- "The old finger in the gun trick" (by which he no doubt means "the old gun in the finger trick") ("Survival of the Fattest")

- "The old flat iron in the hot coals trick" ("A Tale of Two Tails")

- "The old garbage trick" ("Mr. Big")

- "The old gas bomb in the horoscope trick" ("The Decoy")

- "The old gas mask in the fake nose trick" ("How to Succeed in the Spy Business Without Really Trying")

- "The old gun in the camera trick" ("Maxwell Smart, Private Eye")

- "The old gun in the crutch trick" ("A Man Called Smart," Part II)

- "The old gun in the flashlight trick" ("That Old Gang of Mine")

- "The old gun in the hand trick" ("The Decoy")

- "The old gun in the maestro's baton trick" ("The Little Black Book," Part II)

- "The old gun in the peg leg trick" ("Ship of Spies," Part II)

- "The old gun in the rabbit trick" ("A Spy for a Spy") and its variation: "The old lighter in the gun in the rabbit trick" ("A Spy for a Spy")

- "The old hacksaw in the belt buckle trick ("The Little Black Book," Part II)

- "The old hideout under the carwash trick" ("Supersonic Boom")

- "The old inflatable head in the cloak trick" ("The Wax Max")

- "The old long-playing high-frequency ultrasonic stereophonic strike the match against the sounding board trick. Works every time, Siegfried." ("Spy, Spy, Birdie")

- "The old Maxwell Smart silhouette on the windowshade trick" ("The Little Black Book," Part II)

- "The old microphone in the squeegee trick" ("The Mysterious Dr. T")

- "The old mortar in the rocks in the fourteenth hole trick" ("I Shot 86 Today")

- "The old picture in the keyhole trick" ("Diplomat's Daughter")

- "The old Professor Peter Peckinpah all-purpose antipersonnel Peckinpah pocket pistol under the toupee trick" ("Smartacus")

- "The old remote- controlled, self-propelled, spinning doorknob trick" ("Operation Ridiculous")

- "The old secret panel in the bookcase trick" ("Strike While the Agent is Hot")

- "The old secret supply room in the supply room trick" ("Valerie of the Dolls")

- "The old sever the cord of the lamp trick" ("To Sire, with Love," Part I)

- "The old shoe switch" ("Dear Diary")

- "The old sleeping foot powder in the shoe trick" ("Run, Robot, Run")

- "The old spy in the dog suit trick" ("Aboard the Orient Express")

- "The old three-way gun trick" ("The Little Black Book," Part II)

- "The old tiny tape recorder in the trailer trick" ("Dr. Yes")

- "The old Wilbur in the drape trick" ("Maxwell Smart, Private Eye")

8

||||||||||||||||||||||||||||||||||||||||||||||||||||||||||||||||||||||||||||||||||||||||||||||||||||||||||||||||||||||||

CLOSELY WATCHED FRAMES

"Honesty is the best comedy."

—Bruce Bilson

With so many writers and native wits around, it surprised no one that scripting continued into rehearsals and onto the set. Ironically—even with *Get Smart* firmly on top of the ratings—neither writers' quarters nor the stage proved particularly easy to find. As described by Leonard Stern, "This structure was typical of the show. We were the only functioning company in this studio, which was on Sunset at Bronson and Gower. We maintained our offices there, but they didn't have a guard and they didn't have a gate. You didn't come into the office building. You had to go through a tunnel which was under the building, which led to the sound stage, which you had to cross to get to the offices. In the course of our being there, Burt Reynolds did his series, *The Hawk* there, and Chuck Connors did *Branded*.

"To go to work, we had to cross and wait for the green light before we could move on. And because sound carries more at night, when we worked late—if they were also shooting late—they'd come around to tell us 'We can hear you. Keep it down. We're shooting.' This would be in the middle of story conferences. So that in addition to trying to resolve our scripts, we'd have to modulate our voices for the benefit of a series that had nothing to do with us."

Embellishing on this strange and exotic lot that belonged to Paramount but was not Paramount's main lot, Bruce Bilson adds, "Stage 5 at Paramount Sunset had been the original Warner Brothers Vitagraph Studio, where *The Jazz Singer* [the first movie with spoken words] was made. That studio was built to be a sound studio, but when I was small, it wasn't a studio. There were badminton courts on two stages, and up in that big building that looked like a southern mansion with pillars was a bowling alley with fifty-two lanes, the world's biggest bowling alley. At times I'd worked there as a pinboy. My folks used to play indoor badminton there, in this nice place where the wind didn't blow."

Story conferences involved the writers, story consultant, story editor, producer, executive producer, and director, but once the script went to rehearsal, the director took charge of turning the script into footage. The first two directors after the pilot—responsible for several dozen episodes each—were Bruce Bilson and Gary Nelson. Before getting into comedy, Nelson directed dramatic offerings such as *Have Gun Will Travel.* Both Bilson and Nelson had directed *The Baileys of Balboa* (1964–1965) in the season before *Get Smart.* This led to their directing *The Patty Duke Show* (1963–1966), followed by *Get Smart* beginning in 1965. Each wondered at first if directing for a color show would pose any special problems. It didn't, and they fit in immediately.

Get Smart's rehearsal and shooting schedule enabled a director to work more than one series at a time. Says Bruce Bilson, "Generally, we got the script the day before we started preparation. In those days, all the half hour comedies were done basically shooting three days a week, so you could do some *Get Smart*s, then maybe go do three *Hogan's Heroes,* then maybe some *Please Don't Eat the Daisies,* then you'd come back and do some more *Get Smart*s. You moved around."

By the third *Get Smart* season, a reviewer, unaware of their newness to the field, assumed from seeing their names so often that they were old men. He wrote that the industry, instead of playing safe with the "old hats," should dare to hire fresh, young talent.

The average *Get Smart* episode required of the director a day of pre-production (casting, finding locations, and so on), and a rehearsal day, and three days of shooting (four until the network said "too expensive—would you believe three?")

Props were provided by the property master (James R. Harris, Edward Goldstein) and special effects man (Paul B. Byrd, Justus Gibbs, Perzy High, Ted Tillman). Sometimes writers would consult with them during the early stage of a script before pursuing an idea, to be sure it could be done. Otherwise, the question came up at the production meeting with the script itself. These ingeniously competent pros had twin assignments: make this gimmick appear to function, and find a relatively inexpensive way to do it. Usually, writers' imaginations could run wild, and the necessary device would duly turn up on the set: a shoe phone, the Cone of Silence (accompanied by such props as a breakaway desk for it to destroy), an invisible bullet-proof wall in 86's apartment (generally done with pantomime—makeup came off on impact with real glass), or an inflatable female dummy to act as Smart's implausible cover on Lovers' Lane.

Some efforts proved messy but hilarious. Dave Ketchum, as the ubiquitous Agent 13, spent one scene in a washing machine: "They built a complicated machine, a thing on rollers, a nine-foot tube to hold me and spin, and two big guys spun it and me. They put it behind the glass pane of a laundry machine, spinning me, while water and soap squirted in my face. So I tumbled around while talking to Maxwell Smart. It was difficult, because you get disoriented, spinning that way while goo shoots in your eyes and you try to do lines. I infinitely preferred the scene, in another episode, where a lady and Agent 13 passed New Year's Eve inside a hollowed-out sofa."

Not all effects worked according to plan. For "Run, Robot, Run," Dick Gautier couldn't quite compel Hymie to discharge one of his least appealing robotic skills: "One by one, men are killed. One of the guys is killed in the shower. We're bending over him, examining the evidence. Hymie takes the soap, tastes it, bites it, and is supposed to give a chemical analysis of its deadly components. When Hymie says this, his mouth is supposed to bubble with soap suds. That's the gag. Well, we couldn't do it. The thing in my mouth, which

wasn't real soap, wouldn't bubble. In desperation, they told me to do it with real soap, because they didn't know how else to do it. But there's no way to have soap suds in your mouth without making a terrible face, which Hymie as a robot wouldn't make. Finally we had to forget the gag. As I recall, I just looked at the soap or smelled it and commented. The only way we could have done it would have been a profile shot with the tube of bubbles coming up the side of my face, which is always such a tipoff it isn't worth doing. Or inducing some sort of fit to see if I'd slather."

For a darkroom scene between the Chief, Max, and Professor Carlson (Stacy Keach), the gag revolved around Max bursting in and turning on the light. But, recalls Keach, "they forgot to dim the light. We did the scene with the lights on. So how could Max walk in and turn on the lights when they were already on? The mistake got a big laugh, then it became a gag in the script. When you see the scene, Max walks into a lighted room and says, 'Don't you know the lights should be off?' Then he turns them off, and the Chief yells at him, because this is new film specially devised by CONTROL to be processed with the lights on. It only ruins the film if you turn the lights off."

The Cone of Silence caused so much trouble on the set that mishaps inspired the writers. Gary Nelson still shudders at the mention of it: "Every time you saw the Cone of Silence in a script, you wanted to run from it, because it never worked the way it was supposed to. A lot of what it did instead—wound up in scripts."

Props and effects incited a competitive, friendly envy. Says Bilson, "It was almost a little contest. We'd have a production meeting and a rehearsal on Tuesday. We shot Wednesday, Thursday, and Friday. If we worked late on Friday night to finish the show, we'd come walking out past the other stage, where we'd see the props for the next episode. If you saw, for instance, a torture rack, you'd think, 'oooh aaah, why didn't I get that . . . ?'"

With experience, James Harris thought of at least one way to simplify his task. Max, 99, or an enemy agent so often had to push a button, Harris made buttons with double-faced tape on the back. Since the buttons themselves didn't have to activate anything—but only exist to be pushed while easier means moved the array of espionage devices—they could now be positioned and repositioned at will.

Some special effects could be equally painless. A knife sailing at 86 and barely missing him is achieved by reversing the film. The real-life sequence begins with the knife in the wall, Don Adams reacting as though it just hit, and then watching with dubious composure as it's jerked from the wall by wire.

A combination of prop and effect which ended as neither simple nor painless centered around a flooding phone booth. In "All in the Mind," Max and 99 enter a phone booth, then can't get out. As it fills with water, 86 observes significantly, "I've got a feeling this is no ordinary phone booth." To create the scene, special effects man Perzy High had a booth constructed of clear plastic with a metal plate for the door, at a cost of $950. As a security measure to permit hasty escape, someone held a ladder in readiness and the booth had no top. For comfort, High heated the water: "After all, you can't put stars in cold water." Adams, who couldn't tread water and disliked a claustrophobic feeling, steeled himself for the scene.

Bruce Bilson directed: "In the beginning of the episode, a player with a few lines of dialogue steps into an actual phone booth, which we then replace with this tank which has the external hardware of a phone booth. It has to fill quickly to give the impression of drowning her in this very short time. But when Don and Barbara are caught later in the same booth, they have two and a half pages of material, so the water has to rise more slowly.

"I sat down with the special effects man and my script, and I marked five marks, and said, 'Each of these marks is a different place on their bodies for the height of the water. This is halfway up their shins. This is the knees. This is the thighs. This is the rib cage. This is the neck. I'll be watching them, and you watch my hand. I'll signal number one, number two, number three, four, five, and as I do it, you'll bring the water up to these levels.' We spent a lot of time working it out.

"The way we set it up, the booth was at the end of a corridor. We had two cameras, one up and one down on them—one close and one wide—with me by the low camera, and the effects man around the corner from them, gluing his eyes on me. A second effects man positioned himself by the tank and operated the valve. We did the scene, and I followed on the script, followed them with my eyes, and signaled. It was going great—Max remembering he could use his shoe phone, and trying to get his shoe off underwater, then asking 99 for change for the telephone—and I got to cue number five, which meant my cues were over with. So I laughed, because it was funny, and tried to contain my chuckling by covering my mouth with my hand. The effects man, concentrating on my every gesture, took this as another signal, gave the sign to the man at the valve, and we blew Max and 99 out of the top of the tank. They didn't get hurt, but it ruined the scene. We had to redo their hair, their makeup, get a fresh wardrobe, and shoot it all again." As Adams and Feldon climbed from the booth, water splashed up and hit a light bulb. The glass shattered. Fortunately, no one was hurt.

A prop that occasioned a difference of opinion between Bruce Bilson and Burt Nodella—"as big a fight as we ever had"—took the form of a sailboat. Bilson and Nodella each owned one. Each wanted his to be used as the Smarts' doomed honeymoon craft ("Schwartz's Island"), anticipating a rental fee or token in return. Nodella outranked Bilson. Nodella won, then nearly regretted it: "Our film editor came up with the idea of doing a smash cut, a frame-to-frame cut, tying the camera down, getting the same proportion of sea with the sailboat in it, taking the sailboat away, bringing in a raft with explosives on it, and blowing up the raft. When I saw the film, it looked like my boat blew up. To this day, I remember seeing it and getting upset. I mean, I knew, but to see it blasted to smithereens . . ."

Shooting on location gave *Get Smart* much of its broad canvas adventure look, but at a price. Since getting to the location is logistically complex, directors want to be sure they've covered themselves from every angle before they leave. For "Washington 4, Indians 3," Richard Donner, doing his first comedy, shot endless footage. Contributing to its length, Don Adams did not excel at horseback riding. Care had to be taken to avoid capturing on film the dread on Adams's face.

Reza Badiyi directed for Robert Altman and Sam Peckinpah before coming to *Get Smart*, and specialized in news, documentary, and industrial films. Having been around the world three times for another NBC program, he brought a unique perspective to the visual portrayal of CONTROL. For "Snoopy Smart vs. the Red Baron," he showed Leonard Stern some aerial footage originally made for an unsold TV project. These shots of Badiyi's were used in the episode, supplemented by additional dogfight material—photographed by Badiyi while strapped to the body of a small plane.

For a script James Komack wrote and directed, "I liked the name Wax Max, so

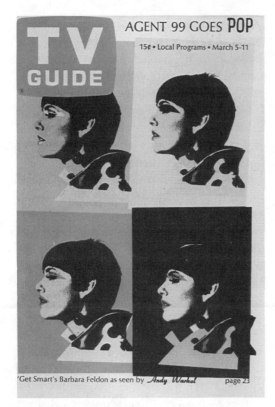 

Get Smart frequently rated the cover of *TV Guide.* Andy Warhol executed the cover on the left. *Reprinted with permission from* TV Guide® *Magazine. Copyright © 1966 (left) and 1967 (right) by Triangle Publications, Inc. Radnor, Pennsylvania.*

I did a story which enabled us to use the Santa Monica Amusement Park, which was opened for us to shoot it. They gave us the run of the place.

"In one scene, Don was going to run around and hide behind mirrors, and the camera was going to follow on one of those little boats. And he couldn't get running the right way and we couldn't get the camera the right way. Finally we decided how we were going to do it. But he got lost totally. Then we got lost with

the camera and crew. It took us half an hour to find each other. That's a lot of time on a set. The camera's gone. The director's gone. The star's gone. Barbara Feldon stood outside watching for us. 'Where are you guys?' We could not get out of the thing.

"It was an amusement park, closed to the public, at our disposal, so there were no guards in there saying, 'Oh, you're lost, we'll help you out.' When I at last found Don, he was at one of those booths where you throw balls at kewpie dolls, waiting."

Because location scenes accounted for major budgetary outlays, people always had an eye out for sets to borrow from another show or a movie. Schwartz's Island was Gilligan's Island, a standing set surrounded by "the lagoon." "Rub-a-Dub-Dub . . . Three Spies in a Sub" utilized the trappings from Paramount's Frank Sinatra picture *Assault on a Queen*. After *Get Smart* moved to CBS Center, sharing a lot with *The Wild, Wild West*, the two series would scout out each other's sets. Says Burt Nodella, "If you look at those shows at the same time, you see the same stairways, the same walls. You'd rent from them, which wouldn't cost as much as building the sets yourself. It might cost $5,000 to build something that would only cost $3,000 to rent.

"Then we shot the one at Pacific Ocean Park before it was ripped down. That was complicated because we had roller coasters and rides and lots of extras, big chases, and so on. But it happened not to be expensive, because they wanted publicity for the park. And we did shows on aircraft carriers, which were complicated, but the Navy would donate them free."

Ted Rich, in charge of postproduction, remembers "when we moved to CBS, the new administration building went up, and they gutted the buildings that were there. It looked like something had been attacked. They started to pour foundations. We saw it, and came up with a scene in which a laundry has been blown up. All that's left when the dust

clears is this area of foundations, with the walls gone."

Casting, accomplished by award winner Pat Harris, covered more bases than usual for a half-hour comedy. Sitcoms as a rule are 90 percent self-contained, and several episodes at a stretch can rely exclusively on the principals, or on the principals, a regular or two, and a walk-on. But *Get Smart*, since it parodied adventures, needed the greater number of players and extras associated with adventure formats. Jay Sandrich, the show's first producer, specifically looked for "not comedy people, but actors, because *Get Smart*'s premise was so stupid that you had to try to put some reality into situations so it wasn't just cartoony all the time."

Pat Harris, a short woman frequently described as "every inch a lady," smoked heavily while always trying to quit, and asserted herself, particularly on the phone. She impressed some agents as being tough, yet took pains to consider the feelings of actors, avoiding emotionally draining "cattle call auditions" whenever possible, relying instead on her instincts and her understanding of script requirements.

Many *Get Smart* players would go on to greater fame on subsequent TV series—among them Barbara Bain (*Mission: Impossible*), Jack Cassidy (*He & She*), Victor French (*Little House on the Prairie* and *Highway to Heaven*), Harold Gould (*He & She, Rhoda*), Gordon Jump (*WKRP in Cincinnati*), Ted Knight (*The Mary Tyler Moore Show, The Ted Knight Show, Too Close for Comfort*), Al Molinaro (*The Odd Couple, Happy*

Days), Leonard Nimoy (*Star Trek, Mission: Impossible*), Regis Philbin (*The Morning Show*), Vic Tayback (*Alice*), and Jason Wingreen (*All in the Family, Archie Bunker's Place*).

Others added an extra dollop of irony to their *Get Smart* rolès by vitue of their previous work. J. Carrol Naish, veteran of three TV series and over 200 movies, with two Academy Award nominations to his credit (for *Sahara* and *A Medal for Benny*), played Sam Vittorio in "The Secret of Sam Vittorio." Martin Kosleck, respected character actor of the movies who portrayed Goebbels in *Confessions of a Nazi Spy* (1939), *The Hitler Gang* (1944), and *Hitler* (1961), and assorted malevolent beings, played the title role of "Weekend Vampire." Gale Sondergaard, a sinister character actress of the same period (*The Letter, Enemy Agent Meets Ellery Queen, The Strange Death of Adolf Hitler,* and *Sherlock Holmes and the Spider Woman*), starred in "Rebecca of Funny-Folk Farm." Vincent Price, filmdom's favorite madman who needs no introduction (*The Tower of London, Dragonwyck, House of Wax, The Fall of the House of Usher* to name a few), drugged the water supply of our national capital in "Is This Trip Necessary?" Bruce Gordon, best known as Frank Nitti from TV's *The Untouchables* (1959–1963), dogged Max's trail in *The Fugitive* spoof "Don't Look Back"—a part he reprised for Talent Associates' series *Run Buddy Run* (1966–1967) which took off on a similar theme.

French leading man Jacques Bergerac (most notably of *Les Girls* and *Gigi*) wooed and nearly wed 99 in the episode "99 Loses Control." Emmy-winning comedian (*The Steve Allen Show*) Tom Poston brought KAOS agents back from dead in "Shock It to Me." Julie Newmar, stunning star of *The Marriage Go-Round* (Tony winner for the Broadway version, then star of the movie version), of the TV series *My Living Doll*, and a popular regular as Catwoman on *Batman*, spied on Max in the guise of a maid and nearly wrecked his marriage in "The Lazer Blazer." The beautiful Gayle Hunnicutt romanced Hymie in the episode "It Takes One to Know One," hot on the heels of her success in the Peter Fonda movie *The Wild Angels*. Angelique Pettyjohn plied the difficult role of CONTROL agent Charlie Watkins—the guy disguised as a bunny club bombshell—in several *Get Smart* episodes. Her previous credits included work on the TV shows *Love, American Style, It Takes a Thief, Batman,* and *The Girl from U.N.C.L.E.*, in the movies *Clambake* and *The President's Analyst*, and as a singer, dancer, comedienne, and occasional bullwhip specialist in Las Vegas.

Some players came through casting calls or Pat Harris's knowledge of a particular performer, while some arrived because a key *Get Smart* figure placed the request. Buck Henry, during his tenure, tried to hire people from the Second City improvisational comedy troupe, and best remembers having acquired its resident wild genuis, Del Close, as a CONTROL scientist:

"I heard Del was in Los Angeles, and I saw a chance to create a really crazy lab scientist. I always wanted to do more with our lab scenes, make it crazier and better, and I felt we could do it if Del wanted to hang around. He played the scientist once and Del, in order to convince Pat Harris that he was the proper character to play this deranged person, put a machine on her desk and two things in her hands, gave her a gimlet-eyed look, and instructed, 'Hang onto these.' As she grabbed them, he sent considerable voltage through her body.

"When her hair had lain down again, she had second thoughts about using Del Close. She told us he frightened her, and I reminded her that he's supposed to, he's Del Close. But we didn't bring him back after that."

Jane Dulo, cast as 99's mother—who never realized that her daughter and son-in-law were spies, and who believes the Chief to be Harold Clark, their boss in the greeting card business—knew Leonard Stern from his Army days: "When they were on leave, he and his buddy used to stay at the hotel across the street from my apartment, which I shared with three other girls. We were their hangout." Before *Get Smart,* Dulo had a regular role on the *Bilko* show, and frequently appeared on the *Dick Van Dyke Show* as well.

Roger Price, Leonard Stern's long-time associate, appeared as CONTROL scientist Dr. Arrick, inventor of the detecto-tune, in "Weekend Vampire." Dave Ketchum, Agent 13, had been before *Get Smart* a regular on *I'm Dickens, He's Fenster.*

Leonard Stern's Aunt Rose—Rose Michtom of the Ideal Toy Company Michtoms*—became a regular walk-on and eventual talisman. She commuted to

*Morris Michtom (1870–1938), "father of the Teddy Bear," founded the Ideal Toy Company in 1903.

"Aunt Rose"—Rose Michtom. Height: 4'11." Weight: 100 lbs. *Courtesy of Leonard Stern.*

work on two buses and sometimes as many as four, had a face seemingly resigned to everything since the world began, and finally changed the spelling of her name to Micktom because away from *Get Smart,* everyone spelled it wrong anyhow. In "Closely Watched Planes," she's the woman across the aisle from Max who sees him speaking to his donut radio, so tries to listen to her donut too. She's a customer buying bread from Regis Philbin in "The Hot Line." She's the photographer's mother and reluctant cheesecake model in "Operation Ridiculous." She's the bag lady—perhaps the first ever in television comedy—in "Run, Robot, Run." She gets out of her wheelchair, offering it to Simon the Likeable, in "And Baby Makes Four," and her photo represents one of Alexi Sebastian's disguises in "Too Many Chiefs." Rose Michtom's *Get Smart* career proved a springboard to further roles in the Aunt Rose vein, for instance a part in *Shampoo* on Warren Beatty's recommendation.

Don Adams had friends and relatives assisting him on the set, and Robert Karvelas and Richard Yarmy (e.g., "The Treasure of C. Errol Madre") turning up in episodes. Max and 99's wedding—the "With Love and Twitches" episode— evolved into a true family affair. Former June Taylor dancer Dorothy Adams (Mrs. Don Adams) accompanied 99 as the bridesmaid. Mace Neufeld, Adams's (and Bill Dana's) manager, played the bridesmaid's husband. The additions cost Adams $400—the price of his wife's gown—while Neufeld provided his own wardrobe. Described by Jane Dulo, "It really was like a family wedding. It seemed like every comedy writer in town, everyone Don knew in his life, was there. And I remember, like a real wedding, we couldn't see Barbara's dress until she came down the stairs with the Chief. It was the big secret of the studio.

We all oohed and aahed when she made her entrance."

James Komack became a triple threat— director/writer/actor—reluctantly: "We needed a gunman. I'd get one actor after another, and Don wouldn't like any of them. 'I've seen this guy too much.' 'He's the wrong type.' And Don kept stalling and stalling. It got to the day when he said, 'I have an actor who will be here tomorrow.' I said, 'I should look at the actor.' Don said, 'You'll love him. Don't worry. If he doesn't work, we can call casting and get someone else.'

"It came time to do the scene, and I asked Don, 'Where is he? I don't see him.' Don said, 'He's here. It's you.' I said, 'What?' He said, 'You're going to do this. Because I don't believe you're a killer. I don't think you look like a killer. You couldn't be a killer. And that strikes me as funny.' He laughed. He thought it was funny. I asked, 'Why is it so funny?' He said, 'You're not a heavy, so you playing a heavy is funny.' I was the guy who shot the silhouette in 'A Man Called Smart.' That's the kind of thing Don did. It's like pulling wings off flies."

The trick in casting Bernie Kopell— whom Leonard Stern brought, and who in turn made a point of advancing the merits of King Moody as Shtarker—revolved around his concurrent ongoing *That Girl* (1966–1971) role: "I didn't have a contract with either show. It was one of those things where I got friendly with the first assistant director and would get scripts as early as I could. Then I'd be able to say, 'Okay, I'm working on Tuesday and Thursday, can we . . . ?' and in all those years, I never once had a problem with it. Extraordinary!"

As *Get Smart* garnered reputation as a hip show, famous friends would advance the notion to Don Adams that they'd like to do a cameo. Steve Allen, Milton Berle, Joey Bishop, Bill Dana, Phyllis Diller, Buddy Hackett, Bob Hope, Martin Landau, among others, played the cameo game. Johnny Carson appeared twice, to be credited one time as "special guest conductor" ("Aboard the Orient Express"). James Caan appeared as Smart's arch foe in the two-parter "To Sire, with Love" on the condition that the closing credits not list his name. Instead they read "Rupert of Rathskeller as himself." Carol Burnett starred in "One of Our Olives is Missing." "That was," recalls Leonard Stern, "a mutual admiration society. I had tried to bring her on the Steve Allen show, without success. She and Bill Dana became friendly, so I think he may have provided the liaison in bringing her to *Get Smart*. I remember her palpable presence, because she brought a sense of fun with her. It was an uplifting experience to have Carol on the set."

At rehearsal, actors ran through the script, made suggestions, and blocked for shooting. Don Adams frequently had ideas, which were often though not invariably accepted. When they weren't, he didn't mind fighting the issue. He wasn't unique in this. At least half those present had strong convictions about their work. Says Bilson, "In the beginning we would fight over a word, and we'd call the of-

With Johnny Carson in a cameo "Aboard the Orient Express."

fice, and the writers would come down, and we'd all pick over things with a fine-tooth comb. It got so that one day, a script arrived with the writers' names and everyone else's on the title page—plus Stern, Adams, Bilson, whoever else—as a joke, and I guess a little bit of a protest."

Gary Nelson recalls the early days when, "the minute we had the slightest problem, Leonard Stern and Arnie Rosen would come right up to the set and solve it. They'd solve it by acting out all the parts. Leonard would take one, Arnie would take another. They'd do the whole scene, work through it, and it would be hysterical. Then they would leave, and the actors would try to do it exactly the same way, and they'd come out sounding like Jewish writers doing the scene."

Sometimes the decision as to what got laughs and what didn't would be referred to script supervisor Dottie Aldworth, whose unique sense of humor led to an inside joke: if Dottie laughs hard at something and shrugs at something else, go with the one she shrugged at.

Don Adams, known for his offstage memory the way Venus de Milo is famed for her arms, nonetheless possessed photographic powers with scripts, learning lines on the spot and a show in two hours. Says Adams, "I would ask Dottie to read the scene to me, and then I'd ask her to read my lines to me. After she did it twice, I had it. I learned by listening rather than reading. If I can hear what is being said, then I know the relationship of the people in the scene and generally, even if the words aren't exact, they're pretty close. It's a kind of thought process rather than a memorizing process."

This from a man famous for forgetting his wife's name; who checked into the elegant Beverly Hills Hotel without cash, checks, credit card, or ID, and had to be bailed out by his attorney/business manager; and who, as Mrs. Dorothy Adams once told the *Saturday Evening Post,* used to drive around oblivious of the garbage cans in his car: "Our old house was on a hill too steep for the garbage truck to go up. So every Wednesday we loaded the garbage in the car, and he was supposed to drop it off at the bottom of the hill before he went to the studio. But every Wednesday he drove to work with the back of the car loaded with garbage."

Adams as a rule preferred not to be wed to a script: "I try hard to keep the spontaneity and it's hard because we shoot and reshoot the scene. I think that takes a little off the performance. It wasn't a matter of rewriting, but of improvising. I'd read it, then I'd go out and do the scene. You'd do it in person once for the cameras, then you'd put in stand-ins for lighting and blocking, and then you figure out how you can make it better or how you can improvise something after that first rehearsal. Or you go through a number of takes. A master shot. An establishing shot. A three-shot or a two-shot. You're constantly doing the scene over again. And in doing that, you sometimes think of things to make it funnier, and you just tell the director."

Ed Platt most often appeared in office scenes, which were generally shot on Fridays because such scenes needed only the regulars and the simple standing set. This meant that if they failed to finish on time, these pieces would be the easiest to pick up later. For these—dubbed by Bruce Bilson as "the Friday Night Follies"—Adams's slight rephrasings had a way of unhinging Ed Platt. Platt frequently carried the burden of exposition: KAOS has a new weapon. The weapon has a fancy name and convoluted functions. A thorough worker nervous about details, Platt originally studied the scripts as written. If a script said "dynamo retrogressor projectile," he mastered precisely that phrase. Then Adams would invert the words—to "dynamic retroprojector" or whatever—leaving Platt to unlearn and relearn the phrase on his feet. He eventually gave up trying to memorize gadget designations in advance.

Adams, sensing a source of fun, took to betting Platt before scenes that Platt would blow a line. Platt's ponderous expositions and lengthy speeches lent themselves to bungling. Yet Platt would bet and lose, and Adams would kid aloud, "Is John Doucette [another balding character actor] available?" The writers, rooting for the underdog and plotting to tongue-tie Adams, started changing difficult lines at the last minute: "Oh, Don. We just changed this password because we have something funnier. Now it's 'the sweet simpering sparrows sit sweltering on the stand.' " Adams, in seconds, would master the new line, then turn to cast and crew to lay odds on the chances that Platt would blow it.

Bernie Kopell thought of the improvising phase as give-and-take: "Stan Burns and Mike Marmer and Leonard and I had a history together, so if I had something that seemed to be a valid idea, or something had happened on the set, we'd throw it in and see how it worked. Sometimes it worked. Sometimes, as in any creative process, you keep spitting it out and rejecting and thinking of other things, and sometimes you hit on something and it works very well. Sometimes what you come up with blows the rhythm, messes it up, and you have to say it doesn't work. The process was

collaborative to a point, without interfering with the original, basic outline of the story."

For Dick Gautier: "We got to play with scripts and make things work for ourselves. Today, there's quite a bit of interference from above, and a script is a script is a script because, once it's been approved, any change means you no longer have approval. Then the other thing is that, because *Get Smart* was a film show, you'd rehearse and shoot one scene, then rehearse and shoot another scene, and the writers couldn't be hanging around for this whole process. Anything you found or played with had to be decided by the actors and the director. So we were able to incorporate things that were born of the moment, like improvisational theater."

Says William Schallert, "All the anecdotal stuff ended up on the screen, so to speak. I worked all the comedy out of my system that way."

Among business developing on the floor:

- Arne Sultan suggesting to William Schallert that when someone hands the Admiral an important message and people ask what it says, the Admiral should answer in his weak, dazed voice, "It says it's an important message."
- Don Adams's suggestion that when Maxwell Smart, out of boredom, tosses crumpled paper into a wastepaper basket in "Maxwell Smart, Private Eye," he should hit his target with the paper both times, and the third

time, sling a plum that splatters against the wall.

- In "Anatomy of a Lover," Hymie has been reprogrammed by KAOS. Max has Hymie's chest panel open, trying to repair the damage. A crew member called out "Why don't you just say 'Hymie, cough'?" It became part of the scene.
- In "The Man From YENTA," Max, the YENTA agent, and KAOS's LeMoco have all disguised themselves to look just like Prince Abu ben Bubbie. The Chief has to tell them apart. During rehearsal, someone on the set joked, "Number one, what is your name?"—the opening gambit of TV's popular game show *To Tell the Truth*. The scene evolved into a riff on the program, from the questions to the inevitable "Will the real Prince Abu ben Bubbie please step forward?"—echoing *To Tell the Truth*'s "Will the real ___ please stand up?"
- For "Schwartz's Island," Siegfried attempts to finish Smart and 99 by leaving them in quicksand. Don Adams, fearing the scene would inspire children to play in quicksand, amended the substance to "synthetic sand."
- For "How To Succeed in the Spy Business Without Really Trying," Bernie Kopell added the thought that Siegfried's young life went awry when his mother wouldn't get him a sled.
- Leonard Stern, from the floor, suggested the original "old ___ trick," "That's the second biggest ___ I've ever seen" and, when "Viva Smart" ran several minutes short, wrote in additional material including a Flamenco dance.
- During one rehearsal, someone looked at a prop that suddenly seemed doomed, and said to someone else, "Don't tell me this gag isn't going to work." Someone answered, "It's not going to work." Snapped the original speaker, "I asked you not to tell me that." No one remembers exactly who said what, but the exchange became a running *Get Smart* joke.

The producer tried to be on the set whenever possible. Says Burt Nodella, "I was always there for master shots. Not necessarily for the coverage, but I wanted to see the masters to see that the gags and dialogue went right. I was there constantly, certainly whenever I could be. First thing in the morning, last thing at night. I loved the process.

The executive producer might or might not have been on hand. Recalls Leonard Stern, "I would visit the set from time to time, mostly to escape from the problems I was having as a writer. I would decide to play producer. And I noticed each and every time I went to the set, the attitudes or the spirit of the company fell short of my expectations.

"I asked Don one day to walk with me. I made a rather flowery speech telling him that comedy had to be performed against a tapestry of joy. Finally he asked, 'What the hell are you talking about?' I answered, 'Well, Don, I have to be honest. Each and every time I've come on the set, I have found everyone uptight and nervous.' And he said, 'Leonard, each and every time you come on the set, we get uptight and nervous.'

"Then I realized I was the father figure. I came on the set, solemn and concerned with my writing problems. They had no opportunity to make this distinction, and thought me displeased with what they were doing. After this revelation, we laughed, and I remembered to come on the set with a smile, or to avoid the set if I was incapable of smiling."

As for the remaining principal players, both Barbara Feldon and Ed Platt distinguished themselves by their willingness not to make waves. Feldon proved herself a good sport as early as the pilot: "We were on the boat with Mr. Big. The men were using machine guns. I had never worked with special effects. I thought they actually had bullets in the machine guns and were shooting them in the air. I was supposed to duck down behind a barrel. A gun went off. Something hit me in the head. It was probably a spent cartridge, but I thought I'd been shot. I played the rest of the scene having an anxiety attack, certain that I'd been shot in the brain, and that I didn't feel anything because severe nerve damage had been done."

Feldon survived the shooting incident, as well as the first in a long line of scenes about water. "Here's what I remember about *Get Smart:* Being wet for five years. Cold and wet. Jumping out of Mr. Big's boat. Drowning in a phone booth. Going through a car wash with the top down. Or getting buckets of water thrown at us. Water is funny. It's also wet and cold, especially at seven or eight in

Barbara Feldon on the set with Linda O'Leary, daughter of Pat O'Leary, Assistant to the Producer. *Courtesy of Pat O'Leary Burkette.*

the morning."

James Komack remembers Barbara Feldon as "a lovely lady, no trouble at all. She could handle herself in any situation. If Don changed a line, took seven lines away from her, added fifteen, it was all fine with her. And what she did on camera, she did so beautifully that maybe viewers didn't see it. Like gravity. You don't think about it, but you couldn't function without it. When you worked with her, that's when you noticed. On film, you're always doing singles and close-ups. You'd go to her singles a lot and say, 'She's funny. Look what she's doing while he's talking.' "

Ed Platt, Komack adds, never failed to be "a journeyman actor and pro. He was around this business before I was around, before Don was around, before Barbara was around. He knew what it was to turn in good work and not get in the way. As a result, he was a very pliable, giving man, who would give you whatever you asked for. If you asked him what he thought about what you asked for, he might say 'I think it's all wrong.' 'Then why are you doing it?' 'Because you asked me to.'

"One time, we were doing a scene that was getting very complicated. Four or five people in the room. I had to cover this and cover that. Smoke coming out of the walls. And I said, 'Gee, I tell you what, Ed. You do this and stand over here.' He said, 'Okay.' I said, 'But I'm still in trouble here. I don't know how to work this thing out. Give me a moment.' 'Okay.' 'Ed, do you have any ideas?' He said, 'I have a very good idea. I shouldn't be in the scene.' I said, 'Now don't be nasty.' He answered, 'I'm not being nasty. I really mean it. If I'm not in the scene, you can get more activity going, because Max won't have to pay attention to my so-called authority as the Chief.' I asked, 'Are you saying this because you're mad?' Ed replied, 'You asked me. You want me to be in the scene? I'll be glad to do it. But I don't think I belong in the scene.' And he was right. Don didn't like my taking Ed out of the scene until I told him it was Ed's idea, and the

reasoning behind it. Then he agreed that Ed had a good idea."

When not on their best behavior, cast members had their share of laughs, as much within scenes as hanging around between them—something which would be impossible in a show videotaped before a live audience.

Adams and Robert Karvelas both used to kid Ed Platt. Says Karvelas, "Ed was the most beautiful man I've ever worked with. Fantastic, a sweetheart. Everybody loved him on the set, and we used to party a lot together, and I'd have fun with him. There was one show that had a shouting match between Larabee and the Chief. They were supposed to stand real close to each other. But I held back. Don asked why. Ed was right there, and I announced, 'I can't work with Ed this close. He's got halitosis, and it's driving me crazy. Can't you get Binaca or something?' The whole set would laugh, and Ed was such a good guy, he'd take it seriously and worry about it."

For "Schwartz's Island," Max and 99 braved high seas in a little rowboat. The crew filmed from a yacht as the water got choppier and choppier. A common question of actors to cameramen is "Where are you cutting me?"—in other words, "How much of me is in the frame?" When the water reached its roughest and both rowboat and yacht bobbed along like corks, Adams hollered across to the crew, "Where are you cutting me?"

In "Back to the Old Drawing Board", Hymie, who had not been built to withstand the effects of alcohol, drinks too much at a party. Max takes him into a closet to scold him. Hymie responds by kissing him on the cheek. But Gautier couldn't suppress his giggles: "Every time I kissed him, looked at him, when we made eye contact, we'd start to laugh. After a while the crew and everyone else was laughing, and we must have done it twenty-two times. What I eventually had to do was not look at him—kiss him from the side of my mouth and look straight ahead—because I couldn't look at his face, at his expression, 'here comes that guy with his lips again.' "

For "Rub-a-Dub-Dub . . . Three Spies in a Sub," Max and Siegfried square off at a submarine periscope. Max has to con Siegfried. Siegfried replies, "The trick is schtupid. . . . The trick is dumb. . . . The trick is . . . working!" The exchange, intended as a two-shot, repeatedly broke the actors up. After entirely too many efforts to capture it on film, the director finally resigned himself to single shots—and sent each actor out of the room while the other spoke.

Recalls Don Adams, "They sent me to my dressing room like a bad little kid. Then they took a single of Bernie. Then they sent him to his room and came for me." Adds Kopell, "We were hysterical, but in the back of my head was this negative fantasy of 'I'll remember today's date because this will be my last day in the business. They will fire me and never allow me to work again because I'm wasting their time and ruining their show.' "

When Don Rickles arrived to do "The Little Black Book," he and Adams managed to waste so much time, it became a two-part episode. The Adams-Rickles friendship had gone back years, with Adams one of Rickles's earliest big boosters. As Rickles acknowledged the debt in *Playboy*, "He's one of my dearest friends, but I wish he'd stop kissing my ring: it loosens the stone. Some guys worshiped Mantle, Gehrig, Williams; I've always been Don's idol. It's a terrible bore, but every so often I break down and spend an evening with him, strictly as a mercy mission."

Though they cut up so much on the set of "The Little Black Book" that the episode had to be stretched to two parts in order to justify its expense in man hours, they ad-libbed more than enough to provide a double show. For the climax, the two are chained to a wall. Recalls James Komack, "They'd been hysterical in the dressing room, hysterical in makeup, hysterical before they went to work and hysterical while they worked. When I said, 'Cut, we're going to go to lunch,' I had them release Don Adams. He said, 'Wait, hold it, don't move anything. I want to talk to you about reshooting this shot.' He came over to me, and I asked, 'What shot do you want to redo?' He told me, 'No shot. Let's go to lunch. But don't release Rickles.' Rickles yelled and screamed, and we left him chained to the wall, in the dark."

For "The Little Black Book," Joey Forman—familiar to *Get Smart* viewers as Harry Hoo, proverb-spouting Hawaiian Charlie Chan-mode private detective—had a scene as Don Adams's and Don Rickles's lawyer. Forman, a Method actor, precisely prepared his

every utterance and emotion. Adams and
Rickles alternated taking director James
Komack aside to confer. After each conference, Komack instructed Forman to
play the scene a different way. Then
while Forman, rattled already, attempted
to do his speech, Adams and Rickles had
private conversations: "Did you see that
girl who came in last week?" "Do you
have crabgrass?" Forman's wife, watching from the sidelines, saw the put-on
and told her husband, who was relieved
to learn that he hadn't been losing his
talent or his mind.

Along with downright silliness came
the comically unexpected. An uninvited
guest flew onto the set for "Maxwell
Smart, Private Eye." Two actors portrayed Peter Lorre (Phil Roth) and Sydney Greenstreet (Berry Krueger) types.
In the course of their two-shot, a fly lit
on Roth's nose. Bruce Bilson, from force
of habit, yelled "Cut!" Adams stifled a
scream: "Why did you do that?" Concedes Bilson, "I've never forgiven myself
to this day."

Accidents that occurred could almost
have come from *Get Smart* scenarios.
For the episode "Perils in a Petshop," a
parakeet cashed in its wings forever when
Adams unintentionally fired his gun too
close to the bird. To his credit, he asked
if the gun was loaded. Someone said no,
but meant that it was loaded with blanks
instead of live ammunition. Adams
pulled the trigger. The parakeet experienced the possibly first and definitely last
shock of its life, swung down dead on the
perch, and had to be pried off by its
trainer.

On location for "The Mild Ones,"
Burt Nodella made the mistake of talking
to stuntmen who had been jousting on
motorcycles: "They asked if I'd ever rid-
den a motorcycle. I said no. They
wanted to teach me. I had on sneakers, I
remember, and we had those motorcycles without self-starters, where you have
to rear up and down to get started. I
reared up and came down with my full
weight and broke my foot."

In "Washington 4, Indians 3," Max
and 99 have to lower themselves down
the side of a steep cliff. Barbara Feldon
did not have fun: "This precipitous cliff
that went straight down didn't look too
bad from below, and indeed, when it
came on screen, it didn't look like anything at all. When Don saw it, it inspired
him. He thought we should just sort of
jump over and skid and slide down the
shale and sharp rocks. I demurred, but
not very powerfully. Don said, 'Don't
worry. I'll be in front of you, Barbara. If
anything happens, you'll just fall into
me. Okay?'

"We were going to get it in one take,
obviously, because there was no telling
what we were going to look like after we
did it. We didn't practice, we just did it.
Don leapt over, carefully, and applied all
the things he'd learned in the Marines. I
shot down. I passed him up. I was all
scratched and bruised. I went head over
heels, right into the cameras, so angry,
mostly at myself."

Burt Nodella asked her later, "Why
did you do it? It was a long shot. You
could have used your stunt double." She
answered, "Don said it would be fun.

Besides, like most actors, you read the script, and you know that on the last page you come out okay."

Fights, properly choreographed, did not necessarily predicate disaster. When Jane Dulo had to belt Jack Gilford (Simon the Likeable) in "And Baby Makes Four," Part II, she pleaded to slap him instead. "I might break his nose." Cameraman, stuntmen, and Gilford helped her. The scene worked without a hitch. Barbara Feldon eventually had all her karate chops taken away from her "because I pulled every punch. They said I would start out like a hatchet and end like a feather. As I got close to the neck, my hand would start getting graceful. I have no strength whatsoever, and it was practically ostentatious of me to think I was a danger to anyone. But I couldn't do it. The only time I did it at all well was when I had to hit a dummy."

At the other extreme, Don Adams, who loved to do his own stunts, was reputed at one time to be Hollywood's clumsiest human, unable to remove his specs without lodging them in his ear or on his nose. He told *TV Guide*, "I trip over things that are not there." To *Newsweek* he admitted, "Smart is dedicated and sincere—he's myself. I guess I'm a bit of a klutz. I would like to be like James Bond, but I knock glasses onto people's laps." Yet like his alter ego Smart, Adams enjoyed living dangerously. He pressed to do his own stunts, with as much fistfighting, fencing, and derring-do as he could wangle. To keep peace, directors would shoot long, drawn-out confrontations, which

they knew would be reduced to size during the editing process.

Adams discharged these scenes so intently that he seemed to have bought Max Smart's self-image. At once a master of comic underplaying and a guy who delighted in rough stuff, he achieved the difficult balance that personifies Agent 86, straight man to himself. Adams could have played James Bond with total conviction, employing the same fisticuffs, and the same savoir faire. William Shallert describes watching Max Smart in action:

"Whatever weapon the villain got, Don grabbed one just like it. They shot at each other. Swung on ropes at each other. They fenced with each other. It was like a Douglas Fairbanks movie. What interested me was that Don wasn't going for humor at all. He became caught up in the serious side of being a good fencer, of wanting to look good doing it. He was very concerned that it not look hokey—doing well at all these things Smart wasn't supposed to be good at in the first place."

The fights would be choreographed, with Adams's stunt double when there was no way around it, otherwise with Adams. Says he, "I remember once, I had to do a big fight in a car wash, with a lot of water and soap and suds and everything, and the car moving on rails. They didn't want me doing it, thought it too dangerous. But the stunt man choreographed it so there was no danger. Our fists never came within six inches of each other, but when you look at it on the screen, it looks like every slug is a direct

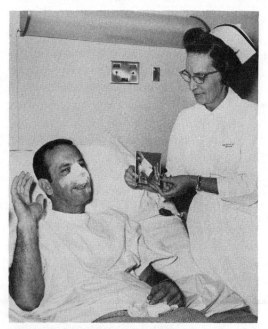

Don Adams recovers from his broken nose, sustained in the line of duty. *Courtesy of Robert Karvelas.*

hit. It's just a matter of positioning, and our people were great at it.

"I did a lot of action scenes and fight scenes and stunt scenes, and mostly did my own stuff until I got my nose broken. Then I stopped for a while."

The nose broke during the fight scene in "Smart Fit the Battle of Jericho." According to Bilson, who directed the episode, "I asked for a rehearsal, and said, 'just do it half speed so we know where all the punches and moves are.' Don was not very good at half speed. He speeded it up, and the other fellow, Steve Gravers, speeded it up, and Don's head came one way as the guy's hand came the other way. Crack. I could hear his nose go up.

That was it. His nose swelled. Had to be set. Closed us down for about a week."

The directors wore the hats of conductor, arbiter, and coach; endeavored to keep Adams from killing himself; worked to keep the comedy honest. Broken noses notwithstanding, they favored playing things too straight over playing them too campy. Bilson found that "one of the traps people fall into on such shows is trying to be funny. The heavy decides, 'This is my chance to be a comedian.' But when heavies tried to be funny, the show didn't work. We had all the good television heavies, and the ones who worked best were the ones who understood the threat had to be there. Everybody has to bring his or her own little something, some sense of humor to it, but not let it come spilling out.

" 'Kiss of Death' may have been the worst episode I did, because I let the heavy get away with it. I couldn't quite control it. We saved the episode for New Year's Eve, because nobody liked it and we thought this way no one would see it. Then everyone in the entire motion picture industry and television business who was waiting to go to a party saw it."

The director also had to concern himself with Adams's and Feldon's "good sides." Feldon wanted to be photographed looking camera left; Adams favored looking camera right. Walking into rooms on camera, he faced one way, she the other. At the Chief's desk, they angled for position. Feldon would stand between them, beside the desk, so that she and Max could each talk to the Chief without either of them having to forfeit the preferred profile. After the scene that broke Don Adams's nose, and after everyone assured Barbara Feldon that he wasn't seriously injured, she found herself wondering whether the accident would alter his profile enough that he'd want to be photographed from the other side of his face. If it did, she'd have to give up her favorite side of *her* face to accommodate him. But nothing changed, neither Adams's sculpted physiognomy nor his love of a good fight scene.

Over the years, directors increasingly grappled with the issue of bringing back Glick. The infectious quality of Adams's "Glick voice"—the ratchet twang that put him on the map in *The Bill Dana Show* and *Get Smart*—had plus and minus aspects. As a plus, it invited instant imitation across the country, and contributed significantly to *Get Smart's* success. As a minus, it encouraged involuntary aping on the set. For one scene, Adams did a line, followed by an actor responding with—unintentionally—the same intonation. The director had to stop the cameras. Without meaning to, he called "Cut" in an identical voice.

Adams deliberately pulled back from Glick: "The first year, I did it almost consistently, but I got to hate it, and the fact that everyone around me was doing it. It was like a contagious disease. People on the set. Actors I worked with. When people impersonate me, they do an exaggerated version, just as my version is an exaggerated William Powell. Gradually I started cutting it down, using a controlled version of it that wasn't as harsh or clipped as in the first year,

and I'd only use it on certain phrases or certain sentences. By the time I got to the last couple of years of the show, I hardly used it at all, except on certain words. If I used it on them, it gave the impression of my using it constantly."

Directors noticed, and urged him, "Don, more Glick." By Glicking, Adams could usually insert humor in speeches that in themselves lacked hilarity. Glicked, even something as simple as "The name is Smart, Maxwell Smart" had devastating comic impact.

With the give-and-take that existed among directors, writers, and stars—and with Adams's active input in every aspect of the series—a new ingredient flavored the stew when triple-threat Don Adams (star, writer, stuntman) became a quadruple-threat: director. Previously, he directed indirectly, expressing his opinions and instincts. Some expressed gratitude that there were only twenty-four hours in a day, or he'd have found more to make suggestions about.

Came the fateful day: "The first year, I wanted to direct so much, because I loved directing, and I kept bugging them and bugging them and bugging them to let me do it. We were on a low budget then. *Get Smart* had one of the lowest budgets of any show on the air at that time, and it was an action show, a one-camera film action show, which today would cost an absolute fortune to shoot. The budget for the show for the whole week was something like $85,000. Today it would be $850,000 to shoot an action show like that, with car chases, outside locations, rooftop things.

"So finally they came to me and said, 'Okay, we have the script for the week.' The director fell out or got sick or whatever. 'So we're going to let you direct it.' I went to the script. About 90 percent of it took place in the Sahara Desert. I said, 'Terrific, when are we going on location? Are we going to Palm Springs? The Mojave Desert? Death Valley? Where?' They said, 'We'll show you,' and they took me to stage seven, and there were two trucks with sand.

"And they had backdrops, cut-outs, of sand dunes against a blue cyc [short for *cyclorama,* a fake sky]. That was my set, and that's what I had to direct. So I had them build me a portable sand dune, which I kept using throughout. I kept shooting it from different angles, except that I couldn't shoot up, because that would be shooting off the set. It was a nightmare. Phony. Of course, they did second-unit stuff, took two doubles out to a real desert. What's amazing is that once you have the second-unit material, the two people out in the vast expanse, the desert with sand dunes and shadows and everything, and you intercut it with what you've shot on the phony set, pretty soon you get the illusion that it's real. No matter how fake it is.

" 'Appointment in Sahara' was the episode. The average script is about thirty-three pages. We were supposed to do eleven pages a day. They were panicky about going overtime. The first day, I did my eleven pages and everyone felt happy and relieved. The second I did two and three quarter pages, and you've never seen such panic in your life. 'We should

never have let him do it! Why, oh why did we let him do it?' I spent two and three quarter pages on a fight scene in a tent. I was experimenting, like Orson Welles with a toy. I had a hand-held camera, all kinds of shots, stunt men, a camera going in, overhead shots, and spent the entire day shooting this one fight scene.

"But I knew that the next day, all the scenes were in the Chief's office or right outside the Chief's office, and would be easy to get. So I finished the show on time, although I had to do nineteen or twenty pages that last day.

"I always loved to direct. I still do. Toward the end of doing *Get Smart,* I was so tired, and I used to go on the set feeling wiped out. I had to push myself out of the chair to do a scene. One day, I was like that and they told me the director was sick and had to go home. I had to take over for him. We start shooting at eight. This was maybe ten o'clock in the morning. I got out of the chair like someone had given me miracle drugs. I was so full of energy. So stimulated. All the tiredness left me. I had to figure out all the shots I was going to do, had to direct the acting, communicate with the cameramen. Suddenly I was raring to go.

"I'm not that stimulated performing or writing, but the director takes the words that the writers write, and takes what the actors do with the words that the writers write, and then he has to make a picture in his mind, has to put the pieces together, has to make it work. In his mind, he's got to be able to run it cut and edited and finished and up on the screen before he does it, and while he's doing it. It's a real challenge.

"I always got paid as a director when I directed because I had to join the director's union, and the union expected me to get paid. But I would have been glad to do it for nothing. As a matter of fact, I would have paid them."

Way back in the beginning when Talent Associates hired Don Adams to be Maxwell Smart, he had the choice of a big salary or a smaller salary and a piece of the show. He opted for the latter, which gave him a third of the series' profit. He reasoned that if *Get Smart* didn't work, he'd have a salary for thirteen weeks and nothing more when it ended—but if the series hit and ran a few years, a piece of the show would support him for the rest of his life. Adams would fall back on this when directors cautioned him that too much kidding on the set cost time, and therefore money. Adams would reply, "Take it out of my third." But no one ever did, and it's highly unlikely that so complex a computation could be made if anyone ever wanted to.

A third of the show might, conceivably, have made him wonder about budgets and inspecting books, "but I didn't. All I knew was every show came in over budget, so I knew I'd have to make the money in syndication. How we got to be over budget didn't interest me until one time, I was directing 'The Treasure of C. Errol Madre.' I don't remember the numbers they told me, but they said the episode would be maybe $15,000 over budget going in. This

means before we even had one set-up, before we took a shot. With an $85,000 budget, this meant we had gone through $100,000 already. Mystifying. So I asked to see the sheets—the first time I ever asked, because I used to get dizzy just looking at them. I got the sheets, and scanned for the big numbers. If I saw $200 or $400, I kept looking. Then I saw this big figure, it might have been $12,000. I said, 'What's this?' They said, 'That's to build the city morgue.' I said, 'A morgue costs this?' They said, 'We need drawers that pull out, lighting, tubs, basins.' I said, 'Take me down and show me the set.' I came up with a few ideas that cost two or three hundred dollars instead of all those thousands.

"What I did was shoot some of it silhouette, through a glass window in a door that had CITY MORGUE on it. Then I did a high overhead shot down on the gurney where a body was lying and the Chief and I stood next to it. Then I shot from the floor through the guy's toe—the tag on the toe coming out from under the sheet—up into the faces of the Chief and me."

Adams attributes much of his directorial style to the influence of Stanley Kubrick in his *Paths of Glory* mode: "He had a style that each scene triggered the next scene. A very fast action style. I can't stand directing with a heavy hand, where the director falls in love with streets or scenery or getting from one place to another. I like the action to move along."

Yet he goes on to characterize his style—along with the styles of most directors in *Get Smart* situations—as "style in a half-hour show is very hard to establish when you're fighting the clock every minute. Most television directors—and we had some good ones in those days—were under a tremendous pressure to bring a show in under three days that it wasn't possible to bring in in three days. Most of the time was spent, really, trying to do that. Bring it in on time and under budget."

Fighting the clock entailed a series of judgment calls on the part of the director, making him in addition to everything else, a referee. The producer and director, sometimes in conjunction with the cameraman, lighting man, and others, would approach dinner time and look at the script. They could quit at dinner time and let things run into another day. Or they could break for dinner, and have everybody come back after dinner at least 50 percent uninterested. Or they could work through dinner and hope to finish fast. Any decision to work late carried a high price tag. Any judgment call that "we can finish in three hours" could be counted on to backfire.

Says Adams, "Three hour estimates were always bad estimates. Actors can blow their lines. A camera shot or boom shot will go out of whack. You'll get hair in the aperture. The sound will go out. You think you're going to struggle until ten o'clock, and you go until one or two in the morning. You're in golden time, and golden golden time. It costs you a fortune. For 'One of Our Olives is Missing,' with Carol Burnett, we were on a plank outside a window doing shtik at

three A.M. because she had prior commitments and couldn't come back the next day or the next week. We had to finish that night. No wonder the show always ran a deficit."

The goal: to shoot two episodes in a week—and between thirty-two and twenty-six a season. But everything presented some obstacle. For Jay Sandrich, "My big memories as producer are just of the complexity of getting the show shot in a reasonable amount of time. Everything held up shooting. Nothing worked the first time. We were always going over schedule. For example, that Cone of Silence was very difficult to light in a way that didn't reflect our stage lighting equipment. It took a long time to shoot.

"And the networks invariably wanted more exteriors. But they didn't want to pay more money for them, so it was hard trying to handle the production requirements for the show and still do it for a budget."

They compromised—going over budget, but not beyond all conceivable reason—putting their money on the screen.

At dailies—when evidence of each day's work first appeared on screen—there was much to laugh at, and plenty to fuss over. As Ted Rich recalls, "When we shot, Don did a lot of funny stuff, pratfalls and things like that. They'd show up in the dailies and everyone would be hysterical. But we'd have to lose them in the edit, either because they made the story too long, or because they threw off the timing. Tempo, particularly with something like *Get Smart,* is all-important."

Watching the dailies for "Rub-a-Dub-

Dub . . . Three Spies in a Sub," Leonard Stern at first couldn't imagine why one of Siegfried's uniformed KAOS commandos seemed so familiar. On closer inspection, he realized why he hadn't been able to place the man's face. It wasn't a man. It was Aunt Rose in a moustache, used in the scene for the dailies only, as a gag.

Leonard Stern watched dailies with intense scrutiny, sometimes to the distress of others: "You're unaware of the patterns you form, but whenever we went to the screenings of the dailies, I'd sit in the same seat, which was against the wall. And I had taught myself not to be negative. But what I was unaware of doing was an unconscious response to things that bothered me. I hit the wall. One time, Arne Sultan had joined the show as producer, and entered the room before me. He took a seat. They told him, 'Don't sit there, it's Leonard's seat.' Arne dismissed the thought, certain that I'm not the sort of person who would reserve a seat. I sat next to him. And something bothered me about one of the scenes. I automatically reached out to the wall and punched it hard, forgetting Arne was there. I missed hitting him by very few inches. He said, 'Leonard, take your seat.' Then they showed me where I had been knocking plaster off the wall, which took me by complete surprise. I thought I had been handling it so well."

One of the scenes that bothered Stern occurred in the dailies for "A Man Called Smart." The scene required Max and 99 to pile into a car when offered a ride. The joke was supposed to be that they didn't realize they only had a few feet to go,

and that it took longer to get into the car than it took to reach their destination. As shot, there were a few seconds of the car leaving, and a few seconds of it arriving. It looked like the car had covered miles. Stern had the scene rephotographed.

For Max and 99's wedding scene, no one realized until a few weeks later that only half the room had been shot. Reza Badiyi, doing second unit direction before he moved up to director, had the responsibility of re-creating the chapel and photographically filling in the blanks.

Badiyi regularly filled in another important blank, that of title visualization: "I wasn't a title maker. It wasn't a question of chosing letters to put across a piece of film. For the opening title, I created what was visually happening behind the scene, to catch the eye. When a viewer is turning the television dial, at that moment, like at eight o'clock, the viewer is shopping. You have to mesmerize viewers right away so they don't keep turning the channel. You have to have a good tap dance going on. By the time they've seen the tease and Max's car speeding down the street, they're hooked, or anyway, it's too late for them to switch to another channel because they've already missed the beginning of the other shows." Along with *Get Smart*, Badiyi's highly recognizable opening visualizations include those for *He & She*, *That Girl*, and *Hawaii Five-O*.

Postproduction would lend the finishing touches to each episode—from adding clip-clop sounds in "Ship of

Spies" (it still bothers Bruce Bilson that he went to all the trouble of photographing wooden shoes clomping along, and then no one remembered to put in the clip-clop) to creating a tease about meeting on the moon. (Leonard Stern came up with it during editing. The moon walk had just made headlines. In the tease, the Chief and Max are on the moon but say they'll have to find somewhere else to meet secretly, now that the astronauts have found the place.)

For some episodes, postproduction continued long after *Get Smart* went off the air. Burt Nodella recalls a time when a joke could not be utilized, as much as Stern wanted to make it work. "I told him we couldn't have done it and still finished the show. It would have taken three more set-ups. So we did it without the joke. I saw him at a party five months later. He said, 'Can we fix that?' I said, 'Leonard, the show is cut. It's on the air.' Years later, I was at a Christmas party with him. I said, 'Why don't we rent a studio? We get everyone back and shoot the scene for you?' Of course, we didn't do it. But Leonard really cares that much."

Admits Stern, "In my mind, I'm still recutting *Get Smart*."

Producers: Chris Hayward, Burt Nodella, Jess Oppenheimer, Arnie Rosen, Jay Sandrich, Leonard Stern, Arne Sultan

Directors: Norman Abbott, Don Adams, Reza S. Badiyi, Earl Bellamy, Richard Benedict, Bruce Bilson, Paul Bogart, Dick Carson, Richard D. Donner, Harry Falk, Murray Golden, Roy Joy, James Komack, Tony Leader, Frank MacDonald, Sidney Miller, Gary Nelson, Jess Oppenheimer, Alan Rafkin, Don Richardson, Charles Rondeau, Edward Ryder, Jay Sandrich, Joshua Shelley, Nick Webster, William Wiard.

9

THE SPY WHO CAME IN FROM THE PHONE BOOTH

"I say, marriage with Max is not exactly a bed of roses, is it?"

—Jack Favell (George Sanders), in *Rebecca*

When the *Get Smart* pilot went into production for NBC, a gorgeous woman in a trenchcoat accosted NBC network executives on the street, slipping messages, clues, and riddles in their pockets to hype the show. Recipients smiled, anticipating a hit. Then NBC tested the *Get Smart* pilot. It tested badly. Horribly. The worst. Leonard Stern suggested that perhaps the test viewers had no frame of reference. The show's style seemed realistic, but action seemed bizarre. Was it a serious James Bond done badly? Or a new kind of joke? The test viewers weren't sure, and whatever their confusion, they weren't having fun. Dan Melnick has said that if NBC had one more middle-class, middle-of-the-road pilot which tested acceptably that year, *Get Smart* might never have gotten on the air.

Fortunately, the affiliates had enjoyed the brief teaser screened in advance of the finished pilot, and Johnny Carson, who saw the pilot, admired it enough to bring Adams on the *Tonight* show, boosting *Get Smart* before its national premiere.

During the early weeks of *Get Smart*, Dan Melnick drove out to Don Adams's house to pick him up for dinner: "We'd already gotten a couple of national ratings and were clearly in the lead. I went to Don's. He was living in a house on top of one of the canyons. Wind blasted up from the desert, and it was so hot, the sweat poured off us. I said, 'Don, the show's the number two show in the country. Why don't you buy an air conditioner?' He said, with his Maxwell Smart twang, 'Not until the third national Nielsen.'"

With its first few episodes, *Get Smart* left no doubt that the world relished its newest spy. Agent 86's catchphrases spread coast-to-coast. People stopped watching for Clark Kent in every phone booth, hoping instead to find Maxwell Smart.

Get Smart's success grew. It knocked CBS's counter-programmed *Trials of O'Brien* off the air in May of 1966, and CBS's equally solid counter-programmed *Secret Agent* in September of the year. The stately closing credits of prestige dramas such as *Hallmark Hall of Fame* would roll to the accompaniment of Don Adams's unmistakable nasality in voice-overs promoting upcoming episodes of *Get Smart*. "This is Maxwell Smart, Agent 86, reminding you to watch . . ." A child wrote God a widely quoted letter, asking whether God let His son stay up to watch *Get Smart*.

Spoof series, once distrusted by network programmers, enjoyed a brief heyday as networks vied to cash in on the popularity of *Get Smart*. Buck Henry's superhero *Captain Nice* (1967–1967) and Leonard Stern's guy on the lam *Run*

Would You Believe

The producers of

Get Smart

would like to herald the show's second season

on N B C - T V September 17

by inviting you and a guest

to a party originally scheduled for

Maxim's
Paris, France

and now changed to

Dinty Moore's
New York City, New York

Four-in-Hand Tie

Motel accommodations, details concerning ferries and pooled cabs, and off-Broadway tickets for your brief stay are being sent to you under separate cover

Invitation promoting *Get Smart*, 1966.

Buddy Run (1966–1967), and his series about an actor who was not at all like his TV Western image, *The Hero* (1966–1967), along with the spies in *The Double Life of Henry Phyfe* (1966–1966) and another superhero, *Mr. Terrific* (1967–1967), had their adherents but lacked longevity. Whether they were ahead of their time, or whether it is nearly impossible to sustain a satire season upon season no matter how good you are, each failed to do what *Get Smart* had done.

On top anyhow, the *Get Smart* team took its steps to ensure sustained high ratings. Their creative minds combined with those of the publicity firm of Rogers & Cowan, engineering parties ("there will be refreshments on counters, should you wish to become a counter-spy, served in glasses, spy glasses of course, followed by dinner. Let your food-taster go first"), public appearances, and Barbara Feldon posing with pigs at state fairs. The first year, cast members appeared on a float in the Rose Bowl Parade. As the impressive display of stars and spectacle rolled past the reviewing stand, the announcer enthusiastically exclaimed that Don Adams and Barbara *Eden* were passing by.

In August 1966, the U.S. Army Counter-Intelligence Corps invited members of the *Get Smart* cast to entertain on the occasion of its nineteenth annual convention banquet. Isobel Silden, the publicist assigned to coordinate, took pains to confirm that the proceedings could be photographed. She even called "the president of the California branch of spies, and he confirmed this. He said spies at a party look different than spies on the job. I thought this was pretty intriguing. I'm not a spy but I look pretty much the same at a party as at the office, give or take a few more layers of makeup."

They found a spy who posed for gag shots with Don Adams, only to find the photos could never be used. So "we all tooled back upstairs trying to find a real spy. Boy, I spotted a great one. Sort of youngish man with the best black goatee you ever saw. I asked him if we could shoot pictures of him and identify him. 'Sure,' he told me. 'I'm an antique dealer from Long Beach.' He was there because the president of the California chapter was his uncle."

They zeroed in on two more spies—one who had subbed for President Roosevelt at the Teheran conferences, and another who had captured Himmler after the world thought Himmler dead—and moved forward with the festivities. Dave Ketchum emceed. Ed Platt sang "Ol' Man River." Barbara Feldon performed a skit about being Agent 99. Don Adams followed with several minutes of material. But the real *Get Smart* sketch transpired behind the scenes.

Before the evening ended, two operatives approached Silden and the press agent, demanding the negatives from the original batch of pictures. They further requested a signed letter saying the negatives had been turned over. The letter was duly executed, with a carbon, but the carbon paper had been reversed. One operative confiscated the carbon paper, immediately burning it in an ashtray. The press agent rewrote the release, addressing it, as before, to a box number supplied by the operatives. The operatives gave a new box number the second time around. Except that there was no Agent 13 under the ashtray, it created an unnerving atmosphere of *déjà vu*.

For *Get Smart*'s second season, Isobel Silden faced the challenge of "topping all those crazy things we did the first year. I did a series of invitations for reviewers and people like that. The first was engraved or embossed on very classy paper.

It said, 'Would you believe . . . you are invited to dinner at Maxim's in Paris?' and pertinent details. For the inside, I had taken my gourmet cookbook and found a string of French recipes that, put together, made no sense.

"About three days later, I sent a second one. 'Would you believe . . . that dinner at Maxim's in Paris has been rescheduled to Dinty Moore's in New York?' The menu was corned beef and cabbage, and Irish beer.

"Three days later: 'Would you believe . . . that the dinner in Maxim's that was rescheduled to Dinty Moore's in New York has been rescheduled to Joe's Taco Palace in Tijuana, Mexico? The menu: tacos, refried beans, chiles rellenos, and lukewarm beer.'

"That was followed by the biggest bag of popped popcorn I could find, and around its belly I had a banner which read, 'Would you believe . . . *Get Smart* returns to NBC' with the date and the time.

"We got appreciative phone calls and fan letters from critics, but one critic did not find it at all hilarious. It seems his wife had a bad habit of going to his office with him and opening his mail. She found the Maxim's invitation, went out and bought a gown, and got all her shots. For years after this, the shows I represented were studiously avoided by this critic, who shall be nameless."

Internally, *Get Smart* changed in minor ways during its years on the air. The red Sunbeam Tiger that turned the corner of an outside set for the earliest opening credits gave way, in 1966, to a blue Carmen Ghia and a location shot (downtown Los Angeles) resembling Washington, D.C. (Adams personally preferred the Sunbeam, which was given to him as his personal car). Beginning with 1968, a jigsaw pattern preceded and followed commercials and in the same year, writers' and directors' credits appeared before, rather than after, each episode. Yet the basics of the opening and its door sequence—despite occasional discussions as to whether to overhaul—suffered scarcely any modification.

By the middle of its five-year run, the series' most dramatic shifts occurred in the realm of action. "In the first few years," comments Mike Marmer, "our idea was to play a violent situation but you really weren't that violent in extricating yourself from the situation. In 'School Days,' Max and 99 are tied to a chair. A bomb is about to explode, as soon as a candle burns down. They have to get Fang to blow out the candle, which they do by singing 'Happy Birthday' to him. The contrast between the danger and their solution contributed to the comedy." After a few years, because Don Adams liked fight scenes and exercised certain clout—and because James Bond movies had become parodies themselves, making it harder to parody the parody—more fists swung, and no dogs blew out candles.

In the 1968–1969 season, because any new idea is never as new in its fourth year as it was in its first, the writers introduced a switch. Max, apparently capable of forming a lasting relationship with a woman, commenced the season by proposing to Agent 99. They tied the knot in November. Their engagement, nuptials, and wedded bliss triggered previously untapped plot possibilities, without ever removing them from their natural sphere of espionage. *Get Smart,* while not the novelty it had once been, continued to surprise. But in those days, networks routinely replaced shows that failed to promise not one but five more years on top of the ratings heap.

At the end of the fourth season, after two successive years of Emmy Awards as best comedy series (1967–1968, 1968–1969), NBC surprised the *Get Smart* team. Leonard Stern, at home when the call came, picked up the phone: "It was Herb Schlosser, a friend, who was NBC vice president in charge of programming on the West Coast then. My daughter Katie used to play with his son Eric. Katie was perhaps ten years old at the time. Herb, who had gone to New York for the meeting where they determine the new fall schedule, started the conversation with, 'Leonard, it's a total shock. I never anticipated this.' I responded, I believe, 'Uh, yes—?' and as Herb went on that he felt terrible, Katie, who had answered the phone, kept asking me, 'Is that Eric's father?' Herb told me that *Get Smart* had been cancelled. Katie told me to give her regards to Eric Schlosser. I promised Katie that I would, then resumed speaking with Herb. Katie wouldn't leave us alone. 'Daddy, you haven't given Eric my regards.' So I had to interrupt myself to give her regards to

The wedding of the season: 86 and the future Mrs. 86, with the Chief as best man.

Eric Schlosser. Herb said, 'Leonard, I'm not calling from California, and Eric is in California.' I said, 'I know, but Katie insists.' Then we were able to get back to our conversation of secondary importance, about the impending demise of *Get Smart.*"

Stern next phoned Dan Melnick in New York. Melnick contacted Mike Dann, head of programming at CBS: "I might be able to deliver *Get Smart* with everybody in it." Dann gave Melnick a provisional order for the show—that he thought he'd take it if the deal could be struck by a certain date. Technically, NBC owned the show beyond this date, and resisted dropping it in a way that might benefit a rival network to NBC's detriment. Negotiations, hinging largely on NBC's stake in maximizing syndication value of the four years it already owned, ultimately released the property.

The deal concluded so swiftly that the principals of the series hardly had to be advised that they were cancelled. It was more a matter of reworking individual contracts "because we're moving from NBC to CBS."

In *CBS: Reflections in a Bloodshot Eye*, Robert Metz records how Mike Dann "played the press like a violin" in using his *Get Smart* acquisition to boost CBS ratings during the sweeps—with the birth of twins to Max and 99—while ratings expert Paul Klein of NBC, "taking his cue from the then current ad campaign for the movie *Rosemary's Baby* . . . sent Dann a note saying, simply, 'Pray for Mike Dann's baby.'"

Dann scheduled *Get Smart* for 7:30

Get Smart wins two of its many Emmies, June 1969. Left to right, Irene Ryan (of *The Beverly Hillbillies*, presenting), Don Adams for best actor in a comedy series, Hope Lange (*The Ghost and Mrs. Muir*) for best actress in a comedy series, Sebastian Cabot (of *Family Affair*, presenting), and Burt Nodella, *Get Smart* producer, for outstanding comedy series. *Courtesy of AP/Wide World Photos.*

Friday nights. The babies achieved what they'd come to do, pulling a large audience for the two episodes ("And Baby Makes Four") in which they were born, while their season was marked by the biggest graphic shake-up ever in *Get Smart*'s opening titles: A combination of action clips from previous episodes and a voice announcing what the evening's segment would hold in store . . . Overhead shots zooming in on landmarks of Washington, D.C. . . . Max pulling up to CONTROL Washington headquarters in a classy gold car . . . And the door sequence, unaltered except for the players' names occupying *two* lines instead of one, filling up the screen, no longer receding but jumping out at the audience.

But by the end of the Sixties, a number of brilliantly daring satirical movies had so completely plundered establishment institutions that little more remained to be pilloried. *Our Man in Havana* (1960) and *That Man from Rio* (1964), *Dr. Strangelove: or How I Learned to Stop Worrying and Love the Bomb* (1964) and *The President's Analyst* (1967), *Catch-22* (1970) and *M*A*S*H* (1970) were tough acts to follow. The established movie spies—from James Bond to Matt Helm—didn't try. Instead they embraced high-tech fantasy and sexual silliness. Even the first Bond didn't like what they had become. Sean Connery took exception to "all the hardware, the people falling through the Eiffel Tower or something, and then getting up and walking away." Maxwell Smart would have been at home in any of them.

Get Smart, in its fifth season, had a big look and strong material, but a spy (or a therapist) will tell you that no one assignment is supposed to last forever. Identify your objective. Do what you have to do. Know when you've done it, and leave. You can assume just so many disguises, kidnap just so many enemy agents, be kidnapped just so many times yourself, before you start to hanker for a different merry-go-round. *Get Smart* said what it had to say, having won seven Emmies, including three by Don Adams, and having outlasted most of the spy series it spoofed. Maxwell Smart's shoe phone stopped ringing. The Chief's migranes went away. Besides, the end had been foretold in the 1967–1968 season episode, "The Little Black Book," Part II, which gave the Chief three years until retirement.

In the year that *Get Smart* left the air—1970—*Lancelot Link, Secret Chimp* sprang up on Saturday morning TV. As described by its co-creator Mike Marmer, "Stan Burns and I did a chimpanzee version of *Get Smart*. The show cost a fortune for costumes and training, but we had these chimps as good guys and bad guys, doing alternating dialogue, and of course they seem to be talking. Bernie Kopell did several of the voices. One was the Baron, patterned after Conrad Veidt. The Baron wore a wing collar, spats, a fur-collared coat, a homburg, and a monocle. Great chimp. He never lost the monocle during the entire shooting.

"We'd have thirty chimps in a master shot, tobogganing and skiing down snow-covered hills. Kids took it for granted that chimps could do this, but

Lancelot Link, Secret Chimp. Courtesy of Mike Marmer.

adults would get together on Saturday mornings to watch the show." In fact, to marvel at the show—the Seventies' equivalent of Dada as applied to the world of espionage.

Meanwhile Don Adams, who had earned a fortune as Maxwell Smart, signed a contract with NBC and Universal to star in one property and produce another. He read and rejected 300 pilots, then drafted three himself. The first teamed him with Don Rickles, but Rickles, committed to CBS, couldn't do it. The second involved a World War II Marine who, after some three decades wounded and lost in New Guinea, has to reenter civilization. The third concerned a tough cop who has to adjust to laws apparently favoring the rights of the criminals over those of the victims.

Universal saw Adams's third approach as the leaping-off point for a detective series with Godfrey Cambridge. Adams agreed, but found in working with Cambridge that "the chemistry wasn't right." Cambridge departed before the show ever aired. Adams told *TV Guide*, "Now he's mad at me. I tried to call and explain, but his manager says he won't take my phone calls." Cambridge responded to *TV Guide* that he thought it best to get out while he still had his original stomach lining.

To replace Cambridge as Adams's co-star, Universal brought in another black actor, Oscar nominee (for *The Reivers*) Rupert Crosse. Adams hoped that this new comedy offering would investigate racial issues between a black cop and a white one working together. NBC and Universal argued otherwise.

NBC launched *The Partners* in September 1971, scheduling it for eight on Saturday nights. Fred Silverman, over at CBS, heard that it tested extremely well and countered by moving one of his stronger shows into the same time slot. *All in the Family*, a mid-season entry that had steadily gathered steam since its January 1971 debut, clobbered *The Partners*. In the week that *All in the Family* recaptured its number one Nielsen rating, *The Partners* secured position fifty-four. Adams may have been right. Perhaps it was the wrong time to back down on social issues.

The Partners folded in September 1972, leaving behind, while not enough episodes to add up to a rerun package, a TV movie called *Confessions of a Top Crimebuster,* derived from the series . . . and memories of Robert Karvelas as Freddie, who constantly bothered the partners by confessing to crimes he didn't commit.

TV Guide proclaimed Adams "a rich man" in 1971, with oil wells, airplanes, and real estate under his belt. He enjoyed new success as a director of commercials, earning further piles of money, along with TV advertising's prestigious Clio Award. No longer obliged to work, he continued to appear on TV occasionally for instance poking his head through a cubbyhole to say "Would you believe . . .?" on *Rowan & Martin's Laugh-In,* or joining a 1971 panel of experts (Albert Brooks, Mel Brooks, Tony Randall, Phil Silvers, and others, hosted by Carl Reiner) to discuss contemporary social attitudes ranging from love to money. His 1974–1975 *Don Adams' Screen Test* restaged famous movie moments, pairing guest stars such as Bob Newhart and Mel Brooks with hopeful future actors and actresses selected from the audience. Adams directed and sometimes performed, frequently for laughs. When Brooks appeared on the show, Adams thanked him on the air for *Get Smart* and the way it launched his career. Brooks answered, "Sorry about that."

Adams and Bill Dana, who with D. William Silverstein formed the adver-tising agency of Adams, Dana Silverstein, Inc., in 1966, had several years of success doing commercials before very profitably selling the company—while their most famous joint creation, "Would you believe . . .?" consistently scored in commercials for other advertisers.

Bill Dana remembers "getting sick every time I saw a billboard using—and even to this day using—'Would you believe?' Once I was on Johnny Carson's show, and we were talking about Don, and I looked into the camera and said, 'Now listen, everyone out there in advertising, marketing, promotion, if you have used that formula, it comes from a copyrighted piece of material, so you must send $25 in stamps and coins,' and I gave our address at the Playboy Building in Los Angeles. I got thousands of pieces of mail, almost all of them 'Would you believe a nickel?' 'Would you believe a dime?' 'Would you believe a penny?' But somebody sent me an envelope filled with ashes, and a little note in it, reading 'Would you believe the check got burned in the mail?' "

During *Get Smart's* run, Don Adams and Don Rickles appeared together on two NBC specials. In 1967, they joined Bob Hope, Johnny Carson, Bill Dana, and others for a spy spoof, "Murder at NBC." In 1969, they sent up California, campus unrest, and memorable moments of old movies for *Kraft Music Hall.*

Adams also, in the wake of *Get Smart,* headlined Las Vegas with a $40,000-a-week act, provided the voice of cartoondom's Inspector Gadget, guested on *The Love Boat, The Fall Guy, Fantasy Island,*

Foul-ups, Bleeps, and Blunders, and *Life-styles of the Rich and Famous* (ironically reenacting the title of a *Get Smart* episode, "Aboard the Orient Express").

Barbara Feldon, rated "one of the few women who have scored big in television" by critic Kay Gardella in 1974, went on to co-host and scout talent for *Dean Martin's Comedy World* (summer 1974), and to host the news and issues programs *Special Edition* and *The 80's Woman*. In addition, she appeared in made-for-TV movies *(Smile, Before and After, Let's Switch!, Guide for the Married Woman)*, and feature films *(Fitzwilly, No Deposit, No Return)*, on the live stage *(Uncle Vanya, A Midsummer Night's*

Barbara Feldon on *The 80's Woman*, with guest Colleen Dewhurst. *Courtesy LIFE-TIME Cabletelevision.*

Dream, Camus's—not Vidal's—*Caligula*), and in a one-person presentation for the college circuit, based on the writings of women authors.

Active in the field of voice overs—having done TV and radio spots for AT&T, Panasonic, Maybelline, Dole Fruit and Cream Bars, and the New York City Opera—she served on the Women's Voice Over Committee. Feldon takes particular pride in the committee's latest achievement: the completion of a major study which substantially disproves the theory that men's voices *ipso facto* outsell women's voices in commercials.

A staunch supporter of the ERA, Barbara Feldon served on the board of the National Women's Political Caucus. An avid reader who enjoys the exchange of ideas more than she ever liked any TV camera, she maintains a "vision of myself when I'm in my eighties, wearing sensible shoes and inviting people in for tea."

Ed Platt, who performed occasionally after *Get Smart's* final year, died at age fifty-eight. He was found dead in his Santa Monica apartment in 1974, apparently the victim of a heart attack.

Bernie Kopell, who has appeared in all of Leonard Stern's series, went on to a lengthy tenure as Dr. Adam Bricker on *The Love Boat;* King Moody assumed the post, unrecognizable as himself, as the clown prince of fast foods, Ronald McDonald. Dick Gautier has done motion pictures, and wrote, produced, and starred in *God Bless You, Uncle Sam*. He appears frequently on stage and in

Ogilvy
&
Mather

2 East 48th Street, New York 10017

Client: **AMERICAN EXPRESS**
Product: **CARD**
Title: **"BARBARA FELDON"** (:10C)
Commercial No.: **XAPM 7011**

BARBARA FELDON: To get to Hollywood, all you need is talent, brains, charm and beauty.

But to shop here you need something more.

The American Express Card.

Don't leave home without it.

Barbara Feldon does an ad for American Express. *Courtesy of American Express.*

Dick Gautier (self-portrait, right) has written a book on caricature. Shown here: *The Art of Caricature,* **published in 1985 by Perigee, a division of the Putnam Publishing Group.**

movies of the week, has guested in TV series from *The Mary Tyler Moore Show* to *Columbo,* and has to his credit one book on cartooning and one on caricature. Dave Ketchum, who in *Get Smart* replaced Victor French as the agent who hid in uncomfortable places, has become a successful writer for a long list of shows—among them *Highway to Heaven,* on which French co-stars.

A huge roster of writers, directors, and producers associated with *Get Smart* went on to further glory, from directors

Gary Nelson (miniseries such as *Noble House*), Paul Bogart (for years, the director of *All in the Family*) and Richard Donner *(The Omen, Superman: The Movie),* writer Alan Burns (creator/producer, *The Mary Tyler Moore Show*), associate producer David Davis (co-creator and executive producer, *Taxi*), to Reza Badiyi, who moved from a credit for title visualization to directing shows ranging from *Police Squad!* and *Sledge Hammer!* to *Falcon Crest* and *Cagney & Lacey.*

One member of the original *Get Smart*

team, Mel Brooks, had, like Don Adams, discovered a knack for commercials. For his directorial debut, he promoted the Bic Banana with a venture considered to be one of the first funny TV ads. Like Adams too, Brooks turned up on a TV panel discussion, this one hosted in 1970 by David Susskind. The subject: Jewish mothers. His conclusions, among others: that David Susskind didn't grow a large nose until he entered showbusiness, and that David Steinberg embodied "the Winesberg, Ohio, of Jews."

Brooks and wife Anne Bancroft had a son in 1972, and named him Max (Maximilian, however. Not Maxwell). For television—ABC finally took a chance on satire—he created the Robin Hood take-off *When Things Were Rotten* (1975–75), with *Get Smart* alumni Dick Gautier as Robin Hood and Bernie Kopell as Alan-a-Dale. Notes Gautier, "Bernie and I have had the honor of being in all of Mel Brooks's television projects—two." For the wide screen, Brooks made/directed/wrote/co-wrote/ and/or/appeared in movies: *The Producers* (1968), *The Twelve Chairs* (1970), *Blazing Saddles* (1974), *Young Frankenstein* (1975), *Silent Movie* (1976), *High Anxiety* (1977), *History of the World, Part I* (1981), *To Be or Not To Be* (1983), and *Spaceballs* (1987). These qualified him, by the close of 1976, as the country's fifth largest box-office attraction—right behind Robert Redford, Jack Nicholson, Dustin Hoffman, and Clint Eastwood. He'd call Burt Reynolds, greeting him with, "Hello, Six. This is Five speaking."

His trademark remains the outrageously irreverent lambasting of whatever begs for it most, whether Hitler in *The Producers* and *To Be or Not To Be*, the Spanish Inquisition in *History of the World, Part I* (nuns doing a Busby Berkeley-type water ballet, emerging from the pool with their heads lit up in a giant menorah, and Torquemada playing Jewish heads like bars of a xylophone), or the *Star Wars* genre with *Spaceballs*. Yet in the early Eighties, he began Brooksfilms, the production company responsible for *The Elephant Man, Frances, My Favorite Year, The Fly*, and *84 Charing Cross Road*. "I'm very proud of all those films," he told *USA Today* in 1987, "but I don't like to get too close, because I think it only confuses the public and the critics. If they see my name in big letters up there next to *The Elephant Man*, they automatically assume it's some kind of wacky comedy."

After *The Troublemaker, Get Smart*, and *The Graduate*, Buck Henry wrote/ co-wrote/directed/and/or/appeared in the movies *The Secret War of Harry Frigg* (1968), *Candy** (1968), *Catch-22* (1970), *The Owl and the Pussycat* (1970), *Taking Off* (1971), *Is There Sex After Death?* (1971), *What's Up, Doc?* (1972), *The Day of the Dolphin* (1973), *The Man Who Fell to Earth* (1976), *Heaven Can Wait* (1978), *Old Boyfriends* (1979), and *The First Family* (1980), to name a few.

---

*For which actor-turned-governor Ronald Reagan was offered either of two roles—a crazed meat inspector, or half of a Siamese twin. Reagan, inexplicably, refused both.

A political satire starring Bob Newhart, Gilda Radner, and Madeline Kahn,
The First Family was written and directed
by Henry, with Dan Melnick as executive producer. Said Melnick at the
time, "Years and years ago, when we
were working on *Get Smart,* I was saying to Buck, 'Hey, wouldn't you want to
direct a movie some day?' And I remember him saying, 'Well, I guess every
red-blooded American boy has to direct
a movie sooner or later.' The first thing I
did when I came to Columbia as an executive was to make an arrangement for
Buck to write and direct three pictures
for the company."

In terms of production problems, *The
First Family* followed in the footsteps of
Get Smart—with torrential California
rainstorms crashing mudslides into,
under, around, and through, any number of the sets.

On television, Buck Henry distinguished himself as a frequent guest
host and recurrent character Uncle Roy
on NBC's *Saturday Night Live.* Uncle
Roy, devoted baby-sitter, gives selflessly
of his time in exchange for the privilege
of photographing little girls in their underwear and jammies. A more recent TV
role completes the circle of his manic
mission begun by *Get Smart:* On *Falcon
Crest,* Angela hired him to drive Melissa
bonkers.

To restaurants around the world,
Henry may be best known for his rubber
chicken. Some years ago, while dining
with George Segal, he happened to mention that he didn't love the food. When
next Segal invited him to dinner, a rubber

**Buck Henry (left) with Chevy Chase
(right) on NBC's *Saturday Night Live.*
*Courtesy of Howard Frank Archives/Person-
ality Photos, Inc.***

chicken covered the plate. Subsequently,
wherever he might be eating, with Segal
or without, he can never quite be sure
that another chicken won't be served. So
far, Segal has zapped him repeatedly in
cities throughout the world. Comments
Henry, "This absurd prank amuses him,
so I pretend not to notice. Also, I find as
the years go by I seem to have an increas-
ing appetite for rubber chicken."

Of the three partners of Talent Associates, David Susskind died in 1986, still
starring in his weekly syndicated *David
Susskind Show* (which evolved from
Open End in 1967). Dan Melnick became production chief of MGM pictures
in 1972, head of worldwide productions
for Columbia Pictures in 1977, and an

independent producer in 1979. He has produced, among other films, *Straw Dogs* (1971), *All That Jazz* (1979), *Altered States* (1980), and *Roxanne* (1987).

Leonard Stern, nominated for writing and producing awards five times by the National Academy of Television Arts and Sciences, five times for writing awards in five separate seasons by the Writers Guild of America (and five separate nominations in one of those seasons), has twice been awarded the Emmy (for *The Phil Silvers Show: You'll Never Get Rich* and *Get Smart.*). Having created, written, produced, and/or directed the sitcoms *I'm Dickens, He's Fenster, He & She,** *Run Buddy Run, Holmes and Yoyo, Diana, The Hero,* and *The Governor & J.J.* in the Sixties and early Seventies, Stern turned to writing, directing, and producing the more dramatic *McMillan and Wife, The Snoop Sisters,* and *Lanigan's Rabbi* in the mid and late Seventies. He wrote and directed his first feature film, *Just You And Me, Kid,* starring George Burns and Brooke Shields, in 1978.

While *Get Smart* was still on the air, Leonard Stern wrote a script for a feature-length film version which became, instead, the three-part "A Man Called Smart" within the regular series. In 1987, he won the unprecedented honor of two simultaneous awards from the Caucus for Producers, Writers, and Directors:

the Distinguished Service Award and the Prestigious Member of the Year Award, representing his lifetime body of work.

In 1979, Universal Pictures announced *The Return of Maxwell Smart,* budgeted at $8,000,000 and based on a script by Arne Sultan, Bill Dana, and Leonard Stern. Initially, Universal planned to release the film theatrically abroad, but to run it as a two-hour TV movie in the U.S. When word got out, overwhelming public response clearly demanded a full-length full-blown flick. Universal, in turn, demanded more of a "movie look" along with other changes, which ultimately diminished the input of the original *Smart* people.

Universal released it as *The Nude Bomb* with only Don Adams and Bob Karvelas re-creating their TV roles. Dana Elcar, the KAOS doctor from "And Baby Makes Four," appeared as the Chief; Bill

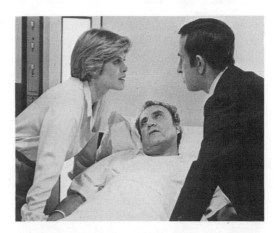

Andrea Howard, Bill Dana, and Don Adams in *The Nude Bomb* (1980). *Courtesy of Universal City Studios, Inc.*

---

*When it won the Outstanding Writing Achievement in Comedy Emmy for Alan Burns and Chris Hayward (May 19, 1968), Mike Dann pronounced it "the best show I ever cancelled."

Agent 86 encounters Bruce the shark on the Universal lot in *The Nude Bomb*. Agent 86 has left, but Bruce can still be seen by tourists taking the Universal Studios Tour. *Courtesy of Universal Studios, Inc.*

Dana, CIA agent Quigley of "Ice Station Siegfried," played Jonathan Levinson Seigle; Joey Forman, Harry Hoo, and a CONTROL lawyer from the TV cast, played David Ketchum's role, Agent 13; Max had a new love interest, and no Agent 99. *The Nude Bomb* generated a profit at the box office—fans really wanted to see Maxwell Smart return— until the reviews suggested that onto

many of the right ingredients, *Bomb* tacked too many of the wrong ones. For example, a lengthy climactic chase scene through the Universal Pictures backlot, obviously designed to highlight the appeal of open-to-the-public tours of the Universal Pictures backlot, earned Vincent Canby's observation in *The New York Times* that the scene "goes on much longer than a commercial should." In the end, *The Nude Bomb*'s long lines at the box office were deemed to be a tribute to what was, not to what it was.

The fans, however, are undeterred by their not having liked *The Nude Bomb* better. In fact, when it rolls around on the TV schedule as, not too amazingly, "*The Return of Maxwell Smart* (original title, *The Nude Bomb*)," they watch and laugh. When the movie made its TV debut, it won its time slot. Good ol' Max. Good ol' Larabee. Good ol' CONTROL—well, not CONTROL. In the movie, it's PITS (Provisional Intelligence Tactical Service), but you learn to overlook things when you reunite with a friend.

Since his brief brush with PITS, Adams has appeared in the 1987 movie *Back to the Beach*—a Frankie Avalon/Annette Funicello reunion of which Roger Ebert has written, "Paramount Pictures refused to hold preview screenings . . . apparently because they feared critics would hate it. The critics loved it, too late to save it at the box office." For the past several years, Adams has starred in the made-in-Canada syndicated sitcom *Check It Out*, but he never entirely abandoned his ties to CONTROL. Using his Agent 86 voice, he treats fans to multiple Max-like moments in TV commercials for advertisers ranging from Chief Auto Parts to the Alabama Transit System, from electronics to beer.

In a spot for Coors Light Beer, Adams tries to relax with a drink at the Silver Bullet Bar. A beautiful blonde sits next to

him, utterly fascinated, but an irritating loudmouth (Ronnie Schell) keeps pestering him with Maxwell Smart impressions. Adams can't even silence the guy with a lapful of brew and an impression of his own, "Missed it by that much . . ."

Bob Fox, Coors Light brand director, describes the thinking behind the commercial: "The Silver Bullet Bar became the main focal point of our Coors Light commercials in 1985. Since this time, our Coors Light commercials have consisted

Don Adams with the cast of *Check It Out*. *Courtesy of CTV Television Network, Ltd.*

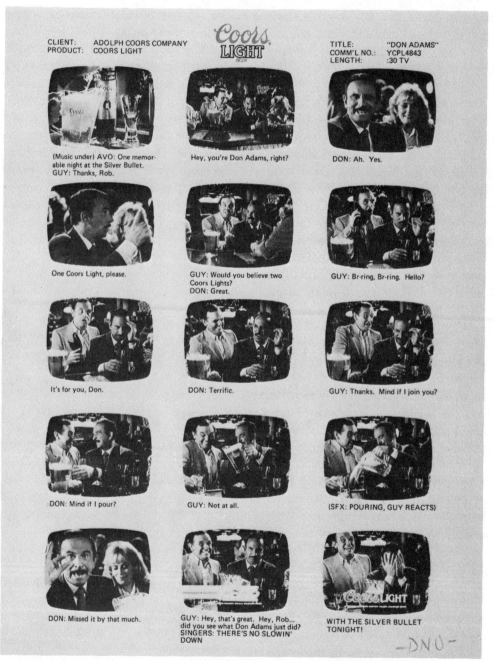

Don Adams in the Silver Bullet—commercial for Coors Light Beer. *Courtesy of the Adolph Coors Company.*

of various real-life situations that may occur in any bar across the United States. We thought it was time for a well-known celebrity to make an appearance in the bar and create a situation on how the customers would react.

"We selected Don Adams to be featured in this commercial because of the natural situation it created about the numerous impressions Mr. Adams receives of the popular and colorful character he portrayed for many years, Maxwell Smart.

"Because of the popularity of *Get Smart*, Don Adams will always be remembered by many as Maxwell Smart, and the many amateur impressionists that approach him to present their version of the character is probably the highest compliment he could be paid. He created a memorable character that will always be near and dear to everyone that has had an opportunity to enjoy *Get Smart*.

"We hope the people viewing our Coors Light commercials will also enjoy and remember this bit of nostalgia."

Indeed today, even with the media growing fuzzy in their details of the legend of Maxwell Smart (*People* magazine, in 1987, mentioned the "shoe phone that never worked." Did too. The phone company should "never work" as reliably), and even with syndicated episodes cut to eliminate jokes and whole scenes (and cameos, and story points), the legion of fans, if organized, could form a sizable cult. Maybe two cults—since a whole subgenre passes out the nickname of "Hymie" to people who look like

Dick Gautier, and stolidly acknowledges Hymie as the original Robocop and the original six-million-dollar bionic man.

According to a 1985 *People* magazine poll, the Best Secret Agent is Maxwell Smart. James Phelps *(Mission: Impossible)*, Napoleon Solo *(The Man from U.N.C.L.E.)*, and Emma Peel *(The Avengers)* trail behind. *Get Smart* continues to rerun, having played on some stations as often as five times a day. When programmers take it off the air, viewers complain in droves, bringing it back. Other TV satires have come along, but not lasted: *Quark*, a space-spoof (1978–78); *Police Squad!*, a cop-riff (1982–82). To date, only *Sledge Hammer!* (1986–   ) could conceivably be a contender in the field of long-running parodies. (*Sledge Hammer!*, created, produced, and sometimes written by Alan Spencer—who is coincidentally a *Get Smart* fan—commemorated its affection for the forces of CONTROL by denoting hotel room doors as 86 and 99 in its first episode.) The national taste for tongue-in-cheek spy yarns may have revitalized itself in recent memory—with Parker Stevenson's *Rockhopper* (1985—Rockhopper being the code name of an agent Larabee), George Hamilton's *Spies* (1987), and Disney's *Double Agent* (1987). Like the Marx Brothers, the Three Stooges, and the Honeymooners, who had to be thought old-hat for a while before being embraced as giants of classic comedy, Max and 99 are due for their resurgence. Like *The Honeymooners*, *Get Smart* even has its share of "lost episodes"—the episodes from the CBS season that only infrequently appear with the rest of the rerun package.

Don Adams once had mixed feelings about *Get Smart:* "I watched I think two shows after it came out, then I never watched it again in all the years we were on. When I watched the first couple of shows, I hated the laugh track. It bothered and annoyed me. I felt like throwing the TV through a window. I hated some of the things I was doing. Then, ten years later, I'd look at the reruns, finally able to look at it objectively, and I found myself laughing out loud."

If even Don Adams has come around, a mood strongly favoring revival is surely afoot. But what's a foot without a shoe phone? And why bother to have spies at all if at least one of them can't be Maxwell Smart?

A new made-for-TV *Get Smart* Movie was planned for Fall 1988 release. Unfortunately, the industry-wide writers' strike began a few weeks before completion of the script. As this book goes to press, and the strike remains unsettled, it's a safe guess that the movie will air sometime later than first planned.

10

||||||||||||||||||||||||||||||||||||||||||||||||||||||||||||||||||||||||||||||||||||||||||||||||||||||||||||||||||||||||||||||

MAXWELLGATE

Jeremiah McAward, a secret agent for the CIA during the Fifties and Sixties, now heads the largest private investigative firm in the United States. His staff consists largely of former federal agents. His black Labrador retriever, named Agent 99, wanders in and out of the offices on something resembling patrol.

The author recently asked McAward how closely *Get Smart* mirrored spying of its day and of our day. The cone of silence descended, and the former agent replied as follows—

SMART'S BOOBY-TRAPPED APARTMENT

McCrohan: What about Smart's booby-trapped apartment?

McAward: Agents had a choice. They could live in their own places, which were not part of their occupation or their station, or they could live in a place that was owned by the agency and maintained by the agency, the agency having been the CIA, or any of the other organizations that conduct clandestine investigations for the United States: the IRS, the National Security Agency, the DEA (Drug Enforcement Agency), or the DIA (the Defense Intelligence Agency), which is as shadowy as the National Security Agency. If you lived in one of their places, it was likely to be rigged up with hidden weapons. You would know that right under the coffee machine there was a fully loaded automatic, or hanging underneath the table there was a very sharp knife with poison on the edge. These would be things the man would reach for if he found himself entertaining a contact or source of information who turned out to be in a killing mode.

McCrohan: In Smart's apartment, they were triggered automatically. For instance, open the desk drawer and a decorative wallpiece brains you.

McAward: It was much safer if you were on station in a particular place, like Santo Domingo or Berlin or whatnot, where you would have your own digs; and you would probably not wire them up with very much except some method to tell if anyone had been there during your absence. If you wanted weapons around, you'd hide them in various places.

But you'd only rig a place if you weren't planning to use it for long, and you wanted it to harm someone who attempted to enter. You could use a few manufactured deadfalls, things like a mat that exploded when he stepped on it, or that would cause a weapon to fire out of a cabinet as he walked in the door. In extreme cases, maybe the floor would open.

There were other methods to determine whether the door had ever been opened; there were hidden TV cameras, real tiny TV cameras; and lenses no larger than a pinhead which could be imbedded in the wall and you wouldn't see it as more than a bubble on the paint.

McCrohan: Smart's fireplace, properly activated, could suck things out of the room.

McAward: The fireplace in the East German Embassy in a nameless European capital was used more than once by the Americans to gain access to the embassy. It was large enough not to suck you up, but to allow you to drop down, aided by a cohort on the roof.

We regularly used the fireplace as a means of gaining entrance. The difficulty was, if they had used the fireplace, one tended to track cinders throughout the building, so you had to vacuum your way out. In other words, the fireplace didn't suck us up, but we had to suck up our tracks before we left.

CONTROL'S HIGHLY ADVANCED TECHNOLOGY

McCrohan: With the exception of devices like the shoe phone, Smart seemed not to reuse weapons.

McAward: Neither did we. For instance, most of the recording devices were throw-away devices. Not that they were any less expensive or any less durable, but if you were bugging the opposition's apartment, you never went back to get the devices. If they were found, you only had to reply, "Hey, wasn't me."

McCrohan: What about recording and listening devices?

McAward: They had one tiny little pill they developed in the Fifties, about the size of a lentil, and it could be ingested with your soup and you wouldn't even know it. It used the heat of the body to generate enough electricity to broadcast a tone, and until you passed it, it would enable you to be tracked.

An olive would not be a good radio,

though, and a toothpick would be a poor antenna, because if the thing were immersed in a martini, you would have a problem. Maybe in the whole dish of olives, in the middle of the plate could have been one that was inedible.

Apart from cocktail parties, they had tiny transmitters that could be worn on your lapel or as a shirt button, quite powerful enough to be broadcast to a repeater which would then enhance the signal and send it a considerable distance.

Today they've gone even further. During the *Get Smart* TV series, they didn't have the satellites they have now, and they can also track via satellite. It's incredible what they can do.

McCrohan: Would this have been available to the public then?

McAward: Not then. Things like these are available to the public now, like the doppler effect microphone, which you can train on a far-off window and convert its vibrations into the sounds made by the people inside, or what they call the big ear, a surveillance dish that goes for $19.95. You just point it, for instance if your neighbor's having a barbecue, you point it and hear the gossip about you. And it's not illegal. All you're really doing is amplifying the sounds that are coming your way. It's entirely different from planting a bug.

McCrohan: That's for picking up sound. What about sending pictures?

McAward: Cameras in shirt buttons are pretty difficult to do, but they did have some really neat pen cameras that were in fact TV cameras. The receiver of course, particularly then, would have had to be a certain size to accommodate the necessary electronics, but the cameras, on the other hand, could be made the size of a ballpoint pen, with everything in it to broadcast to a receiver. The pen could be left in a pen holder, although there would have been devices to detect the transmissions.

McCrohan: In James Bond and *Get Smart*, the agent goes to the lab to select, and be given, appropriate devices and equipment. What would procedure actually have been?

McAward: Real life would be, "Here's the problem, go take a look at it." Or, the person who was there before you would say, "Here's what we need to do. We need that room bugged, and we need to make certain that whenever the guy starts his car, we know about it, and whenever he starts his car when we don't want him to drive it, we can make sure he can't drive it." So you would establish what had to be done, and it might require forty-five different people—tradesmen, technicians, mechanics—to do what you wanted to do, and you couldn't mount it overnight. You might have to mount a huge operation in order to wire one automobile. The FBI in this country is particularly good at wiring— phone booths nearby underworld social clubs, barstools, eyeglasses. Anything that you leave in your office.

They don't often bug clocks because clocks go tick-tick-tick. Even quartz watches make a very audible hum. It's astonishing what they can do.

McCrohan: What about a mechanical fly as a listening device? Smart mistook one for a real fly and destroyed it.

McAward: That wasn't real but we sure thought about it enough. Wouldn't it be wonderful to have a mechanical bird or mechanical fly that would just be there? People don't really swat flies when they're engaged in an animated conversation. I'm sure we worked on it. We worked on some nifty things.

McCrohan: Inflatable people? Smart used one when he stationed himself on Lovers' Lane, in order not to arouse suspicion.

McAward: We'd use inflatable people in automobiles. Inflatable people you could blow up—no pun intended—if someone left the car and you wanted people to think no one had left the car. They looked very convincing. Might not stand extremely close scrutiny, but they were actually look-alikes of the people they represented.

McCrohan: Have you ever seen a shoe phone?

McAward: Until recently, only when I watched *Get Smart*. Now you can buy them for personal use. Some company manufactures them.

HIDING AGENTS IN LOCKERS

McCrohan: Agent 13 did surveillance from post boxes and lockers.

McAward: Someone must not have liked him very much. We didn't hide like that, though you might have hidden in the trunk of a car while sucking air out of a spare tire. That's one of the best methods of surveillance. You don't leave anything in the car that they can find or which would fall off, or which would be unusable if they drove through water. Once you got the car trunk opened, you could put an agent in it with a radio. Then you might want to jam the lock so they don't open the trunk, find you there, and shoot you.

You would then be followed by another car, and you could hear what was going on inside, and report it verbally, along with which direction they were going, which you determined essentially from whether your head banged into the right or left side of the trunk.

People are pretty careless when they're being followed. Even people in espionage, if they think they're home free, they make so many left turns, go down so many dark alleys, never realizing that maybe someone is attached to the underside of the car or there's someone in the car.

Another fairly primitive method, but an effective one for following a car, would be to put a little piece of blue tape over one part of the tail light, maybe an inch in size. If you put it on the tail light, you can spot that car a mile away at night, because red and this violet really travel. The blue and violet travel a lot farther than the red. You know which car it is, even if it's pitch black and there are ninety-five cars in front of you on the expressway. It's on the rear of the car, so the driver doesn't see it, and no one else pays any attention to it.

THE CONE OF SILENCE

McCrohan: CONTROL had this cone of silence intended to protect the privacy of top-secret conversations, but it either caused people to shout at each other to be heard, or smashed through the furniture.

McAward: The real one worked fine.

But it's not a cone. It's a room that's built inside a room, and it's usually lucite with copper mesh imbedded in the lucite to prevent leakage of any electronics used within it, if you were playing a tape recorder, and it prevents microwaves entering to pick up anything. It's on special shock absorbers so that if doppler effect microphones are trained on the surface, they won't work. This lucite room could be lowered over the parties speaking.

They called it a safe room or a sound room and it was used for people who wanted to whisper. The other way to really do it was to go into a swimming pool with someone, up to your neck, and whisper.

McCrohan: Is this a new development?

McAward: They were in existence in the Fifties.

EVERYTHING WAS A KAOS FRONT

McCrohan: Smart couldn't go to a radio station, bookstore, or Chinese laundry without its being a KAOS front. What were some real fronts?

McAward: I know of two agents who set up a bar in the Kenyan jungle, called the Afro Negro Club back when a club could have been called the Afro Negro Club, which would have put it back in the Fifties and early Sixties. It was supplied with liquor that was allegedly hijacked from the U.S. Ambassador's monthly shipment. The Ambassador knew about it, of course, but what they wanted to do was to have a place where these emerging Africans could meet and be eavesdropped upon. Then our agents could know who was going to be the emerging guy, which might conceivably have given us a handle on whom to back. It went on for about five years. These guys would sneak off into the jungle and do their plotting, and we knew everything they said.

ALEXI SEBASTIAN, MASTER OF DISGUISE

McCrohan: Someone like Alexi Sebastian could make himself up to look like anyone alive, from Johnny Carson to Maxwell Smart's Aunt Rose.

McAward: When Jimmy Carter dismantled the CIA, there were a lot of really good disguise experts out there, people who could wear disguise well, people who could create disguise well. And a friend of mine who was in the agency years ago, now retired and living in another country, and I decided we would go into protecting CEOs of large corporations. Here you are, a well-known individual, and you want to go trout fishing in Wisconsin, but you don't want to be recognized, you don't want anyone to see you. Suppose we supplied someone to take your place while you change your appearance very slightly and go fishing?

This replacement would be able to perform all your duties for a week or two weeks or whatever while you get a little R and R.

McCrohan: And look somewhat like you?

McAward: And look exactly like you. Maybe your spouse wouldn't be fooled, but everyone in the office would be fooled.

McCrohan: Are masks that good?

McCrohan: Masks are excellent. Now they have some excellent paraphernalia. But we'd have found a person who had the bone structure and maybe had the same hair characteristics, and start with that. We had a stable of people, some of the finest disguise artists in the world. We got a number of people lined up for this but it never really went anywhere. We found out that the average American CEO wasn't paranoid enough, though we had a couple of Germans who expressed interest.

THE CIA LOVES A GOOD LAUGH TOO

McCrohan: Do you remember any Agency reactions to *Get Smart?*

McAward: I happened to mention to a friend that I would be giving this interview. He had been in the Agency, highly placed, in the Sixties. His reaction was to tell me that *Get Smart* really had the Agency worried, because the show was getting too close to reality. They were particularly worried about the Cone of Silence, because we pretty much had one, which was supposed to be a secret. He said he remembers several discussions among members of his echelon, as to whether they should go to the producers of *Get Smart* with a list of things to stay away from. They never did, which is just as well. The list might have turned up spoofed as an episode of *Get Smart.*

11

UP TO THE SAME OLD TRICKS

"I've never met any secret agents, but I've read articles that James Bond and *Get Smart* started a few ideas that were picked up by government agencies."

—Don Adams

One way to gauge the success of any topical satire is to look back twenty years later and see how accurately it presaged the future. In the late Sixties, both Dan Melnick and Don Adams spent years exploring the possibility of developing and merchandising commercial shoe phones. But microtechnology had not reached its present advanced state, and a Sixties shoe phone would have required a prohibitively expensive, staggeringly large shoe.

That was then. This is now. What *Get Smart* posited as a joke, we've done for real, and more so. Stan Burns said that

the writers liked their spoofs to contain "a little truth, an absurd comment on things." But more absurd than the spoofing was the reality they spoofed. Judging by the following items taken from recent newspapers, magazines, and mail order catalogues, *Get Smart* foreshadowed—from how irrational things already were—precisely how much stranger than fiction they were about to be.

LEAVE THE SPYING TO US

Percentage increase in the number of job applications received by the CIA in 1985: 50 percent.

Percentage increase, since 1984, in the number of job inquiries to the Peace Corps: 22 percent.

Number of times the CIA briefed its

congressional oversight committees in 1985: 500. (*The Harper Index Book,* 1987)

VEE DON'T SHUSSH HERE

A nattily dressed male mannequin stands in the display window of Lane Bryant's poshest New York City store. The mannequin is engaged in feeding correspondence into an office paper shredder.

AND . . . LOVING IT

"Watergate conspirators" Gordon Liddy and John Ehrlichman have become part-time television actors. Liddy has been seen on *Highwayman* and *Miami Vice*. Ehrlichman has done commercials for ice cream and has appeared on *Divorce Court* as a witness.

THE SECRET OF SAM VITTORIO

Federal agents told the *Chicago Tribune* that mob chiefs aren't initiating new members because they fear government spies will infiltrate their inner circle. Attrition is taking its toll. The FBI lists 42 mob leaders in Chicago—down from nearly 200 six years ago. (*USA Today*, July 6, 1987)

KRAZY KODES

"So I take it from what your testimony is, there never came a time when Colonel North said that Paul was sending Aran and the Bookkeeper to the Swimming Pool to get a price so that Orange could send some Dogs through Banana to Apple for some Zebras. Is that correct?" (John Saxon, associate counsel to the Senate's Iran-contra committee, questioning former Pentagon official Noel Koch on code names employed in the secret arms dealings, July 1987)

YOU CAN'T FIRE ME. I KNOW TOO MUCH

"I never said I had no idea about most of the things you said I said I had no idea about." (Assistant Secretary of State Elliott Abrams, to Texas Rep. Jack Brooks at the Iran-contra hearings, June 1987)

WHAT THE WELL-DRESSED SPY IS WEARING

" . . . the Command Cap appears to be nothing more than an ordinary baseball style cap. . . . A conventional hat offers little protection against a bludgeon or bullet; however, the Command Cap can substantially reduce the level of damage from a bullet or blow to your head." (Executive Protection Products, Inc. Catalogue, 1987)

WHAT? NO LAZER BLAZERS?

Price of a fully equipped "terrorist-proof" Mercedes 500 at Washington's Counter Spy Shop: $208,000. (*The Harper Index Book*, 1987)

WOW [manufacturing company] has announced a line of school accessories including Express-It, an answering machine for students' lockers. (*California Magazine*, July 1987)

Available through the mail: *Pictorial History of U.S. Sniping, How To Kill* volumes one and two, *Sneak It Through— Smuggling Made Easier*. (AMOK's *First Dispatch*, 1987)

Moms in France can get a musical warning when baby wets its diaper. (*The Globe*, June 9, 1987)

"The Revenger, a little black box, has become the season's trendiest adult toy . . . You reach for a switch on your dashboard, setting off the shriek of a grenade launcher, the rat-a-tat-tat of a machine gun or the detonating whir of a death ray." (*People*, 1987)

A Defense Department experiment to determine whether lie detectors can weed out spies is useless because there is no way to tell whether people who pass the test are lying, a government analyst said yesterday. (*New York Daily News*, February 19, 1987)

NEVER ANY NITRO-WHISPERIN WHEN YOU NEED IT

About 1,000 heavily-armed troops today surrounded a TV station [in Manila]

where 150 rebel soldiers were holed up. The troops played a medley of Paul Anka songs over loudspeakers to induce the rebels to surrender. (*Reuters*, May 1987)

THE OLD FAKE TREE IN THE FOREST TRICK

In 1980, Soviets revealed that they had discovered a plastic tree stump in a forest near one of their top-secret military installations. Although it was a product of state-of-the-art science, the stump was discovered by security men because it was designed to be an oak tree stump, and the forest where it had been hidden contained only pine trees. (*The Star*, October 22, 1985)

THE RETURN OF AGENT K-13

Seventeen-year-old Fang, a bull dog terrier who cannot retract his tongue, was among the entries in the Twenty-Fifth Annual International Ugly Dog Contest at the fairgrounds in August. Fang was trying to regain the title he lost last year to a Chinese creafted. That dog won because, besides being ugly, it exhibited no personality whatsoever. (*California Magazine*, September 1986)

IT ONLY LOOKS LIKE A PHONE BOOTH

Britain's red cast-iron telephone booths are disappearing from street corners under a modernization program, but have become hot items as greenhouses, shower stalls, and miniature bars. Dudley Moore has one in Beverly Hills, and more than 3,000 of the phone "boxes" have been sold for as much as $2,000 apiece. (*World Press Review*, July 1987)

is an incoming call or when the receiver is removed from the base." (Hammacher Schlemmer & Company Catalogue, 1987)

The Army has set up a toll-free hot line to report suspected espionage—1–800–CALL–SPY. (*Newsweek*, May 11, 1987)

BUT IT DOESN'T LOOK LIKE A PHONE

Remember Maxwell Smart's telephone shoe? Well . . . big deal. Now there's a Puma running shoe (style: RS; price: $200) that comes with a software package compatible with an Apple IIe, Commodore 64, or IBM PC. (*Esquire*, September 1986)

"The Quacking Duck Decoy Phone: Modeled after traditional duck decoys, this unique telephone alerts you with a series of quacks, rather than with a ring . . . the duck's eyes light up when there

REVENGE OF THE NERDS

In a 1987 *Newsweek* article called "Revenge of the Nerds," the FBI estimates that up to a third of Soviet and Eastern-bloc diplomats and representatives in the U.S. are spies working undercover in embassies, missions, and trade offices. A *New York Daily News* commentary about William Casey is entitled "How a Schlep Charmed the CIA." A July, 1987 *Mad Magazine* parody proves that the only way to spoof a successful satire is to repeat what it already said.

A BAD CASE OF THE RE-RUNS DEPT.
Try as you may, when it comes to great spies of the past, it's an impossible mission to…

FORGET SMART

ARTIST: ANGELO TORRES   WRITER: DICK DEBARTOLO

12

PAGES FROM THE CONTROL S.P.Y.* MANUAL

A.A.R.D.V.A.R.K.: Control's Automated Reciprocal Data Verifier and Reaction Computer ("Leadside").

A.A.A.M.M.: Anti-anti-anti-missile missile ("Ironhand").

Absorbo pills: Can dealcoholize liquor if held in the mouth while imbibing ("Double Agent").

ACB: The third spy network (get it?). "The thing that we feared for so long has finally come to pass." When the Chief, 86, and 99 are asked to join or die, Max considers trying it for 13 weeks. ("Die, Spy").

All Night Costume Company: Rents Max his chicken costume in "The Day Smart Turned Chicken."

April 3, 1963: Only the real Joe Froebus knows what happened in Cairo that night ("Someone Down Here Hates Me").

Archer, Melnick: "Put a Red in your bed" Melnick, suspected of selling bedroom sets to Iron Curtain countries, imprisons 99 in his furniture warehouse and substitutes an impostor for her in "And Only Two Ninety-Nine."

Birthmark, heart-shaped: What the real Grillak has on his right knee ("School Days").

Burlington Collection: Leadside steals the "entire Burlington Collection" from

*Specific Procedures and Yarmy.

the National Museum in "Leadside." When *Get Smart* aired in the late Sixties, bedsheets had only just turned to colors and designs. Burlington bed linens called attention to their product with a campaign built around "The Burlington Collection."

CA.44N: Combination of letters and digits on the license plate that opens the trunk of Max's car ("Weekend Vampire").

C.A.D.: KAOS's Contrived Accident Division. Its two experts are Donald Snead and Mrs. Emily Neal ("Run, Robot, Run").

C.O.S. Security Risk: Can only be discussed under the Cone of Silence ("A Tail of Two Tails").

Carioca, Antonio Carlos (a.k.a. The Blaster): Millionaire playboy who annually blows up an important American building ("The Only Way to Die").

Case 1173: Operation Starch (which see). Taken from the CIA and assigned to CONTROL ("Snoopy Smart vs. the Red Baron").

Channel 51: The educational spy channel ("Is This Trip Necessary?"). In the late Sixties, educational channels were just coming into their own, and constituted almost an "in" reference, the way a reference to cable would have been five or ten years ago.

Chez Charles: Skid row bar where Max turns into a wino to trick KAOS ("Double Agent").

Code 4 Alert: All airports, railroad stations, and bus terminals to be covered immediately ("The Return of the Ancient Mariner").

Code 19: Woman being pursued by unknown assailant ("The Girl from KAOS"). Also see Rule 6 on page 182.

Code Z: Cannot discuss the matter with anyone ("One Nation Invisible").

Control Procedure Number 3: Lie and give false information to get what you want ("Classification: Dead").

Curds and whey: Means KAOS agents in the CONTROL singing code (*cigarette* means impostor). ("The Hot Line.")

Danker, Karl: KAOS's #1 killer ("A Spy for a Spy").

Dietrich, Wolfgang: Highest-ranking agent ever to defect from KAOS ("Witness for the Execution").

Disguise HB61: Oriental houseboy ("Casablanca").

The Double Door: The book that triggers the secret entrance, though the safe, in Greer's office ("Greer Window"). Its combination: left to 32, right to 21, left to 0.

Emergency Identification Procedure

#6A: A board of inquiry ("The Spy Who Met Himself").

Emergency Telephone Plan: Speaking to each other from adjoining phone booths ("Our Man in Toyland").

Fargo, Frank: KAOS rendered him amnesiac with a dart-tipped golf ball ("I Shot 86 Today").

Flight 46, Italian Airways: Gino Columbus's Rome to Washington flight, arriving at gate 17 ("Hello Columbus, Goodbye America").

Fong, Lum: CONTROL's top cypher expert and owner of a Chinese laundry ("A Tail of Two Tails").

Formula 6076767: Stolen CONTROL formula with the trade name "dry-up" ("A Man Called Smart").

4th and Vermont: Location of Knight's Stamp Redemption Center ("The Day They Raided the Knights").

Gaul Formula: Taking a leaf from the annals of Julius Caesar, it is, for security reasons, divided in three parts ("A Tail of Two Tails"). Part one resides in a flower shop, part two with the catering service, part three at the bridal salon.

Gemini: Stacked one atop the other, the pair of midget KAOS agents answers to Borgia and operates as a unit. Gemini is foiled when CONTROL agent Munchkin substitutes—undetected by upper Gemini—for lower Gemini ("Hello Columbus, Goodbye America").

Ginzburg Papers: Became the Gottlieb Papers when Ginzburg changed his name ("One Nation Invisible").

Golden Rooster: Burlesque club where CONTROL scientist and bubble dancer Doc Simon performs ("I Shot 86 Today").

Greenbolt Maneuver: Finding and pulling the plug for electric grass ("Satan Place").

Grellman: Code for Washington, D.C. ("Strike While the Agent Is Hot").

Grubnik of KAOS: Dubbed "The Spoiler," Grubnik was traded to KAOS by THRUSH just before the deadline, for a rookie killer and two minor league muggers ("The Reluctant Redhead").

Guild of Surviving CONTROL Agents: Could this Surviving Agents Guild suggest S.A.G. (Screen Actors Guild) in "Strike While the Agent Is Hot"?

Hampton's Fine Food: Restaurant/sidewalk café where Max, using a bugged flower, overhears KAOS agents plotting the return of The Blaster ("The Only Way to Die").

Hathaway, Commander: The Chief's British counterpart ("That Old Gang of Mine").

Item 949: At Knight's Stamp Redemption Center, allegedly the electric toaster but in reality the new stereophonic pistol ("The Day They Raided the Knights").

Jefferson Airplane: The President dreams he disbanded the U.S. Air Force and replaced them with the Jefferson Airplane, which viewers knew to be a popular rock group featuring Grace Slick ("Is This Trip Necessary?").

Kanin Ra, Tomb of: When the Smithsonian returns it to the Cairo National Museum, Max Smart is inside. It doubles as a phone booth, and has graffiti written on the interior walls ("Moonlighting Becomes You").

KAOS Plan 45E: Full-scale attack on Fort Knox ("How to Succeed in the Spy Business Without Really Trying").

Kibbee, Earl: "The Exterminator"—the most cold-blooded, calculating killer who ever worked for KAOS. Also skilled as an accountant ("Witness for the Execution").

Larsen's Shoe Store: Spy ring headquarters ("My Nephew the Spy").

League of Impostors: The KAOS impostor department ("The Spy Who Met Himself").

Left 42, Right 17, Left 58, Right 4, Left 36: Alleged combination of the wall safe in the Bulmanian Embassy ("How Green Was My Valet").

Leviathan, Dr.: Food analyst for the U.S. Department of Agriculture ("Snoopy Smart vs. the Red Baron").

M-4: Complete mobilization raid ("Shipment to Beirut").

Magenta Alert: What the Chief puts CONTROL on after an impression has been made of the key of the conference room door ("KAOS in Control").

Maneuver 14: Asking people straight out, yes or no, "Are you a double agent?" ("Dear Diary.")

Micro-thread: How the plans are transmitted from Richelieu's salon to Beirut for KAOS ("Shipment to Beirut").

NARCO 5-12: Machine gun-like new weapon which emits the energy of 10,000 sonic booms confined in a small area ("I Am Curiously Yellow").

9C: Uncle Abner's shoe size ("My Nephew the Spy").

Obermeyer: KAOS's #1 espionage agent ("Temporarily Out of Control").

101: Shoot on recognition ("Too Many Chiefs").

14783285: Big Eddie Little's number in the race in "Physician Impossible." Max's fantastic total recall recalls it as 14783652.

Operation Baby Buggy Switch: Requires fifteen agents, fails with sixteen, and involves transferring documents from one agent to another by means of pushing baby buggies in geometric patterns which, viewed from above, look like June Taylor Dancers ("Ironhand").

Operation Starch: KAOS's diabolical scheme that destroyed most of the U.S. potato crop ("Snoopy Smart vs. the Red Baron"). Siegfried threatens that after potatoes, it will wipe out broccoli, rhubarb, squash, and kumquats.

Pasteur, Dr. Louis: Impartial doctor who examines Hymie and fails to notice that he isn't human ("It Takes One to Know One").

Petroff: Schnell and he are numbers one and two on CONTROL's most wanted spy list according to the last ratings ("Where-What-How-Who Am I?").

Plan 4A: Walking away to lure an agent after you ("The Whole Tooth and . . .").

Plan 7: Vamp a suspect, invite him to your dressing room, and pull a gun on him ("Casablanca").

Plan 26E: Temporarily blinding an Indian with a mirror hidden in a saddlebag ("Washington 4, Indians 3").

Plan 49K: 99 takes subject to her apartment and keeps an eye on her; 86 follows suspect ("Diplomat's Daughter").

Pomona National Golf Club: KAOS has concealed a mortar under the rocks near its fourteenth hole, the hole nearest the space center. The club has blue golf carts ("I Shot 86 Today").

Project Skyblast: The Army's new antimissile defense system ("Our Man in Toyland").

Rank, J. Arthur: Who Max guesses it is when the Whip sounds the gong ("I Am Curiously Yellow").

Ratton, Doctor: Evil genius who invented Hymie and sold him to KAOS for one million dollars ("Back to the Old Drawing Board").

Rule 6 of Code 19: All CONTROL agents must memorize rule 5 before proceeding to Rule 6 ("The Girls from KAOS").

Schnell: See "Petroff."

Schwartz: KAOS scientist, creator of synthetic islands ("Schwartz's Island").

Section 387B of the Penal Code: Sitting in a chauffeur's uniform next to a rubber dummy. The rubber dummy lobby wants it revoked ("Kisses for KAOS").

Smithsonian Institute, 9 A.M. Tuesday: KAOS code for 11 A.M. Thursday in the park ("Spy, Spy, Birdie"). Correctly speaking, however, it is not Smithsonian Institute but Smithsonian Institution.

Spencer, Mildred: Model turned into a plastic mannequin at Richelieu's ("Shipment to Beirut").

Spy City: Retirement home for CONTROL secret agents ("Dear Diary").

S.S.S.S.S.S.: Spanish Secret Service Strategic Security Staff ("Temporarily Out of Control").

Stanislavski Method: In "Ice Station Siegfried," the method whereby mad scientist Stanislavski plans to freeze the globe. In theater parlance, the Stanislavski Method means "method acting."

Star of India: When it is mentioned in "Leadside" that Leadside stole the Star of India, the question arises whether he stole a fantastic gem, or Sabu (extremely popular teen film star from India in the Forties).

TK800: Tranquilizer bomb formula ("The Amazing Harry Who").

Ten-Four: The code with which Madre (Broderick Crawford) signs off on his mule's shoe phone in "The Treasure of C. Errol Madre." Years earlier, Crawford had made "ten-four" a national catch phrase with his role as Chief Dan Matthews of *Highway Patrol* (1955–1959).

Trent, Helen: One of the most popular soap operas of radio's golden days, *The Romance of Helen Trent* featured a heroine who, "when life mocks her, breaks her hopes, dashes her against the rocks of despair—fights back bravely, successfully, to prove what so many women long to prove in their own lives: that because a woman is thirty-five, and more, romance in life need not be over . . ." When 99 goes undercover on Hannibal Day's radio program using the name "Helen Blake," Day introduces her as Helen Trent ("Moonlighting Becomes You").

236249: Freddie the Forger's number in prison ("Do I Hear A Vaults?").

Vargas, José: Left-handed flamenco dancer and Spanish spy ("Temporarily Out of Control").

XK13074112802 Luger: Max happens to know it only fires six shots, however has trouble counting to six ("Strike While the Agent Is Hot").

X-22: CONTROL computer, fed a deck of cards, now only wants to play poker with the CIA computer ("The Worst Best Man").

Yarmy, Three Fingers: The Shark refers to the famous trick shot of the great pool champ Three Fingers Yarmy in "The Dead Spy Scrawls." Don Adams, in his own life, plays a great game of pool. *Yarmy* is Don Adams's family name.

YENTA: Your Espionage Network and Training Academy—the Israeli equivalent of CONTROL. Their top man is agent 498 ("The Man from YENTA").

Ye Olde Book Shop: KAOS front ("Strike While the Agent Is Hot").

13

CONTROL CASE FILE (EPISODE GUIDE)

Each title is followed by the episode's original air date. Episodes are listed in the order followed by most stations when airing them except that the final (CBS) season is frequently omitted entirely or in part in syndication.

FIRST SEASON

Saturday, 8:30 P.M. September 18, 1965
Mr. Big (pilot)

Mr. Big of KAOS has stolen Professor Dante's inthermo ray, and threatens to use it unless CONTROL forks over a $100 million ransom. Instead, Max, 99, and Fang follow a trail of rubber garbage to a fake garbage scow, Mr. Big's floating hideout. When Mr. Big attempts to use the ray—unaware that the forces of goodness have rewired it—he only succeeds in destroying himself and his evil plan.

Saturday, 8:30 P.M. October 9, 1965
Our Man in Toyland

KAOS is smuggling secrets out of the country in merchandise from Bower's Department Store. Max and Fang investigate as customers, 99 as a salesclerk. She discovers the secret transmission device: Polly Dolly. Fang brings Polly to the Chief. Polly brings a message from Max. Max and 99 fight their way to safety using an arsenal of powerful children's toys.

Saturday, 8:30 P.M. October 30, 1965
KAOS in Control

KAOS has infiltrated CONTROL on the eve of a major peace conference, and has stolen the mind-zapping retrogressor gun.

After both the Chief and Professor Windish have their brains retrogressed, Max takes over, begins the conference, and captures the wrong spy. Then he flushes out the right spy—Alma Sutton—when, pretending to be retrogressed, she makes a slip about watching Captain Kangaroo.

Saturday, 8:30 P.M. October 2, 1965
School Days

Max, looking for a KAOS infiltrator, enrolls in spy school as Alexander Loomis. Fang enrolls too, under the cover name Morris. Max survives a series of assassination attempts without knowing it, then exposes the spy by going after the wrong suspects—and having escaped death with 99 by singing "Happy Birthday" to Fang, who responds by blowing out the flame on the dynamite.

Saturday, 8:30 P.M. September 25, 1965
Diplomat's Daughter

Max and 99 are assigned to protect Princess Ingrid, a wild twenty-year-old blonde bombshell. But all three blunder into the lair of the Claw, a fiendish Oriental villian who has one good hand and one magnetic mauler. Max declaws the Claw by flipping a drawer of cutlery onto his malevolent magnet.

Saturday, 8:30 P.M. October 16, 1965
Now You See Him—Now You Don't

Dr. Haskel has escaped from KAOS with his secret invisibility ray. KAOS overtakes him, and offers the ray to Smart's government in exchange for $10 million. KAOS kidnaps Smart, who cons them into taking him back to his booby-trapped apartment. The ray is a phony, a KAOS plot, and Max nearly demolishes himself on his own booby traps, but with 99's help, he triumphs over the forces of rottenness once more.

Saturday, 8:30 P.M. October 23, 1965
Washington 4, Indians 3

A band of Indians demands the return of all lands taken by the U.S., otherwise they intend to declare war. The Joint Chiefs of Staff discuss blasting Arizona back to the Stone Age, or offering the Indians New Jersey, then decide that Max will infiltrate disguised as an Indian. Max, after flirting with Chief Red Cloud's daughter to avoid torture, finds an enormous arrow disguised as a missile—the second biggest arrow Max has ever seen.

Saturday, 8:30 P.M. November 20, 1965
Our Man in Leotards

CONTROL's new drug, immobilo, has been stolen, presumably to be used by Emilio Naharana—dancer and political activist—against Don Hernando, the Ambassador of Pinerovia. Both 86 and 99 pass themselves off as dancers to penetrate the Naharana dance troupe, burst in on the Ambassador, demand that he eat a peach (peaches counteract immobilo) to save his country, and force Naharana to expose himself and his plot.

Saturday, 8:30 P.M. November 6, 1965
The Day Smart Turned Chicken

Smart reports that a dead cowboy in his bed warned of a plot to poison the Morovian Ambassador. The cowboy disappears, reappears, and Max's insistence persuades the Chief that Max is goofy from fatigue. Thinking a costume party is in progress at the Embassy, Max dresses up as a chicken and descends on the soirée. No costume party. No poisoned punch. When Max goes to court to testify against KAOS, they cite recent events to impugn his credibility—until Max proves that everything was staged precisely to make him look nutty.

Saturday, 8:30 P.M. November 13, 1965
Satan Place

Under Max's vigilant eye, the Chief is kidnapped and held for $200,000 ransom while KAOS's Dr. Harvey Satan freezes the Chief, preparing him for a surgical procedure to render him pro-KAOS. Max passes himself off as the surgeon, and 99 as his nurse. Together, they spring the Chief by freezing Satan and his men. Just as well, since CONTROL had only managed to raise $600 towards the Chief's ransom.

Saturday, 8:30 P.M. November 27, 1965
Too Many Chiefs

Max hides Tanya Lupescu in his apartment until she can testify against KAOS and convey the intricacies of its code system. But KAOS master impersonator, Alexi Sebastian, gets to her by disguising himself as the Chief. The real Chief arrives too. Max establishes the faker by shining a light in his face. Alexi blinks, betraying his identifying trait of weak eyes.

Saturday, 8:30 P.M. December 4, 1965
My Nephew the Spy

Max, simply trying to buy shoes, doesn't suspect that the shoe store is a KAOS front. But KAOS, thinking he knows, tries to eliminate him. Simultaneously, Max's Uncle Abner and Aunt Bertha come to visit. Max and 99 do their utmost to subdue the KAOS culprits without betraying to Abner and Bertha that they're spies—while Max's apartment obligingly springs its booby traps on them.

Saturday, 8:30 P.M. December 18, 1965
Weekend Vampire

When agents are found murdered with mysterious puncture wounds on their necks, a vampire panic grips the city of Washington. The trail leads to the spooky manor of Dr. Drago, who apparently sleeps in a coffin. 86 and 99 invade it by passing themselves off as honeymooners. They discover that the coffin leads to Drago's lab, and that Drago, a former CONTROL scientist, has been bent on destroying the agency since it discharged and humiliated him.

Saturday, 8:30 P.M. December 11, 1965
Aboard the Orient Express

After several CONTROL couriers fail to transport a payroll briefcase, Max is assigned to the task. Double agent Krochanska—a German Shepherd going by the cover name Cyril—almost spirits it away, but Max and 99 keep it secure, forging yet another link in the great chain of victories for CONTROL union benefits around the world.

Saturday, 8:30 P.M. January 8, 1966
Double Agent

Max gambles, drinks, picks a quarrel with the Chief, and goes to seed hoping KAOS will recruit him. They take him—and 99 for good measure—ordering Max to kill her to prove his switched loyalty. Max and 99 bean and shoot a number of KAOS operatives in succession, only to learn that each and every one is an agent working undercover for the U.S.

Saturday, 8:30 P.M. December 25, 1965
Survival of the Fattest

An Arab prince, who has to weigh 300 pounds to keep his kingdom, is kidnapped under Smart's watchful guard by Mary "Jack" Armstrong, the world's strongest female spy. Mary Jack drugs Max with his own truth serum, threatens him with her vast strength, and reduces the prince's weight to a mere 240 pounds. But no problem. The prince's new size makes him a matinee idol in his kingdom, enabling him to retain his title and throne.

Saturday, 8:30 P.M. January 15, 1966
Kisses for KAOS
99 vamps KAOS art dealer and saboteur Rex Savage, but she can't get his finger prints because he almost never takes his gloves off. She lures him to dinner, employing various ID devices from Professor Parker's lab, but KAOS intervenes. Savage, 99, Max, and KAOS artist Mondo next find themselves in Savage's gallery—trapped by a floor bathed in explosive paint. They escape and Max borrows some paint to redecorate his apartment.

Saturday, 8:30 P.M. January 22, 1966
The Dead Spy Scrawls
The Shark, a pool whiz and KAOS kingpin, intercepts and decodes CONTROL messages with a highly sophisticated computer hidden inside a pool table. In order to be able to pass himself off as a pro, Max takes lessons from a pro, doing the man considerable bodily harm in the process. Luckily, Professor Parker comes through with a remote control cue ball which 99 can manipulate with her lipstick. Smart unwittingly opens the pool table computer by shooting the correct combination of balls, then KOs the Shark with his trick ball.

Saturday, 8:30 P.M. January 29, 1966
Back to the Old Drawing Board
KAOS acquires Hymie, the invincible robot, to capture Max Smart and Professor Shotwire. Hymie, passing himself off as a CONTROL agent, goes to a party with Smart and 99 to protect the professor, then proceeds to take Max's every word literally and ape his every move. He abducts 86, 99, and Shotwire to a KAOS hideout—then turns on KAOS instead, because only Max has ever treated him like a real person.

Saturday, 8:30 P.M. February 5, 1966
All in the Mind
A neighbor of Smart's who works for a psychiatrist calls Max to report a KAOS link, then drowns in a phone booth. Max pretends to be a disturbed colonel, and 99 purports to be a secretary. They infiltrate successfully, are caught by KAOS and nearly drowned in a phone booth, which KAOS has rigged for just such occasions.

Saturday, 8:30 P.M. February 19, 1966
Smart, the Assassin
An attempt is made on the Chief's life at the exclusive Regency Club, and only the keen eye of club employee Cedric Devonshire prevents the catastrophe. But Devonshire works for KAOS, abducts Smart, pharmaceutically hypnotizes him to kill the next person who says "checkmate" (which the Chief is certain to say, because he always beats Max at chess). Then Devonshire watches the match, becoming so impatient with Max's slow game that he blurts out "checkmate" and is shot by Max.

Saturday, 8:30 P.M. February 12, 1966
Dear Diary
Retired agent 4 has been keeping a detailed diary of all his years in the secret service. Now Gaffer is gone—kidnapped by enemy agents who want his diary. Max's only lead: "Birds of a feather flock together." A handful of old spies falls under Max's suspicion—one of whom is in fact the culprit.

Saturday, 8:30 P.M. February 26, 1966
I'm Only Human

Fang is a pathetic shadow of his former self since his forced retirement from CONTROL, but Max pushes to have him reinstated in an assignment involving the infiltration of a KAOS kennel. KAOS blanks out Fang's TV transmission collar to lure Smart into a trap, thereby ambushing the Chief. They also brainwash Fang and every important dog in Washington, making them efficient killing animals. Fortunately, Max turns the tables on KAOS, blowing up the forces of evil with its own strategem.

Saturday, 8:30 P.M. March 5, 1966
Stakeout on Blue Mist Mountain

Max goes to the airport to investigate a steady stream of 338 KAOS agents pouring into the country. It appears that each agent is bringing in one part of a bomb that will be assembled at Blue Mist Mountain. Smart penetrates Blue Mist Mountain in the guise of a KAOS agent, then Max, 99, and the Chief burst into the mountain cabin to find and deactivate the bomb. Max succeeds by getting his necktie caught in it.

Saturday, 8:30 P.M. March 12, 1966
The Amazing Harry Who

Hawaiian detective Harry Who assists Max and 99 as they follow a trail of agents and laundry tickets into the Claw's carefully crafted trap. Max accidentally knifes Who and nearly loses his head in a steam press, but ultimately cracks the Claw's operation—a chain of Chinese laundries doubling as KAOS fronts.

Saturday, 8:30 P.M. March 19, 1966
Hubert's Unfinished Symphony

CONTROL agent/violinist Hubert is killed while trying to leave the name of KAOS's new Mr. Big. Max poses as a music critic to find the assassin—a Mr. Badeff, whose name is encoded in Hubert's symphony. Badeff captures Max and 99, but Max escapes with the aid of his heliocoat—just in time to prevent the pianist from striking the keyboard and inadvertently blowing up the concert hall by playing Hubert's Symphony.

Saturday, 8:30 P.M. April 2, 1966
Ship of Spies (Part I)

Max takes to the high seas on the freighter *Evening Star* to recover stolen plans for a nuclear amphibian battleship. 99 follows. Their clue: a clip-clop sound. Unfortunately, everything on the ship makes that sound—a flamenco dancer's castanets, a man with a cane, a wheelchair. Max falls overboard into shark-infested waters while exchanging gunfire with one of the mysterious clip-clops.

Saturday, 8:30 P.M. April 9, 1966
Ship of Spies (Part II)

Max goes to the captain for help. The captain vows to assist but doesn't do much, since he—with his clip-clopping wooden leg—is the rotten apple. Agent 44 tries to warn Max and 99, but someone shoots him before he gets the words out. Max finds out the hard way, at the business end of the captain's peg leg. Max overcomes the captain, and discovers that the nuclear amphibian battleship plans are in the form of scale-model ships in bottles.

Saturday, 8:30 P.M. April 23, 1966
Shipment to Beirut

Thinking to find stolen plans after getting a tip from a model, Max buys, and shreds to ribbons, a number of astronomically expensive designer gowns. When he finally contacts the right model, KAOS turns her into a plastic mannequin. When Max identifies the mannequin for the Chief, the Chief questions Max's sanity and deactivates his status as a CONTROL agent. 99 goes under cover in the same salon and is likewise grabbed and plasticized by the forces of evil. Max solves the case and revitalizes her for the forces of niceness.

Saturday, 8:30 P.M. May 7, 1966
The Last One In Is a Rotten Spy

An endangered female agent named Verna phones Max from a swimming meet. Max and 99 go to her rescue, passing themselves off as a trainer and a chaperone. Max has trouble picking her out because all of the Russian team members' names sound alike to him.

SECOND SEASON

Saturday, 8:30 P.M. October 1, 1966
A Spy for a Spy

Siegfried knocks out and replaces a magician, then kidnaps the Chief as part of a magic act on the Chief's birthday. Siegfried demands the X-11 as ransom for the Chief. Rather than pay the ransom, CONTROL starts kidnapping agents to swap; KAOS follows suit. Soon only Max and Siegfried haven't been kidnapped. They meet, return all agents to their proper sides, seem to be even—except that Siegfried kidnaps CONTROL's bus driver before driving away.

Saturday, 8:30 P.M. October 8, 1966
The Only Way to Die

The Blaster, planning to destroy the U.S. Internal Revenue building, is due in with

"the lover." CONTROL allows everyone to believe Max has been killed in the line of duty. 99, though in mourning, accepts an assignment to protect Antonio Carlos Carioca aboard his $2-million yacht, *El Amador*. Max, realizing that *el amador* is Spanish for "the lover," boards the yacht dressed as 99's old aunt. He prevents Carioca from triggering the bomb, then triggers it himself while explaining the mechanism to the Chief and 99.

Saturday, 8:30 P.M. September 24, 1966
Strike While the Agent Is Hot

Before dying, agent 47 gives Max a clue— "the little red tractor that huffed and puffed"—along with the task of head negotiator for the new labor contract between CONTROL and its agents. Max zealously pursues negotiations with the Chief, and other than its giving him insight into KAOS contracts, fares less well on his case. When KAOS corners him, Max uses his imminent demise to pressure the Chief into signing the new contract, then disarms the KAOS man— believing (inaccurately) that his gun has no shots left.

Saturday, 8:30 P.M. October 15, 1966
Maxwell Smart, Alias Jimmy Ballantine

When an armored truck delivers towels to a barbershop and opens fire on Max, CONTROL suspects foul play. The shop proves to be a KAOS clearing house for everything— from information to heists. Max, passing himself off as master safecracker Jimmy Ballantine, is sent by KAOS to rob the Federal Reserve Bank—which he succeeds in doing only because the Chief orders every Washington area bank to leave its vaults open.

Saturday, 8:30 P.M. September 17, 1966
Anatomy of a Lover

KAOS has rewired Hymie to kill the Chief. CONTROL orders Max to junk Hymie. Instead, Max repairs him, hides him in his apartment, and fakes out CONTROL with a sack of parts from a washing machine. While hiding, Hymie meets the Chief's niece, Phoebe, who becomes smitten. Knowing Max plans to take Hymie to dinner, KAOS jumps him and reprograms him to shoot the next person who says "waiter, the check please." This results in Hymie shooting himself when Max asks for the check in Spanish, and Hymie translates for Phoebe.

Saturday, 8:30 P.M. December 31, 1966
Kiss of Death

Smart rescues madcap heiress Tracy Dunhill, but she's really a KAOS plant. She is in fact the daughter of the founder of KAOS's U.S. branch. Max killed him a year ago; she's determined to destroy Max on the stroke of midnight on the anniversary of his death. Convinced that Max can't resist her, she arms her lips with poison lipstick. But Max outwits her—by taking the precaution of wearing plastic lips.

Saturday, 8:30 P.M. October 22, 1966
Casablanca

Instead of taking his vacation as ordered, Max pursues the Choker to Casablanca. The Chief assigns 99 to the case, but she doesn't know Max is there, and he doesn't know she is. They spend more time spying on each other than they do on the Choker—and suspect each other of being the Choker—until the Choker tries to choke Max and 99. Max bests the Choker with the old false neck trick.

Saturday, 8:30 P.M. November 19, 1966
The Greatest Spy on Earth

When agents die violently at the circus, Max and 99 follow their only clue—a diamond ring. No sooner do they find further evidence of KAOS diamond smuggling than Max is captured and groomed to be a human cannonball, while 99 will be forced into the lion's cage as a lion tamer. They locate the diamonds and defeat the men from KAOS with the help of Hondo the strongman and the Chief, disguised as a clown.

Saturday, 8:30 P.M. November 5, 1966
Hoo Done It

Colonel Forsythe is murdered by an exploding birthday cake in a densely overfoliated tropical hotel. Max, aided by Hawaiian sleuth Harry Hoo, questions the suspects. In a send-up of Agatha Christie's *Ten Little Indians*, the island is suddenly cut off from all contact with the mainland while, one by one, every suspect but Smart and Hoo dies. Smart and Hoo solve the crime—but it's 99, arriving just in time, who saves them from the killer.

Saturday, 8:30 P.M. November 12, 1966
Rub-a-Dub-Dub . . . Three Spies in a Sub

While investigating KAOS's computer-enhanced piracy, Max and 99 are captured by Siegfried and taken into his sub. This puts the Chief in the awkward position of having to decide whether to blow it up with his agents on board, or let the enemy go in order to spare them. The Chief decides to torpedo. Fortunately, 99's quick thinking compels Siegfried to surrender first.

Saturday, 8:30 P.M. October 29, 1966
The Decoy

CONTROL tricks KAOS into believing that Max is carrying CONTROL's new code.

Hugo from the newspaper stand gasses him with a horoscope book and turns him over to KAOS. KAOS tries to break him with sexy femme fatale Greta. When she fails, they use truth serum, but since Max knows nothing, he has nothing to reveal.

Saturday, 8:30 P.M. December 3, 1966
Bronzefinger

Max brushes up on art restoration and 99 becomes a museum tour guide in order to flush out the diabolical art thief Bronzefinger. No sooner does Max line up three suspects than, one by one, they die. Bronzefinger captures 86 and 99 intending to encase them in molten metal. But they shed their bonds just in time, thanks to 99's razor ring.

Saturday, 8:30 P.M. December 24, 1966
The Whole Tooth and . . .

Traveling with microfilm plans for a nuclear reactor in the cap of his tooth and realizing KAOS has tailed him, Max stashes it in the mouth of a strange man—whom he soon discovers to be a convict on the way to Joliet State Penitentiary. Max has himself arrested to recover the tooth. The success of his mission wins him the Spy of the Year Award, but getting him out of jail won't be so easy. Besides, CONTROL has a policy against hiring ex-convicts.

Saturday, 8:30 P.M. November 26, 1966
Island of the Darned

Hobbyist and KAOS assassin Hans Hunter hunts down homo sapiens in his island jungle, and now has his sights set on 86's life and 99's remaining with him on Schwartz's Island. He gives them a knife and the promise that if they survive until sundown, they'll be set free. When he corners them

leaving no way out, 99 prompts Max to destroy him with an exploding bazooka butt cigarette.

Saturday, 8:30 P.M. December 10, 1966
Perils in a Pet Shop

Max tracks a talking parrot who seems to know all about KAOS. The trail leads to Kilmen's Pet Shop and Melnik the smiling killer. When both Max and a KAOS henchman are shot by a tranquilizer gun intended for Fang, they have a violent fist fight—in slow motion—giving the Chief and 99 just enough time to rescue Max.

Saturday, 8:30 P.M. January 7, 1967
It Takes One to Know One

When Octavia, the gorgeous spy, destroys a series of CONTROL agents by driving them mad with desire, Hymie—a robot, impervious to emotion—is appointed CONTROL's #2 man to thwart her. But because she too is unexpectedly a robot, Hymie falls hard and prepares to give her vital information. Max and the Chief intervene. Octavia self-destructs. Hymie attempts to rebuild her, creating a robot that looks perfect but talks like Max.

Saturday, 8:30 P.M. January 14, 1967
Someone Down Here Hates Me

Siegfried puts Max on the KAOS hit list with $250,000 on his head, and says that if Max is still around in forty-eight hours, the annual KAOS bingo party and barbecue is kaput. Max becomes a nervous wreck who suspects, and jumps, all sorts of strangers. The reward leaps to $500,000. Max learns of a Dr. Noodelman, a surgeon capable of performing instantly healing plastic surgery. Turns out Noodelman has been doing the KAOS killers who attacked Max—now

Noodelman wants to do *in* Max himself, for the $500,000 reward.

Saturday, 8:30 P.M. January 21, 1967
Cutback at CONTROL

Max and the Chief testify before a Senate investigating committee which has cut back their funds and is close to disbanding CONTROL entirely. Smart accepts a KAOS job offer in hopes of finding a big double agent and convincing the Senate of CONTROL's worth. While attending a KAOS training school, Max hears the phrase "the jig is up"—which leads him to stumble on the identity of the double agent, who is none other than Dietrich, head of the Senate committee.

Saturday, 8:30 P.M. January 28, 1967
The Mummy

KAOS is shipping agents to America in mummy cases. An operative at the Metropolitan Museum receives them, and returns kidnapped CONTROL agents in their place. The museum's attractive assistant curator lures Max into a trap. The curator wraps him head-to-toe in bandages, and all but has him crated when the Chief rescues him and drops him several times in a row.

Saturday, 8:30 P.M. February 4, 1967
The Girls from KAOS

Miss USA, the daughter of a famous scientist, comes to Max for protection from kidnappers. Max complies by following her to the beauty pageant where, the Chief guesses, one of the entries is a KAOS plant. The plants are Miss Tasmania, her chaperone (actually, her husband, KAOS agent Dmitri Sokoloff in disguise), and Miss Formosa. The three assassinate each other, leaving Smart and Miss USA unscathed.

Saturday, 8:30 P.M. February 11, 1967
The Man from YENTA

Max, with the help of Agent 498 (Israel's top man from YENTA) must safeguard the life of Arab Prince Abu ben Bubbie, though KAOS's villian and master of disguise Le Moco eludes them at every turn. At one point, 86, 498, Le Moco, and the prince are all dressed exactly alike—and it takes pulling beards and educated guessing to narrow down the field.

Saturday, 8:30 P.M. February 18, 1967
Smart Fit the Battle of Jericho

Buildings of the U.S. space agency blow up mysteriously as soon as construction is completed. Max infiltrates the KAOS-supported Joshua Construction Company in the guise of a construction worker, and learns that KAOS is imbedding nitro in each building.

Saturday, 8:30 P.M. February 25, 1967
Where-What-How-Who Am I?

Smart overhears a KAOS scheme to blow up space scientists, then has an auto accident—courtesy of KAOS—before he can report the details. He wakes up in a hospital that refuses to release him, because they *are* KAOS. They give him amnesia pills, causing him to forget everything. Each time he's about to remember, he takes a pill and goes blank. Then 99 remembers Smart's wrist recorder, which he had on when he heard the plot. She plays it, finds KAOS men Petroff and Schnell, and with Max, saves the world by stopping them.

Saturday, 8:30 P.M. March 11, 1967
How to Succeed in the Spy Business Without Really Trying

Siegfried offs a KAOS agent to save Max,

then asks to join CONTROL. With Shtarker's help, he stages his own mock assassination, drops hints about an attack on Fort Knox, tricks the Chief into deploying CONTROL agents to Kansas, and prepares to gas the unguarded chiefs of CONTROL at their banquet. This time, Smart smells a rat, outwitting Siegfried by wearing a gas mask in a false nose.

Saturday, 8:30 P.M. March 4, 1967
The Expendable Agent
British agent Chain helps Max guard rocket fuel scientist Professor Whitaker in Max's apartment. KAOS wires the apartment to explode at midnight. When that fails, KAOS has a woman pose as Whitaker's niece and shoot him. But the man Max thought was the professor was the expendable agent, a decoy; and the man he took for Chain was the rocket whiz.

Saturday, 8:30 P.M. March 25, 1967
Appointment in Sahara
KAOS, becoming the first private organization to own a nuclear bomb, demands the total disarmament of all the world's nuclear nations, and Max and 99 have less than seventy-two hours in the Sahara to find and stop KAOS. KAOS finds them first, parched and dying on the sands. KAOS feigns hospitality, only to stake Max and 99 exposed to the burning sun. A dancing girl rescues the two CONTROL agents, freeing Max to rescue the world.

Saturday, 8:30 P.M. April 1, 1967
Pussycats Galore
When important scientists have been disappearing from Pussycat key clubs, Max and 99 pose as German scientists Fritz and Greta Braun, while male agent Charlie Watkins dis-

guises himself as a stacked blonde woman and takes a job at a Pussycat Club. KAOS tosses Watkins in a freezer and drugs 99, but Max feigns a trance till the right moment—then polishes off his assailants with a little help from CONTROL.

Saturday, 8:30 P.M. April 8, 1967
A Man Called Smart (Part I)
Max negotiates a $25,000 bribe for information on the KAOS agents who snatched a lake-evaporating formula from the CONTROL labs. But his informant, character actor Russell Bedioyskin, is shot before he can divulge his secret. The Chief and 99 take Bedioyskin to the hospital. Max, sent as a decoy, rolls out of a KAOS ambulance and down the street while strapped to a gurney.

Saturday, 8:30 P.M. April 15, 1967
A Man Called Smart (Part II)
The urgency of KAOS's ransom demands brings the ancient Admiral back to CONTROL's helm. The Admiral goes on TV to reassure the nation. Aided by the Admiral, Max and the Chief discover that Bedioyskin is the nearly identical brother of formula inventor Dr. Smith. In a hospital shootout, the Chief is hit and passes out limp, perhaps dead.

Saturday, 8:30 P.M. April 22, 1967
A Man Called Smart (Part III)
As the Chief recuperates, KAOS dries up Niagra Falls. Max and 99 follow Bedioyskin's clues to the Three Brothers Omniwash, a KAOS front for illegal gambling, and to Panamint Studios' Stage 7 in Los Angeles—and an all-out showdown of guns, fists, bottles, furniture, and foils between Max and Otto Hurrah.

THIRD SEASON

Saturday, 8:30 P.M. September 16, 1967
Viva Smart

Max and 99 visit San Saludos, a corrupt Latin American dictatorship run by General Diablo Pajarito. CONTROL wants to return the imprisoned ex-president Don Carlos to power. Max and 99 dress in the costumes of and perform as Flamenco dancers Conchito and Conchata, are apprehended and thrown in jail, bribe the firing squad (after haggling their price down to $60 and then getting a rebate since only half the firing squad could be reached in time), escape with Don Carlos and his daughter, and are recaptured by soldiers who can't wait to tell them the good news—Don Carlos is Prez again.

Saturday 8:30 P.M. September 23, 1967
Witness for the Persecution

A KAOS football which contains both a bomb and a coding device implicates Mr. Tudbury as a KAOS operative. Tudbury retaliates by ordering KAOS to "Get Smart" before he can testify against him at the trial. Max holes up in his apartment, protected by an arsenal of new gadgets from CONTROL's lab. 99 moves in to help out. KAOS attacks. Max repels them, destroying his apartment and getting himself evicted in the process. He eventually makes it to the trial without getting killed—no thanks to the cop who ticketed him for jaywalking as he dodged bullets to cross the street.

Saturday, 8:30 P.M. October 7, 1967
The Spy Who Met Himself

KAOS strikes with its League of Impostors. One of its members impersonates Max, even down to the recent bruise on his ankle. The real Max confronts the fake one in the Chief's office. The wrong Max is established as the real Max before a board of inquiry. The right Chief bursts in, shooting the wrong Chief, leading the wrong Max to shoot the right Chief and the real Max to shoot the wrong Max. We hope.

Saturday, 8:30 P.M. October 14, 1967
The Spirit Is Willing

Max meets informer Ann Ferris in a graveyard. She promises to deliver evidence against Paul John Mondebello, disappears in a twinkling, but leaves her headstone in full view. Max learns that Ann Ferris was the name of Mondebello's last victim, so decides to hold a séance to contact her again. The spirit of Ann requests $50,000. Back in the graveyard, Max discovers that Ann faked her death to raise money and run away with her defecting KAOS lover. Mondebello gets the drop on Max and 99, but Ann's mother reappears from the dead and saves them.

Saturday, 8:30 P.M. October 21, 1967
Maxwell Smart, Private Eye

In this spoof of Bogart flicks, Max and 99 moonlight as private eyes because CONTROL is experiencing another budget cut. Seemingly by coincidence, they're hired by KAOS agents Mr. Sidney and Mr. Peter to protect the very woman CONTROL has assigned them to. In so doing, Max becomes a security leak. Then, trapped, he gets the drop on two agents and tricks the third into leaving by the fire escape—when there isn't any.

Saturday, 8:30 P.M. October 28, 1967
Supersonic Boom

KAOS attacks CONTROL headquarters with a supersonic boom, then goes on TV to demand $50 million within forty-eight hours, otherwise New York City will get the next blast. Max and 99 trace the source of the boom to a carwash. But KAOS, using an illusion room, convinces them that the device has been moved to South America. Contacting the Chief, Max has U.S. military resources mobilized against Argentina, then, discerning that he's been tricked, stops the supersonic boom single-handedly, then uses it on the Chief's office by mistake.

Saturday, 8:30 P.M. November 4, 1967
One of Our Olives Is Missing
A double agent hands Max a miniature radio, built into an olive. Western singer Ozark Annie swallows it. When KAOS uses the transmitter, Annie's stomach talks. Max takes her home for protection. Siegfried follows, disguised as a CONTROL doctor. Max's rescue attempts are at first helped, then hindered, by Annie's developing a crush on him.

Saturday, 8:30 P.M. November 18, 1967
When Good Fellows Get Together
KAOS has created the ultimate robot, Gropo. It's up to Hymie to destroy him. But Hymie refuses to be reprogrammed for badness. He'd rather be Gropo's friend. In a showdown at a Western ghost town, Hymie realizes that Gropo is not a nice piece of metal and, with Max's help, disposes of him in a deep well.

Saturday, 8:30 P.M. November 25, 1967
Dr. Yes
A missile launch goes awry, sabotaged by the Fu Manchu of KAOS—Dr. Yes. Max and 99 masquerade as "stupid, harmless, fun-loving vacationers" at Lost Lake, reputed to be near Yes's hideout. Yes orders them eliminated but they escape his trap and discover his underwater power station, only to fall

into his evil clutches yet again. This time, Max tricks Yes into poking himself in the face with his poison-tipped fingernail.

Saturday, 8:30 P.M. December 2, 1967
That Old Gang of Mine
After subduing the Scar with the old gun in the flashlight trick, Max and 99 proceed to London's Crashing Boar pub in search of British CONTROL. Max takes on the Scar's identity to infiltrate the Scorpion Gang, nail their leader, and uncover the mastermind behind the gang's plans to steal the royal jewels. Both the mastermind and her boyfriend, who work for British CONTROL, surrender when Max threatens them with nitro.

Saturday, 8:30 P.M. December 9, 1967
The Mild Ones
The Purple Knights, a hippie motorcycle gang fashioned after King Arthur's Round Table, kidnaps a foreign prime minister for KAOS. Max and 99 infiltrate as "Wheels" and "Legs." Max and the gang leader joust on motorcycles, using mops for lances. The leader's sweetie falls for Max. The gang fails to draw and quarter Max with motorcycles.

Saturday, 8:30 P.M. December 23, 1967
Classification: Dead
Poisoned while romancing a KAOS agent, Max is doomed to die at 1:00 P.M. CONTROL's Dr. Steele can duplicate the poison but can't find the antidote. Max tracks down Mr. Hercules, the man responsible for poisoning him. Hercules wants to swap the antidote for CONTROL's new code but, with seconds to live, Max poisons him. The two grapple over the antidote and pass out, but the Chief arrives just in time to save Max.

Saturday, 8:30 P.M. December 30, 1967
The Mysterious Dr. T
An important CONTROL scientist dies,

confessing before he goes that a Dr. T actually masterminded his greatest work. Max and 99 for CONTROL—and Siegfried for KAOS—beat the bushes for the mystery whiz, finally discovering him to be the twelve-year-old Tyler J. Tattledove.

Saturday, 8:30 P.M. January 6, 1968
The King Lives?

In a take-off on *The Prisoner of Zenda*, Max bears such a striking resemblance to the King of Caronia that he is able to sub for him to thwart an attempted assassination. The king's half-brother, Basil, wants the crown, and kidnaps 99 to obtain it. Max, suddenly a throwback to the nineteenth century, rescues 99, the crown, and Caronia with a surprising display of swordsmanship.

Saturday, 8:30 P.M. January 13, 1968
The Groovy Guru

The Groovy Guru has launched a massive, drug-and-music-induced freak-out in Washington, D.C., with plans to go national on television. He intends to incite them to anti-CONTROL insurrection. The show starts, but doesn't air, thanks to Max and 99.

Saturday, 8:30 P.M. January 27, 1968
The Little Black Book (Part I)

Sid, Max's buddy from the Korean War, arrives unexpectedly just as a KAOS defector tries to sell Max a book full of secrets. Sid, finding it, mistakes it for a "little black book" and uses it to fix up dates for himself and Max. The dates are with female KAOS agents. When Max gets the drop on the ladies at a restaurant, Sid disarms him, thinking him totally bonkers.

Saturday, 8:30 P.M. February 3, 1968
The Little Black Book (Part II)

Max convinces Sid that he's a secret agent, then with him finds KAOS's villanious Maestro, who captures them, chains them in the cellar, and nearly succeeds in eliminating them with a cannon timed to the "1812 Overture." Instead, they turn the cannon on the Maestro, freeing Sid to date 99.

Saturday, 8:30 P.M. February 10, 1968
Don't Look Back

In this spoof of *The Fugitive*, a Max Smart look-alike robs a bank and kills a guard. When KAOS plants evidence in Max's apartment, Max is arrested and tried for the crime. Not at liberty to reveal his CONTROL agent identity, Max does the next best thing—he defends himself by attempting to bribe the foreman of the jury. Sentenced to death, Max escapes from Sgt. Gronski, goes on the lam in pursuit of the one-armed man who can prove his innocence, and exonerates himself in a showdown at Baltimore's Main Street Hotel.

Saturday, 8:30 P.M. February 17, 1968
99 Loses Control

99 resigns from CONTROL to accept handsome, wealthy casino owner Victor Royal's proposal of marriage. Taking the alias "Max Wheel," 86 considers a job as Royal's bodyguard. Max discovers that Royal works for KAOS, and springs 99 while they still have their lives.

Saturday, 8:30 P.M. February 24, 1988
The Wax Max

When Max quotes Genghis Khan at an amusement park shooting gallery, 99 wins a kewpie doll. Then the two go through the tunnel of love. Weapons just miss them, while Max blithely eats a sandwich. They escape the tunnel to discover the park has been emptied except for the KAOS agents firing on them. The kewpie doll, it seems, is a KAOS device for delivering plutonium. Max and 99 duck into the chamber of horrors, where the exhibits come to life—they're KAOS agents—and attempt to guillotine Max. Max outwits them, thanks to the old inflatable head in the cloak trick.

Saturday, 8:30 P.M. March 2, 1968
Operation Ridiculous
Max has to make CONTROL look good for a *Week News* magazine article. Reluctant to rely only on Max's natural stupidity, KAOS compounds his inevitable blunders. Under Max's protection, the magazine reporter experiences a series of painful accidents. 99 discerns the plot, makes CONTROL look great, and gives all the credit to Max.

Saturday, 8:30 P.M. March 9, 1968
Spy, Spy, Birdie
A little old man in red earmuffs—Albert Pfister by name—appears at Max's apartment and pleads with him to sign a petition against noise. Max rebuffs him. Pfister retaliates by systematically and noiselessly blowing up the world. CONTROL assumes that KAOS is behind the explosions; KAOS accuses CONTROL. Max and Siegfried join forces to find Pfister, who has a menagerie of carrier pigeons armed with nitro-whisperin and ready to be released. Max disarms Pfister by noisily striking a match, then has to prevent Siegfried from taking up where Pfister left off.

Saturday, 8:30 P.M. March 16, 1968
Run, Robot, Run
When the Chief puts Hymie over Max on a case, Max smarts—briefly—then accepts Hymie's analysis of how to preserve the country's honor at an important track meet. Snead and Neal, of the CAD division of KAOS, temporarily put the free world's track stars out of commission, meaning Hymie has to compete in their place. Despite CAD interference, Hymie of the West wins with effortless, wooden panache.

Saturday, 8:30 P.M. March 23, 1968
The Hot Line
Using the Chief's hot line and a voice that sounds like the President's, KAOS phones CONTROL, ordering Max to take over, and to open CONTROL files to a KAOS plant. Tactlessly but happily, Max replaces the Chief—who has to penetrate KAOS, and flush out the truth, in the guise of a singing waiter.

Saturday, 8:30 P.M. April 6, 1968
The Reluctant Redhead
The Krispin Papers contain the names of every politician, army officer, and dentist who owes allegiance to KAOS. Krispin will swap the list in exchange for his wife, Amanda Krispin. With no Amanda on hand, CONTROL recruits her look-alike, Mimsi Sage, whom Max romances to assure her loyalty. When the time comes to make the trade, Mimsi reveals that she's the real Amanda, steals the papers at gunpoint, and is subdued only because Krispin's statuary garden is full of CONTROL agents dressed as statues.

Saturday, 8:30 P.M. March 30, 1968
Die, Spy
A KAOS agent quit when refused a promotion, tried without success to join CONTROL, then formed his own band to destroy both agencies. Max, along with a new recruit named Samuels, travels the world in search of this nemesis who has changed his face through plastic surgery but can be flushed out by his passion for Ping-Pong. The episode echoes *I Spy*, with *I Spy* star Robert Culp in a cameo as an Istanbul waiter.

FOURTH SEASON

Saturday, 8:00 P.M. September 21, 1968
The Impossible Mission

In a tease parodying the opening of *Mission: Impossible*, Max is assigned to find the Leader—KAOS's top agent—before the Leader uses Hellman's Theory to obliterate the human race. Both 86 and 99 go undercover, he as a trumpet player and she as a dancer. When it looks as if the two are trapped with no hope of rescue, Max tells 99 that he'd marry her if they weren't about to die. She thinks of a way to get out, thereby trapping Max for life.

Saturday, 8:00 P.M. September 28, 1968
Snoopy Smart vs. the Red Baron

KAOS's Operation Starch has destroyed most of the U.S. potato crop, but the U.S. has suppressed the news by substituting look-alike edible foam rubber. 86 and 99 go to Idaho to investigate, managing to stop off and visit 99's mother on the way. There they find Siegfried—the key to Operation Starch—with his World War I crop duster. Max and Siegfried duke it out in a WW I-style aerial dog fight, which Max wins by leaping out of his downed plane onto Siegfried's.

Saturday, 8:00 P.M. October 5, 1968
Closely Watched Planes

Max, assigned to protect a courier and attaché case after several of them have disappeared, loses both mid-air, then volunteers to be the next courier. With 99 backing him up as an airline stewardess, he discovers—the hard way—that the couriers all fell through a trap door in the floor of the lavatory. Max bests the KAOS pilot and co-pilot in a fist fight, leaving no one able to fly the plane.

Saturday, 8:00 P.M. October 12, 1968
The Secret of Sam Vittorio

Max and 99 pose as gangsters Connie Barker and Floyd Darrow in hopes that dying mobster Sam Vittorio will confide to them the whereabouts of his loot. Vittorio catches on, just as the real Connie and Floyd arrive. He bumps off the genuine articles believing them to be Max and 99, then spills his secret with his last breath: "Crime doesn't pay."

Saturday, 8:00 P.M. October 19, 1968
Diamonds Are a Spy's Best Friend

Max, buying 99's engagement ring, blunders in on a jewelry robbery. The jeweler, rather than surrender his best diamond, sells it to Max for $80. The Chief, suspecting that Max either stole it or sold out to KAOS, insists on returning to the jeweler to verify the story. Clues at the jewelers lead them to a bowling alley, where KAOS agents are smuggling diamonds which they keep stashed under their wigs.

Saturday, 8:00 P.M. October 26, 1968
The Worst Best Man

KAOS is systematically removing CONTROL agents one by one as Max asks them to be best man at his wedding. Rather than lose more agents, the Chief orders Max to ask Hymie, who is indestructible. KAOS plants a bomb in Hymie, intending to detonate it during Max's bachelor party, but Max detects it, and dismantles it with Hymie's instruction.

Saturday, 8:00 P.M. April 12, 1969
A Tale of Two Tails

The Chief assigns 99 to pick up the three parts of the Gaul Formula, while 86 substitute teaches at spy training school. As a practice exercise, Max tells two students to tail 99. She takes them for KAOS agents. But it's Max who rescues her from the real KAOS agent—by dressing as Santa Claus in the middle of the summer, and dueling with a flat iron in a Chinese laundry.

Saturday, 8:00 P.M. November 2, 1968
The Return of the Ancient Mariner

With Hymie away on an important case, the Admiral is set to be Max's best man. The Chameleon, KAOS's latest master of disguise, poses as Larabee, snatches the Admiral, and assumes his identity to infiltrate a top-secret conference. There, the Chameleon becomes 99, and makes a clean getaway.

Saturday, 8:00 P.M. November 16, 1968
With Love and Twitches

Dr. Madre, who intercepted the map of the Melnick Uranium Mine, transfers it to Max in the form of a drink-induced rash. The map will only come out clearly if Max hangs from a hook on a door through his wedding night. With KAOS after him and his map, Max barely makes it to his wedding—which is only slightly marred by fistfights with KAOS men in the aisles.

Saturday, 8:00 P.M. November 30, 1968
The Laser Blazer

On the Chief's instruction, Max goes to a Hong Kong tailor shop. The tailor gives him a sports jacket which the Smarts' new maid sends out to have cleaned. Only after the jacket is gone does Max learn that it's a secret laser-equipped weapon. The blazer destroys a few cleaning shops, and the maid is exposed as a KAOS operative.

Saturday, 8:00 P.M. December 7, 1968
The Farkas Fracas

Max surprises 99 by inviting the Chief over for dinner. Caught without dessert, 99 accepts a chocolate mousse from her next-door neighbor, Naomi Farkas. Farkas is a KAOS agent, and has mildly poisoned the mousse to get the Chief and Max out of the room. This much of her scheme succeeds, then she and her husband steal the wrong attaché case.

Saturday, 8:00 P.M. December 14, 1968
Temporarily Out of Control

Hours before Max's belated honeymoon, KAOS arranges to have Max and the Chief called up for active Naval Reserve duty. In the reserves, Max outranks the Chief. When the two need to leave ship to crack a case, the captain refuses, never having heard of CONTROL. By the time they do reach their destination, 99 has already foiled KAOS and restored things to perfect order.

Saturday, 8:00 P.M. December 21, 1968
Schwartz's Island

Honeymooning by sailboat with 99, Max sinks the sailboat and the survival raft. They swim to the safety of an island on which sits the world's first giant nuclear magnet. The magnet, operated by Siegfried and Shtarker, can suck the entire U.S. Sixth Fleet from mid-ocean and run it aground. The Chief is captured with Max and 99, but all three escape by inflating the Chief's diving suit (with the Chief in it) and using it as a raft.

Saturday, 8:00 P.M. December 28, 1968
One Nation Invisible

KAOS has stolen the vitally important Ginzburg papers. Max, using Dr. Canyon's new invisibility formula, penetrates KAOS headquarters security. The formula wears off. Max reappears, but still believes himself invisible. KAOS prepares to force him into suicide, when a real invisible CONTROL agent comes to his aid.

Saturday, 8:00 P.M. January 4, 1969
Hurray for Hollywood

Max and 99 take minor roles as the butler and Lady Fannie in a theatrical work which KAOS is using to pass information. Letting the spotlight go to his head, Max comes on like Mr. Hollywood—Laurence Hollywood, in fact—wrecks the stage, forgets lines, and hams badly. KAOS decides to eliminate him during a performance by substituting a real gun for a prop. Before long, not only Max and 99, but also KAOS agents and the Chief, are on stage doing battle and accepting resounding applause.

Saturday, 8:00 P.M. January 11, 1969
The Day They Raided the Knights

Budget cutbacks at CONTROL have forced 99 to look for another job. Becoming a salesgirl at Knight's Stamp Redemption Center, she unintentionally distributes arms for KAOS—because the shop is really a KAOS munitions depot. When 99 catches on, she alerts the Chief, who along with Larabee, dresses in drag to penetrate KAOS's ruse. KAOS captures 99, the Chief, and Larabee, and Max miraculously springs them.

Saturday, 8:00 P.M. January 18, 1969
Tequila Mockingbird

Max and 99 are sent to Mira Loma, Mexico, to keep the priceless Tequila Mockingbird out of KAOS hands. Max poses as a bad doctor, 99 as a dancer. They find an ax with a red W on it, which 99 concludes to mean a red wax candle. The clue leads to the bird, and to a confrontation with KAOS, which is averted by the Chief, who's been hiding under a serape and sombrero.

Saturday, 8:00 P.M. February 1, 1969
I Shot 86 Today

Suspecting that KAOS golfers have been lobbing nuclear golf balls at space centers and blowing them up, the Chief assigns Max and 99 to take lessons and keep an eye on pro Chuck Cramer, particularly at 4:00 P.M. when the adjoining space center will test the M-14 rocket. Max stops by the secret lab of CONTROL's Doc Simon for magnetic golf balls and trick clubs, and good thing, too. After 86 stumbles on the old mortar in the rocks in the fourteenth hole trick and engages in a spine-tingling golf cart chase, he uses the magnetic ball to stop the nuclear one mid-air.

Saturday, 8:00 P.M. February 8, 1969
Absorb the Greek

Ordered to tail the Chief, Max and 99 learn that he's taken up computer dating, and are scandalized by the age of the attractive young woman he's seeing. 99 would much rather fix him up with her mother. As it happens, the Chief's dates are a cover—the woman has been advising him of a secret anti-aging formula. KAOS attempts to derail the meetings, but kidnaps the wrong woman—99's mom.

Saturday, 8:00 P.M. February 15, 1969
To Sire, with Love (Part I)

For security reasons, Max and his perfect double—the King of Caronia—change places at a costume ball. For the next few days, the King exploits the resemblance by romancing 99. The King's enemy, Rupert of Rathskeller, discovers the switch and sends his men over to Max's apartment with a giant tarantula.

Saturday, 8:00 P.M. February 22, 1969
To Sire, with Love (Part II)

Max tests 99's fidelity by pretending to be the King. She bites, then catches on, and turns the tables on Max. Then he catches on, and turns the tables on her. Meanwhile, Rupert's men are kidnapping the king, whom Max must swashbuckle free.

Saturday, 8:00 P.M. March 1, 1969
Shock It To Me

KAOS's formerly dead Dr. Zharko has found a way to bring himself and fellow deceased agents back to life. Max and 99 hunt down Zharko, who responds by preparing them for suspended animation. Max, who often misses the obvious in the simplest situations, knows enough about electricity to free himself and 99, and enough about explosives to put an end to the mad doctor and his weird flunky, Bruce.

Saturday, 8:00 P.M. March 8, 1969
Leadside

In a take-off on *Ironside*, wheelchair-bound Leadside and his two assistants plot the destruction of CONTROL and the death of Maxwell Smart. Having wrecked CONTROL's computer, Leadside zeroes in on Max, who as usual is protected by his booby-trapped apartment. Leadside, who can jog but can't walk, sprints into Max's apartment and fences with Max from his wheelchair. Max prevails by opening the door, letting Leadside sail through it and crash.

Saturday, 8:00 P.M. March 15, 1969
Greer Window

Max, having been shot where he sits, is issued armed crutches and has to stay home. In the manner of *Rear Window*, he watches the office across the street, uncovers a KAOS plot to steal top-secret blueprints, and defends himself more successfully than usual—thanks to the old gun in the crutch trick—when bad guy Greer comes to call.

Saturday, 8:00 P.M. March 22, 1969
The Not-So-Great Escape (Part I)

Twenty-two CONTROL agents, including the Chief, have been kidnapped—many through a revolving airport phone booth—and interned at a KAOS P.O.W. camp near Passaic, New Jersey. Max penetrates the camp disguised as Major Kessler of KAOS high command. Siegfried catches on to him, and imprisons him with the others.

Saturday, 8:00 P.M. March 29, 1969
The Not-So-Great Escape (Part II)

Max has to spring the prisoners before the real Major Kessler can take them behind the iron curtain, brainwash them, and return them to CONTROL as KAOS pawns. Despite the presence of an informer in their cell, and Max digging an escape tunnel that leads back to the cell, Max secures the prisoners' freedom. In digging the tunnel, he damages a power line, which brings all the utility companies to the rescue.

FIFTH SEASON

Friday, 7:30 P.M. September 26, 1969
Pheasant Under Glass

Max and 99 have to rescue nuclear genius Professor Pheasant from an impregnable glass chamber. But Max bungles it, and when 99 tells him that he's going to be a father, he babbles to a reporter that he's a secret agent. He has his face changed and accompanies opera singer Rosa La Costa to KAOS headquarters as her pianist. La Costa's high note fails to shatter the professor's glass walls, but she's big enough to beat them down by dint of her bulk.

Friday, 7:30 P.M. October 3, 1969
Ironhand

KAOS has been taken over by IH Industries, whose president, Ironhand, has one good hand, and one iron fist. Ironhand plots to steal the AAAMM plans, which Max and

99 transport in a rapid-fire automatic, armed baby buggy. Ironhand gets the buggy, then knocks himself senseless when Max tells him the stock market fell twenty-one points.

Friday, 7:30 P.M. October 10, 1969
Valerie of the Dolls
Believing it to be a KAOS front, Max and the Chief enroll in Miss Valerie's School for Expectant Fathers. Max unintentionally swaps his practice doll for one containing part of a secret formula. KAOS agents recover it at gunpoint, then fly to Los Angeles from Washington, D.C. Max, 99, and the Chief beat them to the airport by taking a faster mode of transit: while KAOS was stacked up over L.A. airport, CONTROL took the train.

Friday, 7:30 P.M. October 17, 1969
Widow Often Annie
Although 99 is within days of giving birth, the Chief orders Max to romance and marry Ann Cameron, a professional twelve-time widow of CONTROL agents. The Chief presides over the ceremony, so that it won't be legal. As anticipated, Ann has Max sign over his insurance to her, then attempts to kill him on their wedding night. The Chief, 99, and Larabee stop her. Max regrets the brevity of their fling.

Friday, 7:30 P.M. October 24, 1969
The Treasure of C. Errol Madre
When KAOS hijacks CONTROL's bankroll, CONTROL has to move its offices into an elevator and lay off its entire staff. Max acquires the half-map of prospector Froggsy Debs, then links up with C. Errol Madre in Mexico, who has the other half. They find the gold. Banditos find them. Max saves Madre, who isn't Madre but an agent for KAOS, then Max agrees to split the gold

with the government of the head bandito, who is really an agent in the Mexican secret police.

Friday, 7:30 P.M. October 31, 1969
Smart Fell on Alabama
Max attempts to switch secret codes on Bohrman, a KAOS agent on her way to delivering an important code book to Colonel Kyle K. Kirby in the Deep South. When Max fails, he has to infiltrate the Colonel's top-security plantation, aided by a trio of convict commandos released from the penitentiary in exchange for assisting CONTROL.

Friday, 7:30 P.M. November 7, 1969
And Baby Makes Four (Part I)
Max must keep KAOS agent Simon the Likeable from stealing Pentagon documents. In observing Simon, he manages to walk away with his quarry's coat, so that he has the map to KAOS's new lair, and Simon has the map to the hospital where 99 will have her babies. When the time comes, Max drives 99 to the wrong hospital.

Friday, 7:30 P.M. November 14, 1969
And Baby Makes Four (Part II)
Realizing they're in a KAOS sanitarium, Max and 99 break away and get to the right hospital. The Chief, Larabee, and Simon the Likeable are already there. The Chief, Max, and Larabee find Simon too adorable to arrest, but 99's mother slugs him unconscious for bumping into her and causing her to drop a handful of change.

Friday, 7:30 P.M. November 21, 1969
Physician Impossible
When Max wings Big Eddie Little, an escaping con, Big Eddie vows revenge. Eddie's thugs go to the hospital, kidnapping a doctor to treat Eddie. But the "doctor" and his

"nurse" are Max and 99, dressed in sterile hospital masks and gowns to look in on their newborn twins. CONTROL surrounds the hideout. As Eddie and his thugs drop their guns, the weapons fire, wounding all the hoods.

Friday, 7:30 P.M. November 28, 1969
The Apes of Rath
One after another CONTROL agent receives bananas in the mail, then is brutally murdered. Evidence points to an ape as the culprit, but actually, it's CONTROL agent Armstrong, an ape transformed to human appearance by the evil Dr. Rath. Max's banana comes up next. Meanwhile, Armstrong cuts his finger, and 99 bandages it. Shades of *Son of Kong* and *King Kong*—now Armstrong wouldn't hurt her for the world, but gleefully carries her to the roof of Max's building. In the end, it's beauty kills the beast: Armstrong slips on a Beauty brand banana peel and falls off the ledge.

Friday, 7:30 P.M. December 5, 1969
Age Before Duty
For $100,000 CONTROL defector Felix agrees to unleash his invention, Dorian Gray paint, against every agent of CONTROL. His procedure is to dab his voodoo paint on their photos, which instantly ages them. When Felix turns Max, 99, and the Chief into doddering old fools, they fight fire with fire, aging him with his own paint. Then they discover the antidote in common cleaning fluid.

Friday, 7:30 P.M. December 12, 1969
Is This Trip Necessary?
Smart, 99, the Chief, Larabee, Congress, and the President all had bad dreams the night before, each induced by KAOS's mad pharmacist, Jarvis Pym. Pym is demanding $50 million blackmail via TV plea. Max and

99 track him down to the Dartfoot Spring Water Company, where Pym has been expecting them. Overpowering them with the old mortar (military) in the mortar (pharmaceutical) trick, he imprisons them in a giant capsule, but they get the drop on him, putting an end to his hallucinogenic reign.

Friday, 7:30 P.M. December 19, 1969
Ice Station Siegfried
The planet is freezing over, stranding Max in Miami under twelve feet of snow. The Chief sends 99, and the CIA sends top agent Quigley, to the North Pole, where Siegfried and Shtarker have quit KAOS to join the Mounties. Siegfried and Shtarker lure the two into frozen wilderness, then abandon them; but the stalwart 99 and Quigley stumble onto and dynamite Stanislavsky's igloo-mounted giant electric fan, thereby returning the world's climate to normal.

Friday, 7:30 P.M. January 2, 1970
Moonlighting Becomes You
Max messes with Cairo's National Museum and microfilm imbedded in a stick of gum, while in Washington 99 asks the Chief to give her important assignments. Though the Chief fears that living with Max has made 99 accident-prone, he sends her on an undercover job with Hannibal Day's radio show— a show that transmits coded messages for KAOS. Joining her as the sound effects man, Max massacres the noises but nails the KAOS agent.

Friday, 7:30 P.M. January 8, 1970
House of Max (Part I)
Max and 99 join forces with Inspector Sparrow of Scotland Yard after twelve people are brutally murdered, ostensibly by the original Jack the Ripper. In fact, Jack is made of wax, and is the creation of ghoulish Raul

Duval of Duval's Cave of Wax. With a simple injection, Duval can bring any wax figure to life. To protect his interests, Duval sends the werewolf of London after Max and 99.

Friday, 7:30 P.M. January 16, 1970
House of Wax (Part II)
Hoping to expose Duval, Max substitutes for the figure of Adolf Hitler in Duval's museum. Duval returns, catches on to Max, and brings all the museum dummies to life to destroy him. Max escapes them—even dummies of W.C. Fields and Laurel and Hardy—and when he has also escaped Duval's cauldron of 400-degree boiling wax, the dummies hold a celebration until they harden again.

Friday, 7:30 P.M. January 23, 1970
Rebecca of Funny-Folk Farm
CONTROL arranges for a storm to hit the spooky mansion of Hester Van Hooten so that Max and 99 have an excuse to retrieve an important parcel from her roof. 99 bears a striking resemblance to Mrs. Van Hooten's dead sister, Rebecca. Sebastian, Rebecca's crazed former lover, is murdered. Here's a twist: The butler did it.

Friday, 7:30 P.M. January 30, 1970
The Mess of Adrian Listenger
Six CONTROL agents are murdered—two-thirds of a baseball team on which Max, the Chief, and Adrian Listenger played during their days at CONTROL training school. Max and the Chief remember that when Listenger flunked spy school, he vowed revenge. They track him down, but he's dead, leaving Max and the Chief no choice but to suspect each other.

Friday, 7:30 P.M. February 6, 1970
Witness for the Execution
KAOS brings in the Exterminator when a top-ranking agent defects to testify for CONTROL. The Exterminator, disguised as a plumber, finds him—disguised as a fat red-headed woman, baby-sitting for the Smarts. Max stops the Exterminator by accidentally shooting plaster onto his head. Unfortunately, the same plaster brains the defector, causing him to forget what he knows about KAOS.

Friday, 7:30 P.M. February 13, 1970
How Green Was My Valet
In order to recover stolen rocket fuel, Max and 99 get work as a maid and valet at the Bulmanian Embassy in Washington, D.C. The Ambassador, a KAOS man, keeps the fuel in his wine cellar, and the key to the cellar around his neck. Max gets the key by intoxicating the Ambassador, locates the fuel, and actually succeeds in keeping it out of KAOS clutches.

Friday, 7:30 P.M. February 20, 1970
And Only Two Ninety-Nine
Max returns home to an impostor 99, who fusses over him with enough food to feed an army; while 99, kidnapped by the forces of Melnick Archer, communicates with the Chief by means of a fingernail phone. She learns that the impostor is poisoning Max with his meals, while framing the real Mrs. Smart for murder. 99 escapes, confronts the faker, exposes her as the one with makeup covering a shiner, and decks her.

Friday, 7:30 P.M. February 27, 1970
Smartacus
Eccentric KAOS agent Montague Leach, who runs a chain of "Roman Baths" spas, sweats secrets out of big shots with his truth steam. The Chief checks into a spa as Senator Van Horne, escorted by Maxwell Smart. Under the influence of truth steam, they exchange pent-up hostilities, then proceed to

elude certain death with the aid of a laundry cart, a melted locker key, gladiatorial gear, and statuary.

Friday, 7:30 P.M. April 24, 1970

What's It All About, Algie?

Algernon DeGrasse, proprietor of Algie's Nursery, numbers Washington's most prominent citizens among his clients. When one CONTROL agent disappears, Max replaces him, disguised as a Japanese gardener. De-Grasse suspects, but 99 warns Max, who won't have to be dinner for a man-eating plant after all.

Friday, 7:30 P.M. May 1, 1970

Hello Columbus, Goodbye America

Max and 99 foil a daytime robbery in an art museum, only to discover that the robbers work for Gino Columbus, the direct descendant of Christopher and current owner of the country. Smart, assigned to keep Gino as happy as possible, blunders into and foils a KAOS kidnapping. Once Gino is safe, Smart poses as Gino, is again kidnapped by KAOS, and stalls for time while the real Gino signs the country over to the President.

Friday, 7:30 P.M. May 8, 1970

Do I Hear a Vaults?

The Chief has hidden the vitally important "Who's Who in CONTROL" in the public library. He reclaims it; KAOS will stop at nothing to get it. After Max and Larabee transfer the book to a bank vault, Max manages to lock the Chief and Larabee *in* the bank vault. He has Freddie the Forger released from prison to spring them—since Baffles the safecracker has just been given the juice.

Friday, 7:30 P.M. May 15, 1970

I Am Curiously Yellow

Smart has been compromised by the Whip's gong—the Whip being an inscrutable Oriental agent, and the gong inducing a powerful posthypnotic suggestion. No sooner is Max assigned to protect the only working model of NARCO 5-12 than the Whip instructs him to steal it. Surveillance equipment catches Max in the act. Then Max, taking an antihypnotism pill, returns to the Whip to capture him. The Chief, 99 and Larabee arrive. Larabee strikes the gong-putting the Chief in his power.

Don Adams as a mannequin in *Shipment to Beirut. Courtesy of Howard Frank Archives/ Personality Photos, Inc.*

INDEX